STEEL CITY R
READING FOR PLEASURE
IN SHEFFIELD, 1925–1955

LIVERPOOL ENGLISH TEXTS AND STUDIES 100

STEEL CITY READERS

Reading for Pleasure in Sheffield, 1925–1955

MARY GROVER

LIVERPOOL UNIVERSITY PRESS

First published 2023 by
Liverpool University Press
4 Cambridge Street
Liverpool
L69 7ZU

British Library Cataloguing-in-Publication data
A British Library CIP record is available

ISBN 978-1-80207-858-9

Typeset by Carnegie Book Production, Lancaster
Printed and bound by CPI Group (UK) Ltd, Croydon CR0 4YY

Dedication

This book is dedicated to the 65 men and women who shared their reading histories with the community history group 'Reading Sheffield' between 2011 and 2019. They are listed by date order of the year of their birth and by the name by which they chose to be referred to in this book. Most of the married couples were interviewed together. Jean H, Winnie Lincoln and Joan T were interviewed twice: once on their own and then as a group of friends.

Both audio records and transcripts can be found on the 'Reading Sheffield' website: www.readingsheffield.co.uk and in the Sheffield City Archives.

Ted 1919
Wynne 1919
Irene Hailstone 1921
Mary Soar 1921
Florence 1923
Mary Brothers 1923
Mary Robertson 1923
Winnie Lincoln 1923
Margaret G 1924
Barbara 'Betty' R 1925
Betty B 1925
Elsie Brownlee 1925
Eva 1925
Ken 1925
Jean Mercer 1925
Malcolm Mercer 1925
Jean H 1926
Jocelyn 1926
Pat Casson 1926
Pat Cymbal 1926
John D 1927
Alma 1928

Edna 1928
Kath 1928
Dorothy H 1929
Hazel 1929
John Y 1929
Peter Mason 1929
Jean A 1930
Peter B 1930
Norman Adsetts 1931
David Flather 1931
Dorothy Latham 1931
Doreen Gill 1934
Dorothy Norbury 1934
Margaret C 1934
Betty Newman 1935
Jean Wolfendale 1935
James Green 1936
Shirley Ellins 1936
Meg Young 1936
Erica 1937
Sheila Edwards 1937
Mavis 1937

Yvonne Bland 1937
Frank Burgin 1938
Chris 1939
Judith G 1939
Julia Banks 1939
Noel 1939
Bob W 1940
Christine 1940
Madeleine Doherty 1940
Gillian Applegate 1941
Joan Challenger 1941
Joan T 1941
Maureen L 1941
Adele 1942
'Delia' 1942
Josie Hall 1942
Alan 1944
Anne 1944
Barbara Green 1944
Carolyn W 1944
Margaret H 1945

Contents

Illustrations

Acknowledgements

I dedicate this book to the readers who volunteered to be interviewed by 'Reading Sheffield'. I would like to thank them all for trusting us with their memories and for the photographs that illustrate their histories. The history of reading and of the city in which they became readers has been enriched by their participation in our project.

Without the 'Reading Sheffield' team these memories would never have been recorded: thank you to Sahra Ajiba, Jan Chatterton, Trisha Cooper, Jean Gilmour, Liz Hawkins, Loveday Herridge, Clare Keen, Ruth Owen, Sue Roe, Alice Seed and Peter Watson. Their interviewing skills were rooted in their understanding of the communities in which they have lived and worked. They gave the interviewees the confidence that they would be heard and understood. Many of the interviewers also helped to transcribe the interviews. Audio and transcribed records of all the recorded interviews can be found on our website: www.readingsheffield.co.uk and in the Sheffield City Archives.

The initial project depended on the generosity and trust of several donors. Sheffield Hallam University has been a constant support, especially Professor Chris Hopkins, who, as head of the Humanities Research Centre, has obtained funding for our annual events, engaged with the project personally and given us invaluable advice. Sheffield's oldest charity, the Sheffield Town Trust, gave us our initial sizeable grant, which funded our equipment and training. It also funded work done with artists and poets in the community. Without their support these histories would not have been collected. Clare Jenkins and Stephen Kelly trained the 'Reading Sheffield' team, giving us the benefit of their extensive experience in taking oral histories.

Alongside the interviewees whose memories were formally recorded, I have also collected memories informally from members of many community groups. I would like to say a particular thank you to these readers. I met many at gatherings hosted by Sheffield Library Services, whose staff have always made us welcome. The Sheffield Red Hats, a group of retired Sheffield librarians, have shared their knowledge and enjoyment of their work in Sheffield Library Services. Relatives of initial interviewees, including Kathryn Austin, Maureen Burgin, Jane Ferretti, Margaret Morlan, Ruth Potts, Frances Soar and Sally Wilson, continue to share invaluable information about family members. Stephen McClarence's articles in the *Yorkshire Post* and the *Sheffield Daily Telegraph* attracted media interest and new participants to our project.

Much of the material we have gathered can be found on the website, which was set up by Dennis and Lizz Tuckerman. Lizz is also an artist and it is to her and Dennis that we owe the attractiveness and usability of our website. Photographs of our readers as adults were taken by Tom Stayte and others. Lizz and Tom created a photographic record of the images shared with us by our readers. In 2017 Lizz's exhibition 'In Praise of Libraries' gave us a rich opportunity to bring our readers together to celebrate their reading histories.

I am grateful to Picture Sheffield for permission to use the images of the Red Circle library and Woodhouse Children's Library. I appreciate that no fees have been charged by the archives of Boots UK for the images from the Boots Book-lovers' archive. I would like to thank the Senior Archivist of Boots UK, Judith Wright, and her colleague, Sophie Clapp, who have been my guides. Other archives used include those of the Workers' Educational Institute in Sheffield and the AQA archives in Manchester. I am grateful to all the librarians who have helped me in my explorations.

This book owes its origins to the encouragement of three people in particular: Loveday Herridge and Sue Roe, my 'Reading Sheffield' colleagues, and Janet Atkinson. All helped to unlock my initial fear of beginning this writing project.

Historians and people who know this city exceptionally well have been generous with their knowledge. I am particularly grateful to John Baxendale, Clyde Binfield, Sylvia Dunkley and David Price for their interest and advice. Richard Caborn helped me understand the changing patterns of employment in the city over the twentieth century. I constantly learn from the research of the Sheffield-based 'Reading 1900–1950 Reading Group', some of which can be found at https://reading19001950.wordpress.

I am grateful to our son, Jay Grover, to our friends and to fellow researchers in this field who have discussed various aspects of the project with me. The book has benefited hugely from their critical engagement.

Drafts of particular chapters have been read by my sister, Eleanor Watts, and by Loveday Herridge, Sue Roe and Val Hewson, all three from 'Reading Sheffield'. Val Hewson's knowledge of Sheffield's library history is exceptional. I have constantly used her research when considering the way in which Sheffield City Libraries served our readers. She is now chair of 'Reading Sheffield' and is developing the nature of the project.

It was a particular joy that the poet Eleanor Brown responded to the experiences of our readers in her collection *White Ink Stains* (Bloodaxe, 2019). Eleanor has also read drafts of several chapters of this book. Her poems are a testament to the eloquence of our readers.

This book has attracted more practical support than any author has a right to expect. My first draft was read by Chris Hopkins and Jan Montefiore, and later drafts by Karin Barber and Steve Loveman. I hugely appreciate their time, encouragement and criticism. Christine Kenyon Jones and Faye Hammill helped me decide how and where I should try to publish this book. Its existence in print owes much to their advice. I would like to thank Christabel Scaife at Liverpool University Press for all her help and encouragement. Many thanks also to Sarah Warren, Senior Production Editor at LUP, and the team at Carnegie Book Production for making the text fit for publication.

My final draft was read by Alison Light. It is to her that this book owes its final form and much of the way it connects with British culture beyond Sheffield. Above all, she has continually affirmed the value of the 'Reading Sheffield' project and of the men and women whose histories are at the heart of this book.

The publication of this book has depended on the financial generosity of all those who contributed to the cost of the Open Access fee. These include local firms Gripple and J.S. Neill and the 'bibliomaniac' Robin Ince. Thank you all and thank you to Margaret Bennett and Val Hewson who orchestrated the JustGiving campaign.

My final and inexpressible thanks are to my husband Derek, whose active encouragement, reading and rereading made this possible. Though I do not dedicate this book to him, he knows how much it owes to him and to his shared commitment to the city in which we are lucky enough to live.

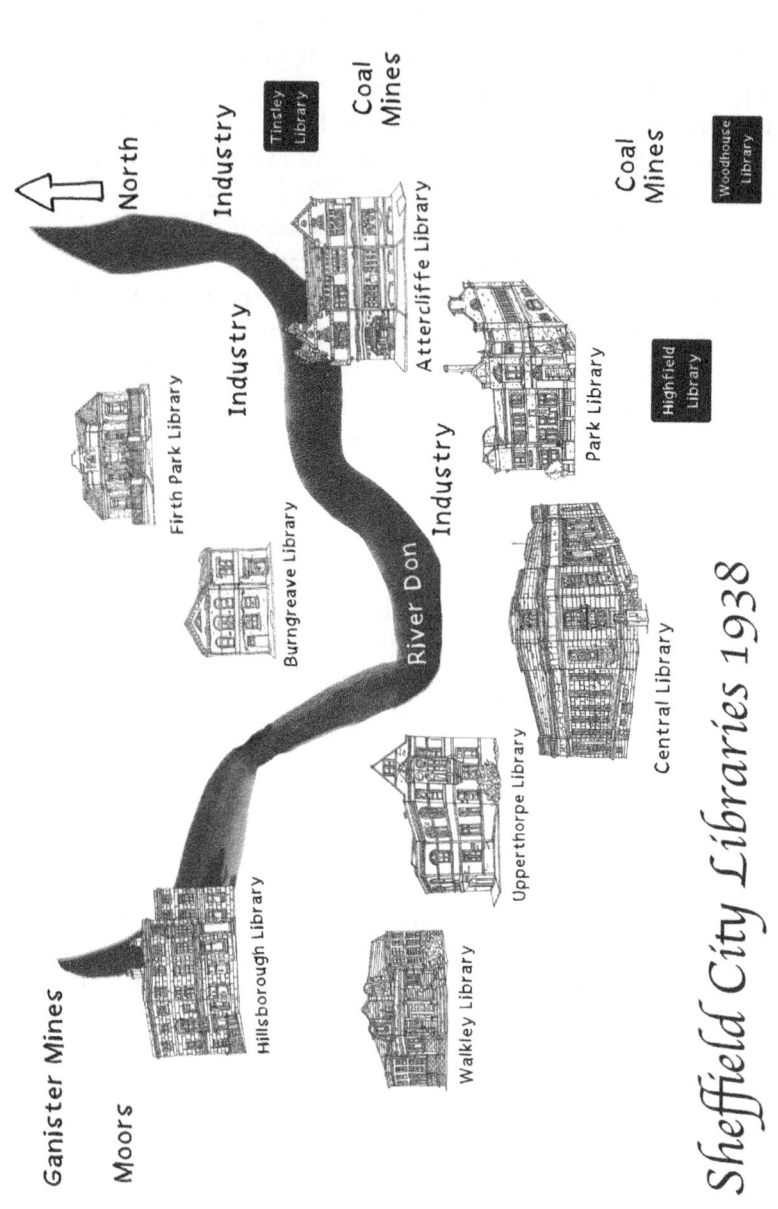

Sheffield City Libraries 1938

1 Map of Sheffield's libraries in 1938. Illustrations and design by @Mdale_art aka Jack Martindale

Introduction

Reading: 'I saw no living in it'

Irene Hailstone, born in 1921, is pictured here with her mother and brother:

> I could read quite early. I was never stopped from reading but my mother didn't read and my father read a paper and that was it... I sometimes got shouted at because I should have been doing something else... My husband used to get Westerns and if I had nothing else to read I used to read those and he got them from a bookstall in the market and if he took them back you got so much knocked off the next one... If there was nothing to read, I would read anything.[1]

1 Irene Hailstone, born 1921, interviewed by Susan Roe, 28 February 2012.

Irene's mother may not have been a reader but she nurtured her children's educational development. Irene's reading was tolerated, but Adele's was actively defended by her mother from the mockery of her father. Born twenty years later than Irene, in 1942, Adele was the only child of a painter and decorator and a mother who had been in service, Adele remembered her teenage reading.

> Mum would be in the kitchen getting tea ready when Dad came home and he said, 'Oh look at her. She's sitting reading.' And I can distinctly remember my Mum saying, 'Leave her alone. She's enjoying it.'[2]

In spite of her father's active hostility to reading, Adele just couldn't help herself. She had to read: 'Something gets hold of you, doesn't it?' Adele marvelled at her compulsion to read and pondered on how it was that books had become essential to her happiness.

That compulsion was shared by the 65 Sheffield readers whose experiences are at the heart of this book. All were born before 1946. Their reading memories were collected by the community history group, 'Reading Sheffield', between 2011 and 2019. These readers were born in a time of economic depression followed by wartime and post-war austerity. They grew up in an industrial city which for most of the twentieth century set little store by bookish or clerkly skills. Yet they developed a habit of reading that changed their lives, personally, culturally and economically. How and why did this happen?

The low estimate put on the economic value of book-learning in Sheffield was not misguided. One of Sheffield's most famous products was stainless steel, developed by the remarkable Harry Brearley at the beginning of the twentieth century. In 1883 the frail 12-year-old joined the steel works of Messrs. Thos. Firth and Sons to wash bottles in the chemical laboratory. He arrived at his job addicted to any comic he could lay his hands on. His boss, the chemist James Taylor, tried to take the boy's education in hand. 'He offered me a copy of Roscoe's *Chemistry*, which I honestly tried to read but with a total absence of either pleasure or understanding.'[3] Despite this setback, Harry did decide that reading was the way forward and plunged into a course of self-education, finding books and educated men who could guide him.

2 Adele, born 1942, interviewed by Liz Hawkins, 19 July 2012.
3 Harry Brearley, *Stainless Pioneer: Autobiographical Notes*, Solihull: British Steel Stainless and The Kelham Island Industrial Museum, Sheffield, 1989, 26. The work lent might well have been *Roscoe's Lessons in Elementary Chemistry* (1866), which was widely circulated in Britain and across the world.

Ruskin's *Unto This Last* was 'a revelation'. Brearley had read a library copy of this radical critique of capitalist economics, published in 1862, but he craved ownership: 'I dare not steal it and I could not afford to buy it. So, I copied it out in my most careful hand-writing and bound it in cloth boards with leather back and corners.'[4] Despite Brearley's resourcefulness, as a young adult his passion for literature was checked not simply by the meagre supply of affordable books but by the employment opportunities available in Sheffield at the turn of the nineteenth and twentieth centuries.

> This excursion into literature excited an appetite which will never be satisfied. But I saw no living in it... There was some prospect of becoming an analyst which I could not afford to neglect.[5]

The clarity with which Brearley thought through his decision to direct his extraordinary gifts towards the study of metallurgy rather than literature is characteristic of the man. None of our readers, who came to adulthood in the mid-twentieth century, describes such an explicit choice, but even during this period of increasing literacy very few men or women would have judged there to be a 'living' to be had from reading in Sheffield.

Had Irene or Adele grown up in Manchester, Leeds or Birmingham, cities with a far greater range of trades, their parents might have been more encouraging of their children's absorption in books. Sheffield's heavy reliance on the metal and mining industries meant that there were fewer clerkly jobs than there were in cities associated with cloth manufacture, the law and commerce, for example. The economic historian Sidney Pollard confirms a commonly held view that, in the twentieth century, Sheffield was 'the biggest proletarian city in Britain'.[6] There was a low proportion of jobs in white-collar work and a high premium on jobs that were physically demanding, highly skilled and only done by men. There were fewer avenues for women to become independent wage earners than there were in the textile mills to the west and north of Sheffield.

It is possible that there was less prejudice towards print in late eighteenth- and nineteenth-century Sheffield. Working-class men made great efforts to read during this period and created reading communities

4 Brearley, *Stainless Pioneer*, 29.
5 Brearley, *Stainless Pioneer*, 29.
6 Sidney Pollard, 'Labour', in *The History of the City of Sheffield 1843–1993, Volume 2: Society*, ed. Clyde Binfield, Roger Harper, David Hey, Richard Childs, David Martin, Geoffrey Tweedale, Sheffield: Sheffield Academic Press, 1993, 260.

in the workplace. In 1794 the radical newspaper *The Sheffield Register* had a circulation of 2,025 but was read by far more. The widow of its editor, Joseph Gales, records that not only was it read 'in every house of respectability', but that 'one at least was taken in every manufacturing Shop, so that it was read by at least 10,000 persons of that class, as they clubbed to pay the subscription'.[7] Winifred Gales also described how men would read aloud to one another and share books or newspapers until they fell apart. This entrepreneurial and cooperative reading among fellow workers was fostered by the small scale of 'little mester' metalworking workshops on which the cutlery trade depended, and the period of radicalism that preceded William Pitt's repressive measures in the 1790s.

The 'Reading Sheffield' project recorded no account of communal reading in the twentieth century, except in the household of Mary Soar whose father was a printer. Books were generally regarded as of economically low value and held little cultural status, often being associated with 'pudd'n burners', women who neglected their household tasks in favour of God knows what frivolity. Though the father of Yvonne Bland himself read Westerns, the filesmith was nevertheless irritated by his young daughter's reading in the 1940s: 'Put that book down. Get something in your fingers.'[8] A book was not 'a thing', nor was command of the written or spoken word, especially for women. On the other side of the Pennines, the son of the proprietor of a corner shop in the 1920s recalls a similar identification of reading with female idleness. In many homes in the mill town of Salford, books and magazines were prohibited 'on the grounds that they kept women and children from their proper tasks and developed lazy habits'.[9]

Despite prejudice against the 'gobby', the glib and the 'tall poppies' who appeared to be asserting their superiority to others by voicing an opinion out of turn, many of our female readers did in fact, eventually gain employment, notably in the 1960s and 1970s, as a result of their command of the written and spoken word. Gillian Applegate had a second chance to connect with the kind of education that she had hoped for when she first attended grammar school in the 1950s. Her mother

---

7 Winifred Gales's 'Recollections' in the Gales Family Papers at the University of North Carolina, https://finding-aids.lib.unc.edu/02652/#folder_1#1. I am indebted to Loveday Herridge and Susan Roe for sharing the results of their research into Sheffield reading cultures in the eighteenth and nineteenth centuries.

8 Yvonne Bland, born 1937, interviewed by Susan Roe, 24 June 2019.

9 Robert Roberts, *The Classic Slum: Salford Life in the First Quarter of the Century*, Harmondsworth: Penguin, 1973 [1971], 166.

had insisted that she leave school at 16 in order to prepare for life as a wife and mother. In the 1980s, with the encouragement of her husband, Gillian joined her local Further Education College as a library assistant and studied for a qualification in library work. To her astonishment she got merits and distinctions, but her husband was unsurprised: 'Oh, I knew you'd pass. It's as if you were rehearsing all your life.' Her private passion for reading had been a rehearsal for public competence.[10]

Whether or not a reading habit eventually became an economic asset, books helped our readers to become eloquent narrators of their own lives. The books they sought and held and read are images of different stages in their lives, chapters in their autobiographical narratives. Many readers came to their interview with documents to hand that were the groundwork of such narratives: reading diaries or notes of books read by their friends. By asking Sheffield readers how they became readers, despite lack of encouragement, despite the apparent absence of any use or value, and despite the pressures of courtship, marriage, parenthood and work, we learn a lot about the inner compulsion to read. Sheffield's very lack of bookishness makes it an excellent place to explore what it is that 'gets hold of us' when we cannot be without a book.

We have not found comparable projects in Britain or in other English-speaking countries. The invaluable histories of reading by Christopher Hilliard, Helen Taylor and others rely principally on library records, questionnaires and interviews with those providing books.[11] Surveys such as A.J. Jenkinson's study of children's reading, *What Do Boys and Girls Read?* (1940), gathered contemporary information drawn from questionnaires issued to school teachers and librarians.[12] That survey is fascinating because it is contemporary with the readers whose tastes it examines, and also because it reflects the values of a particular cohort of English teachers in the 1930s. The questionnaires produced apparently quantifiable data, usually in the form of lists: 'How many books do girls read?' for example. It is clear, in fact, that the material was consciously mediated by the English teachers in each school. Jenkinson notes, 'Some authors who write for adults and are quite often read by adolescent girls

---

10 Gillian Applegate, born 1941, interviewed by Mary Grover, 3 May 2012.

11 Christopher Hilliard, *To Exercise Our Talents: The Democratization of Writing in Britain*, Cambridge, MA, Harvard University Press, 2006; Christine Pawley, *Reading Places: Literacy, Democracy, and the Public Library in Cold War America*, Amherst, MA: University of Massachusetts Press, 2010; and Helen Taylor, *Why Women Read Fiction*, Oxford: Oxford University Press, 2020.

12 A.J. Jenkinson, *What Do Boys and Girls Read?*, London: Methuen, 1940.

are omitted from these lists, such as E. Phillips Oppenheim, "Sapper", and Edgar Wallace' in part 'to keep the lists short'.[13] Any list can create the illusion of finality or comprehensiveness.

This is not simply a history of reading in a particular place or time; it is a contribution to the histories of people who did not expect to write or make history. Many of our readers came from families with few possessions of any kind. In her introduction to *Common People*, Alison Light describes the challenges faced when historians try to write personal or communal histories when there is a lack of a 'treasury of biographical objects which might stand in for their lives'.[14] Irene Hailstone was born in 1921 and was brought up in Grimesthorpe, a short distance from Firth Brown's, the huge steel manufacturer where her father worked. The family also ran a dairy and ice-cream business from their house. When we interviewed Irene, the shelves around her were filled with a rich selection of modern fiction and non-fiction, but she had laid out on the table in front of her carefully preserved story books and annuals, gifts from ninety years earlier. When she became an independent reader, Irene was sent annuals of all sorts. 'One old lady' used to send her *Pip, Squeak and Wilfred* annuals, spin-offs from the strip cartoons to be found in the *Daily Mirror*. 'I think the earliest one I got was 1926 which I still have. I read that.'

> Occasionally my mother would read a comic to me of a Saturday morning but she was the daughter of a farmer who couldn't read or write so well and he didn't agree with her reading so I don't think she ever read a book in her life.

But thanks to the gifts sent to her by friends and family, Irene read early, arrived at school well equipped for study and gained a place at grammar school. Each annual marked another stage in Irene's life. They were the most durable of her childhood possessions, still immaculate and still counting for much. Many of the books shown to us by our readers were gifts from members of the family who had had better luck than the reader's own and were witness to a child's value to her wider family: a 'treasury of biographical objects' indeed.

Jonathan Rose, the pioneering author of *The Intellectual Life of the British Working Classes*, comments, 'It is significant that when the "inarticulate masses" write their own history, they have quite a lot to

---

13 Jenkinson, *What Do Boys and Girls Read?*, 185–6.
14 Alison Light, *Common People*, Harmondsworth: Penguin, 2014, xxii.

say about their reading.'[15] As these interviews testify, our readers were anything but inarticulate, and in describing what they read they mapped their personal histories. Though our readers were usually unguided, they were far from passive in the way they read. They learned what genres appealed and which authors spoke to them. As Sheffield City Libraries became more abundantly stocked in the 1930s, selecting what they read became an arena of choice in the lives of people who, otherwise, had little choice. In spite of their limited educational and economic opportunities they developed the power to discriminate in this private sphere. They relished their own resourcefulness in tracking down authors who met their needs and in establishing a domain defined by these purely private pleasures. The reading identities they created were usually of little interest to anyone else. When Adele's father came back from a day of hard physical labour to find his daughter sitting and reading instead of helping his wife cook the tea, he was irritated by the fact that his daughter read at all, not by the nature of her reading choices. This left her free to develop her reading choices without a cultural censor. The very constraints of our readers' lives created a particular kind of freedom.

The methods used by 'Reading Sheffield' to gather and map their patterns of choice are, we think, unique. If this study prompts other projects of this kind, rooted in different social and cultural contexts, we shall learn more about how the habit of reading develops and the varying ways in which it is nurtured. A wealth of such projects will sharpen our sense of how our environment shapes the way we read.

The 'Reading Sheffield' project

'Reading Sheffield' was founded in 2011 with financial support from Sheffield Hallam University and Sheffield's oldest charity, the Sheffield Town Trust. Our first project was to record the reading memories of Sheffield men and women who came to adulthood in the mid-twentieth century. We recruited and trained a team of co-investigators. Most of the other investigators had, like myself, spent the greater part of their working lives fostering the habit of reading and extending educational opportunities in Sheffield.

All the readers interviewed grew up in and around Sheffield. They were born between 1919 and 1946. They had all developed the habit of seeking

---

15 Jonathan Rose, *The Intellectual Life of the British Working Classes*, New Haven, CT: Yale University Press, 2001, 34.

out books before television became a dominant source of narrative and information and before Sheffield ceased to rely so exclusively on the metal and mining industries.

Of the 65 people interviewed, 52 were women and 13 were men. This imbalance owes much to the nature of the community groups from which they were recruited: library discussion groups, social groups in residential homes and exercise groups for example. There were more women than men in all such groups. They were not a scientifically selected sample and they were all white.[16] Our first readers were recruited by the librarians of the Mobile and Housebound Library Service, a service critical to the happiness of its users; all these users were women. I then tried to fill in the geographical and social gaps by visiting a range of community groups in different parts of the city, inviting members to be interviewed if they felt that reading had been an important part of their lives.

We tried to discover the occupational background of the chief wage-earner in each reader's family of origin. We were told of the occupations of the parents for all but six of our readers: three of these six never knew their fathers and were supported, in difficult circumstances, by their wider family or, in two cases, by a mother able to earn a living. Of the remaining 59 readers, 28 were the children of men who were manual workers; eleven of these were in metal manufacturing and ten in mines. Men in the metal and mining trades had a huge range of skills and earned anything between 21 and 52 shillings a week, wages rising significantly during the Second World War.[17] The next biggest group of wage-earners were thirteen managers or professional workers (a high proportion of whom were engineers of some sort working in mines or steelworks). There were also five retail workers, five clerks (two working in steelworks), two salesmen, one carter and one policeman. The wealthiest fathers were four factory owners; three of these were in metal manufacturing and flourished in the 1940s, while the fourth, who produced mother-of-pearl goods, had to close his business during the Second World War when the market for such work collapsed. It is clear that the vast majority of our readers were the sons and daughters of men whose livelihoods, in the 1930s and 1940s, depended on the dominant industries in Sheffield: mining and metalwork. Their backgrounds reflected the pattern of employment of

16 Most migrants to Sheffield from other countries arrived after the Second World War.

17 Sidney Pollard, *A History of Labour in Sheffield*, Liverpool: Liverpool University Press, 1959, 303.

Sheffield in these decades. For most jobs, general reading would not have been an asset, and only one of our readers had a parent who had made a living closely connected with her love of books: Betty, whose mother had been a teacher. The book-filled nursery that Betty's mother established was unique in the mining village of North Staveley where Betty grew up. Many of these books were sent to her mother by a family friend and not acquired in Sheffield.

The process of recruitment deepened our understanding of the cultural environments of our readers and of how, on a very local scale, where we live influences how we read; location was as important as parental occupation to understanding the nature of a child's access to books. The seven rivers of Sheffield divide its population into areas that are still quite separate from one another. Coalmining communities to the east were often semi-rural, set apart from metalworking communities nearer the centre of Sheffield. Steelworkers tended to live in the crowded and blackened terraced houses on the hillsides above the vast corridor of steelworks along the valley of the Don. Both sets of manual workers lived in relatively homogeneous communities defined by shared occupations and distance from people with other kinds of job. In the more affluent and semi-rural areas to the north-west of the city, by contrast, there was more diversity of occupation.

A recruiting mission to the Slightly Sprightly exercise group in this north-western suburb introduced us to the diverse community of Wadsley. This exceptionally mixed community was on the rural edge of the city but close to its industrial heartlands. Miners of ganister, used to insulate blast furnaces, lived alongside poachers, gamekeepers, mental health nurses from the vast local sanatorium and 'little mesters' working metal on a small scale, with connections, of course, to the huge industrial enterprises just a mile away in the valley. We also learned of two local politicians from opposing parties living civilly alongside each other, and perhaps both using the newspaper table cannily introduced by the proprietor of the local general stores to lure his customers into dawdling another ten minutes before returning to their daily chores. I interviewed three friends who either grew up in this community or moved there as young adults. Winnie Lincoln married the son of a farmer who made his living in a variety of occupations connected with the refractory industries. She was very impressed when she moved out to Wadsley from the working-class terraces of inner-city Upperthorpe to find that the vicar was himself an author, a respected local historian. The Revd H.A. Kirk-Smith's *History of the Village of Wadsley* is still worth reading. The interviews he conducted with his parishioners for this book must in themselves have given them a sense that writing books was a serious trade and one that could connect directly with their lives.[18] The exceptionality of this socially diverse semi-rural suburb, where the bookish and unbookish lived alongside each other, will be borne out by my later discussion of the monolithic nature of Sheffield's other urban villages, where a neighbour with books, let alone one capable of writing one, was a rarity.

Reading distance: 'nobody was called Penelope where I lived'

For most Sheffield readers, the world as represented by the books they read was, on the surface, geographically and socially remote. Born in 1928, Alma, like the majority of our readers, grew up in an exclusively white working-class community. Her father was a steelworker. When she was a girl, she came across 'Angela Brazil books, of course, which were about schools and things which we knew nothing about'.

> There was this girl called Penny-lope. I always read her as Penny-lope and it was only years later that I realised it was Penelope. [laughs] I guess nobody – nobody was called Penelope where I lived.[19]

Alma laughed, but unapologetically. She didn't distance herself from the pleasure of those early reading experiences either by mocking herself or the books themselves. Her memory of misrecognition is shared by many of our readers and so is her matter-of-fact account of making mistakes when negotiating a world so remote from her own. None of our Sheffield readers, whatever their social background, remembered coming across a book that described the lives they lived in the 1930s and 1940s. It is not surprising because there were few, for either adults or children. The absence of books that reflected the social world around them is rarely commented on by our readers, but their hunger for books needs to be set in this context of absence. If social self-recognition was not one of the pleasures derived from the predominantly realist tales they read (fantasy as a genre hardly figured), then what was the reading pleasure that hooked them and made them habitual readers?

18 H.A. Kirk-Smith, *History of Wadsley, 1800–1957*, Sheffield, 1957.
19 Alma, born in 1928, interviewed by Liz Hawkins, 8 November 2011.

'Not from round here'

In writing this book, I have of course been influenced by my own childhood experiences of reading, my education and my residence in Sheffield. Yet, as my Sheffield school pupils occasionally reminded me, I am not 'from round here'. As a child I was geographically far more remote than these Sheffield readers from the fictional worlds I explored, yet I never felt that they were alien. I grew up in the country then called Burma, my family's little library having been carefully selected in 1950 to sustain us all for the next seven years. Into the black tin trunk to join us after our six-week sea voyage went the complete works of Charles Dickens, Jane Austen, Dorothy L. Sayers, a selection of the novels of P.G. Wodehouse and my first reading primers. Underneath the creaking fan my father would labour over the first English-language textbooks to be published in Burma after the Japanese invasion in 1942, and I would be learning to read from the pages of 'Old Lob', the guardian of a farmyard of enchanting English beasts.

Nobody was called 'Old Lob' or Jeeves in the country where I lived nor in the England to which I returned at the age of seven. But unlike Adele, who was in no doubt that she and Pene-lope would be forever worlds apart, I was equally sure that the worlds of 'Old Lob' and Jeeves were in some way 'home'. Every inch of my reading journey was shared with my parents and, to a great extent, scripted by them. We were a family of readers who have all made our living out of teaching. So the way I encountered new texts could not have been further removed from the unguided explorations of our Sheffield readers. As a child, I never came across a book by chance; my choices were made for me and independent quests to the market or the library were impossible. And I grew up with a strong sense that books were profitable baggage.

Since 1982 I have lived and worked in Sheffield, teaching English. During the 1980s I taught in the first purpose-built comprehensive school in Sheffield, then in the 1990s in a further education college with a large cohort of trainee engineers and electricians, and finally, for the last fourteen years of my career, at Sheffield Hallam University (previously Sheffield Polytechnic) teaching twentieth-century literature. In school and further education college, very many of my students were doubtful about the worth of the subject I taught. A qualification in English or Communication Skills had a temporary, merely transactional value. There were few spaces on the curriculum of any course I taught where students who had the reading habit could share their tastes with others.

If possible, I borrowed from students their personal favourites, but there were all too few opportunities to encourage personal and independent reading. As any teacher knows, it is the habit of reading that delivers fluency and confidence with the written word, and the courses I taught were never designed to create that competence.

When I went on to work in a university, I taught the kind of twentieth-century literature that demands a great deal of its readers. Virginia Woolf or James Joyce, for example, defined themselves against the kinds of texts that you could read at a gallop and thereby establish an ease with the written word. Although it gave me great pleasure when a seminar group took to Woolf's masterpiece *Mrs Dalloway*, it was the negative attitudes of Woolf and other intellectuals in the first half of the twentieth century to the popular reader that came to dominate my own research. The cultural snobbery of the 1930s was my focus. I explored the texts hostile to 'mass culture' and the novels that were thought to epitomise its ills.[20] What I was unable to do, because such readers do not tend to record their views, was to hear the voices of the 'masses' whose taste for such novels was regularly condemned.

'Mental dramshops'

My attention to the voices of these Sheffield readers is a response to the ways in which cultural commentators, over many years, have denied the value of such reading lives. In the 1930s and 1940s, when our young adult readers were absorbed by writers as diverse as A.J. Cronin, Daphne du Maurier, Charles Dickens, J.B. Priestley and Edgar Wallace, their pleasures were being identified by a wide range of commentators as substandard, uninteresting and uniform. Indeed, their tastes were held to be symptomatic of an encroaching mass culture which threatened the values of civilised society. At a time when those values were indeed under threat throughout Europe, it is no surprise, but deeply disturbing, that intellectuals turned on the ever-growing number of people who were, thanks to improved education and library provision, being given, for the first time in the history of their families, the opportunity to become habitual readers.

20 Mary Grover, *The Ordeal of Warwick Deeping: Middlebrow Authorship and Cultural Embarrassment*, Madison, NJ: Fairleigh Dickinson University Press, 2009; Erica Brown and Mary Grover, eds, *Middlebrow Literary Cultures: The Battle of the Brows, 1920–1960*, Basingstoke: Palgrave Macmillan, 2012.

Fear and criticism of this new reading public came even from librarians. The headline for a report on a Library Association conference in Sheffield in 1913 was 'Young Librarians' Contempt for Fiction'.[21] These 'young' librarians were set to become the senior staff of the libraries used by our readers in the 1930s. The *Sheffield Daily Telegraph* reported that members of 'The Sheffield Libraries' Committee were afraid that novels were getting too great a hold upon the people, and to some extent they discouraged the use of them as far as possible'. A total ban on any fiction in free libraries was advocated, Mr Proctor from Leeds arguing that the intellectual life of the working classes was imperilled by the 'mental dramshops' of libraries stuffed with intoxicating fictions.

At least these early twentieth-century librarians implied that the working classes had intellects that could be nurtured. They placed the needs of the reading public at the heart of their debate. The rhetoric of later commentators on the evils of popular fiction conflated the supposed shoddiness of popular fiction with the inferior nature of its consumers, which was apparently intrinsic to their social class and suburban environment, the kind of suburbs that were not extensive in the overwhelmingly industrial city of Sheffield in the 1930s. The tastes of the urban working class were not, in fact, the target of the scourges of mass culture.

Readers of popular fiction have always been vilified, but most vehemently in the interwar period. Intellectual distaste for the tastes of 'the masses' united commentators of every political complexion: Marxists, modernists and those suggesting that the study of the great works of English literature would counter the moral and cultural decline caused by industrialisation. The Marxist György Lukács discussed in 1923 the evils of the culture industry which peddled misrepresentations of reality, such as works of popular fiction. These were designed to foster a 'false consciousness' that concealed the ways in which their oppressed consumers were exploited by capitalism.[22] Chris Hopkins notes that British Marxists in the late 1930s tended to respect the nineteenth-century canonical novel because of its wide social scope and its dramatisation of the incoherence at the heart of the bourgeois model

---

21 'Mental Dramshops: Young Librarians' Contempt for Fiction', *Sheffield Daily Telegraph*, 18 September 1913, 7.

22 György Lukács, *History and Class Consciousness: Studies in Marxist Dialectics*, Cambridge, MA: MIT Press, 2000 [1923].

of social order. In contrast, popular contemporary fiction was considered narrowly generic and apolitical.[23]

Like many other intellectuals in the 1930s, Graham Greene characterised readers of popular fiction as ignorant and passive. In 1936 he addressed such readers directly and with contempt: you read 'while you wait for the bus, while you strap-hang, in between the Boss's dictations, while you eat your A.B.C. lunch'. Clearly 'you' are female and more vulnerable than a male reader to the corrupting influence of novels 'written without truth, without compulsion'.[24]

The modernist novelist Virginia Woolf was relatively comfortable with the masses whose tastes were confined to fictional dope. Her venom was reserved for those readers who deluded themselves that a novel could be both readable and serious. From a position of inherited cultural capital, Woolf only tolerated popular fiction readers when they were locked into an addiction to genres of the most predictable and lurid sort, riding what Rebecca West called 'the tosh horse'[25] in a merry and unthreatening way: unthreatening because such readers were, in Woolf's opinion, unlikely to advance into the literary territory she commanded. Woolf violently denounced readers she characterised as 'betwixt and between', those who, like our readers, had a taste for a range of fiction, whose tastes were not exclusively lowbrow.[26]

Class-ridden and anti-democratic though these attitudes were, none were as complex as those influenced by the Cambridge academics F.R. and Q.D. Leavis. Though rarely discussed on English literature courses today, these campaigners for a reform of English teaching had far greater influence in the grammar schools of the 1940s and the 1950s than did Woolf or Marxist critics of the culture industry. Like the Marxists, the disciples of Q.D. and F.R. Leavis promoted the value of the great Victorian realist novels, in part because their authors were hostile to the effects of industrialisation. The commercialised culture produced by an industrialised society was preceded by a supposedly Golden Age when the reader was closely connected to nature and heir to a rural folk

---

23 Chris Hopkins, 'Thrillers and Dystopias: Leftists and Thrillers: The Politics of a 1930s Sub-Genre', in Chris Hopkins, *English Fiction in the 1930s*, London: Continuum, 2006, 123–37.

24 Graham Greene, *Journey without Maps*, London: Heinemann, 1936, 14–15.

25 Rebecca West, 'The Tosh Horse', in *The Strange Necessity: Essays and Reviews*, London: Jonathan Cape, 1928, 319–25.

26 Virginia Woolf, *The Death of the Moth and Other Essays*, London: Hogarth Press, 1942, 127.

culture. This Leavisite hostility to contemporary popular fiction affected secondary modern and grammar school pupils differently. Margaret Matthieson observes that those teaching

> able children ... responded to Leavis's conviction by investing great value in their pupils' capacity to respond sensitively to great literature. Those involved with less able pupils, particularly from working-class backgrounds, have turned to pupils' creativity to compensate for the inadequacies of industrial society.[27]

The truth of this was borne out by my experiences of teaching English in a non-selective boys' secondary school in inner-city London in the early 1970s. The reading act was usually to be followed by a creative rather than a critical response, the authenticity of the text unlocking access to an authenticity in the reader. Yet the boys had never been encouraged to acquire a familiarity with print that might have helped them develop a written language of their own and that would have fitted their creative purposes. None of my English lessons were designed to encourage reading for pleasure, a habit which, more than anything else, gives us ease with the written word.

The Leavises inspired a cohort of committed teachers, but pupils were actively discouraged from reading what simply happened to come to hand. For the grammar school child, each reading act should be an act of discrimination, of rejection or of virtuous choice: how to tell diamond from coal. The title of Margaret Mathieson's book about English teaching in the first half of the twentieth century rightly characterises the Leavises and their followers as 'Preachers of Culture', who equated skills in literary discrimination with moral superiority and promoted 'the redemptive power of English'.[28] The Leavises inspired many of their 'disciples' to teach in secondary modern as well as grammar schools.[29] Unfortunately such recruits were urged to be conscious of their moral and intellectual superiority to the mass of those they taught. In 1932 Q.D. Leavis asserted her membership of 'the sensitive minority' set apart

---

27 Margaret Mathieson, *The Preachers of Culture: A Study of English and Its Teachers*, London: George Allen and Unwin, 1975, 96.

28 Mathieson, *Preachers of Culture*, 96.

29 As a teacher in a boys' comprehensive school in 1970s London, I owed much to the quality of books inspired by Leavisite ideals: Raymond O'Malley and Denys Thompson's poetry anthology, *Rhyme and Reason* (1957), and David Holbrook's two-volume collection of short stories, *People and Diamonds* (1962). But it should be noted that Holbrook would never have called himself a 'Leavisite'.

from benighted readers of all classes who, in misattributing value to shoddy writing, were colluding with an attack on 'the world of letters which is quite unprecedented'.[30]

The implication that members of the majority cannot be 'sensitive' is misguided and unpleasant, but it is important to acknowledge that mine and other readership studies owe a huge amount to Q.D. Leavis. Leavis actually read the novels she anathematised: bestselling novels such as Warwick Deeping's *Sorrell and Son* (1925) and Gilbert Frankau's *Gerald Cranston's Lady* (1923), for example. She examined information from many sources that would help her understand how 'the herd' was reading: responses to competitions in the *Sunday Dispatch* newspaper, the *Cambridge Daily News* in 1930 which prompted readers to share their literary tastes, marketing from the Book-of-the-Month Club and sales figures of various sorts, and a range of contemporary writing. She set her 1930s study in a historical context of popular reading in the preceding centuries. Her intellectual energy and passionate engagement with her theme are never in doubt. She is never dull. Though she may not have respected the readers of popular fiction, she afforded them her full attention. What she never did was to address, interrogate or listen to such readers.

Telling the story

The principal aim of the initial 'Reading Sheffield' project was clear: to record how two generations of Sheffield readers described the way in which they became habitual readers. It is important to acknowledge what the project was not. It was not setting out to construct a definitive map of what was read by a particular class, in a particular kind of city at a particular moment in history. My study does indeed examine how an individual's reading tastes were the product of societal circumstances. Each narrative is understood in the context of historical sources of many kinds, but my chief interest has been in how these stories have been told. I hope future researchers in all sorts of fields might find the nature of this project useful.[31]

---

30 Q.D. Leavis, *Fiction and the Reading Public*, London: Bellew, 1990 [1932], 67.

31 I value two American studies of reading in a specific time and place: Frank Felsenstein and James J. Connolly's *What Middletown Read: Print Culture in an American Small City*, Amherst, MA: University of Massachussetts Press, 2015; and Christine Pawley's *Reading Places: Literacy, Democracy, and the Public Library in*

At the beginning of our interviews, we elicited factual information about our readers' backgrounds and then helped them recall the contexts of the different stages of their reading development. These developmental stages shaped the structure of each interview and the structure of this book. The interview prompts (to be found in Appendix 1) were tools to aid narration. We were prepared to abandon a prompt if it caused confusion or distress, as could happen, and to stay with an approach that a reader found comfortable or exciting.

Less useful than the series of prompts were lists of authors that readers might be familiar with. We had prepared these lists as an aid to recollection, but they often closed down the process of self-reflection. They could trigger a reader's anxiety that he or she was lacking in some way. Mary Robertson, pulled out of school at 14 to attend to the needs of her family, was shown our list of 'Classics': 'Nope, I never read Jane Austen or the Brontës. I should have done.' Or if, in scanning our list of bestselling authors of the 1930s and 1940s, a reader 'confessed' that she had not heard of Mary Webb or Hugh Walpole, for example, she could feel she had failed some sort of test and fall silent. The list could also trigger an acceleration in pace, setting interviewer and interviewee on a rapid gallop through all the authors listed and interrupting the unfolding narrative of discovery. When we realised that our list could cause our readers to lose control of their own narrative and suppress their individual voice, we came to use it sparingly. Above all, we sought to enable our readers to map their own reading journeys in terms, and in a sequence, with which they felt at ease.

Though common patterns of influence emerged during the course of the project, it was difficult to resist the delight in what was least expected. Alongside the appetite for pleasures desired for their very predictability (Angela Brazil, Edgar Rice Burroughs and then Enid Blyton, for example), there were many reading choices that appeared to be acts of pure serendipity. Such literary encounters were, perhaps, the most unpredictable pleasures experienced in our readers' day-to-day lives.

Cold War America, Amherst, MA: University of Massachussetts Press, 2010. The nature of the evidence collected by both studies differed from the Sheffield oral history data but, in different ways, we are all seeking to reflect the experience of the general reader in a particular social context. When we shared the 'Reading Sheffield' project with academic groups, the Society of the History of Reading and Publishing, Roehampton University's Centre for Book History and the Oral History Society for example, we did not hear of comparable projects in Britain or in other English-speaking countries.

And these moments of revelation had been rarely shared. The eloquence of many of our readers and the pleasure they seemed to experience as they recounted their reading histories derives in part from the privacy of their reading experiences. It is difficult for those of us who have read for a living or who have grown up in the age of the reading group to appreciate that for the greater number of our readers, whatever their social class, reading was a private pleasure: sometimes even concealed from others, certainly rarely discussed at home, school or work. This means that the men and women we interviewed had had few opportunities to rehearse or mythologise their lives as readers. They often took time to respond to a prompt or question. With one exception, we listened to narratives which were in the making, not made earlier. Nearly every speaker had their own repeated phrases that signalled that their account was, in some ways, tentative: Frank's 'funnily enough', Winnie's 'I think so', Peter Mason's 'It's just my opinion', Wynne's 'it might have been', Erica's 'I don't remember but ...' and many more.

It is interesting to compare the self-presentation of our readers with the kind of personal myth-making examined in Raphael Samuel and Paul Thompson's *The Myths We Live By* (1990).[32] Many of the narrators of the autobiographies described in that book were placing themselves in relation to a past that was difficult, dangerous and public. Migrants recounting a past that enabled them to live with dignity in a community with no recognition of the cultures from which they had been displaced, or political activists seeking to reconcile themselves to their part in the failure of the revolution on which they had set their hopes, were under enormous pressure to mythologise their pasts. Much less was at stake for our readers in the telling of their lives. Most of them had never expected their reading to be chronicled. Our readers were not seeking to locate their lives in history. This does perhaps make their narratives a more reliable reflection of their lives than are the narratives of those who know that their stories will be exposed to possibly hostile scrutiny.

Though every oral history is shaped by pressures to conceal, elaborate or possibly to invent, by contrast with the narrators discussed by Samuel and Thompson, our readers gave us a sense of a story unfolding rather than one being handed over. This sense of process, of a story in the making rather than ready-made, was enhanced by the reading backgrounds of the team of twelve interviewers. All but two were the first in their

32 Raphael Samuel and Paul Thompson, *The Myths We Live By*, London: Routledge, 1990.

family to have been able to access higher education. That access had in large part been gained because they were confident, independent and habitual readers. A shared sense of the personal significance of acquiring a reading habit frequently contributed a sense of collaborative dialogue during the interviews.

The subject matter of our project, as much as the way it was conducted, contributes to the huge range of ways in which our readers told their stories and the props they used to illustrate them. We were attending to aspects of their lives that they had rarely talked about. If, for example, we had been exploring with them their experiences of the Second World War, it would have been difficult to escape the individual myth and how it played into a shared national myth, because so much has been asked, shared and written about the interplay between individual and collective memory in relation to that event. What is perhaps most unusual about our project is that it was about private pleasure, and it gave pleasure to all who participated in it, as our readers' engagement with our annual gatherings testifies.

Though many of you will read this in digital form, at every stage of the project the power of the book as a physical object was demonstrated. We are often invited to share our project with community groups, which we do with the aid of physical copies of the books our interviewees read and loved. A copy of the 1937 *Girls' Crystal Annual*, the cover of *Anne of Green Gables* or an illustration from *Just William* have the power to trigger memories so strong that years of silence can be broken. We are frequently told that group members have spoken for the first time in a meeting as they lay their hands on a copy of a book whose physical familiarity plunges them back into the past. The physical copy evokes the place in which the book was read, the feeling and thoughts it excited, the people who gave, lent or read it aloud and the people with whom it was shared. Its power derives from a sense of permanence; the object that might now have vanished did, at one time, seem all one's own and is now lodged forever in the mind.

The next seven chapters are based on the different stages of development in the reading lives of the men and women we interviewed, each stage being dealt with in turn. The final two sections of the book are different. Chapter 8, '*Anna Karenina*, you know, and all the normal sort of things', spans the first three or so decades of our readers' lives and asks how authors now regarded as in some way canonical came into their hands, if indeed they did. As 1930s readers, did they read 'thirties' authors? Did they have a sense of what was a classic and what was not? The patterns revealed would soon begin to change as, from the 1950s onwards, a more extensive radio service, a developing television service, wider educational opportunities and greater affluence increasingly influenced the way reading choices were made.

In my final section, three of our readers, Mavis, John D and Malcolm Mercer, have 'The Last Word'. I never discussed with interviewees my own reading background or underlying research questions but, occasionally, my personal interests and perspectives were directly addressed. I am grateful to all three of these readers for deepening my understanding of why I asked the questions I did.

CHAPTER ONE

At Home with Books

Mary Robertson, born in 1923, was one of the few of our readers whose family could afford a holiday in Bridlington. Not only did her older sister take her paddling, she also read to her from the books on the family shelves. Her father was an industrial chemist with the renowned steel firm of Vickers Armstrong, a leading Sheffield employer in the 1930s. The family lived on the smoke-free hills on the western side of the city.

> On Sunday we always had the roast lunch, Sunday lunch time, and the fire would be [pause] and we always read after Sunday lunch. We had lots of armchairs and that is where we always read. Mother, my sister and I, I don't think my brother did.[1]

1 Mary Robertson, born 1923, interviewed by Susan Roe, 7 March 2013.

A story with no beginning

I remember one book. I can see the front cover: it had a little girl on it. At the end a fairy had three wishes and she had to choose one. One was a purse that always had another penny in it, one was a book that when you got to the end always had another page to read – I can't remember the third wish. I always chose the book that never ended.

Joan Challenger[2]

When our readers were asked to recall the very first books they had read to them, they were often ill at ease, wanting to be accurate but unable to recall what those first books might have been or whether indeed they were ever read to. None of our readers could share the opening chapter of their reading story. Together we tried to tease out the probable pattern of their first encounters with books. As our readers retrieved memories of their first books, they also called to mind the friends and family members who put those books into their hands, and, if they were lucky, read to them. The process of retrieval was coloured by the feelings aroused by those adults and by the physical nature of the books themselves.

Those of our readers who came from families without the means to buy infant books were the most emphatic in their conviction that they were never read to as infants. Mary Brothers, the daughter of a miner, was born in 1923. She declared that nobody read to her when she was young: 'I don't think it was something people did back then. There were so many jobs to do around the house. My mum took in washing.'[3] Dorothy H, born in 1929 and the daughter of a butcher, was also sure that she was never read to: her mother 'hadn't got time. There were eight of us.' She reflected on that endless sequence of pregnancies: 'They went in for it in those days, didn't they?'[4]

It was obvious to Mary and Dorothy that they could not have been read to: no parental time and no books to hand. Our readers from homes where they might have been read to were more puzzled and uncertain: 'they must have read to me' and 'they probably read to me' was a recurring refrain. Though Maureen L cannot remember being

2 Joan Challenger, born 1941, interviewed by Jan Chatterton, 9 March 2012 (summary only).

3 Mary Brothers, born 1923, interviewed by Ruth Owen, 21 March 2013 (summary only).

4 Dorothy H, born 1929, interviewed by Susan Roe, 7 May 2013.

read to she has been handed down a story that demonstrates that she was.

> They must have done, because my mum used to tell me I always cried when she read Little Bo Peep, so she stopped reading it. I think I had it on a handkerchief and she threw it away because I got upset about these sheep being lost! So, they must have done.[5]

Experiences before the age of three and a half are irretrievable for most of us. Yet events from these earlier years can be rescued from what psychologists call 'childhood amnesia' in all sorts of ways. Material objects, books for example, can come to enshrine what 'must have been', unless, like the Little Bo Peep handkerchief, these objects have been thrown away or handed on. By telling and retelling the story of her daughter's sorrow Maureen's mother created the illusion of memory, the image of the handkerchief reinforcing its reliability. Maureen's vivid recollection of her mother's story, not the object itself nor the experience of being read to, illustrates the power of what has been called 'the maternal narrative', the version of a child's past that is relayed by others and then becomes the stuff of imagined memories.[6]

Any parent can be this narrator, a guardian of family legend, a legend that acquires force if there are props to back it up with: a handkerchief, a photograph or a book. The attempt to retrieve a memory of being read to often woke a sense of loss. Some readers found it difficult to revisit a childhood where the absence of books was so clearly linked to the absence of parental time and attention. Parents from working-class families in the 1930s, 1940s and 1940s rarely had the time to share any activity that was purely recreational or private. The physical labour of earning a living and providing warmth and food for a family meant that the time that needs to be invested in reading any book to an infant was in short supply. Few of the men and women we interviewed had been read to as children.

Hazel B, who like Mary and Dorothy was born in the 1920s, was destitute as an infant. Her father died in 1931, when she was two years old. She struggled in response to the question, 'So there was no money for books?' because it led her straight back to desperate times. 'I don't

---

5 Maureen L, born 1941, interviewed by Mary Grover, 30 April 2012.
6 Qi Wang and Sami Gülgöz, 'New Perspectives on Childhood Memory', Special issue, *Memory*, 27.1 (2019), 1–5; and P.J. Bauer, *Remembering the Times of Our Lives: Memory in Infancy and Beyond*, Mahwah, NJ: Laurence Erlbaum Associates, 2007.

know what we'd do without me grandma. There were no books, no, no money for anything ... food either.' Somehow an elder sister found some reading matter to share with her younger sister: 'I think she'd read to me and I think I would be asleep before she knew. You know, it were like a sleeping tablet. She were kind to us.'[7]

Even if a family had the means to buy books for children, they would have struggled to find them; few were published. It was not until the production of the Little Golden Wonder Books in 1942 that a plentiful supply of affordable picture books began to be available. Interwar children's books were often marketed on the high quality of their illustrations, which were costly to produce. Beatrix Potter's ever-popular tales sold for 1/6. They were only ever mentioned by middle-income families who possessed rather than borrowed them.

Where were the libraries?

When we first started interviewing, we assumed that families with few or no children's books of their own must have found some in the junior sections of the city libraries. 'A Survey of Children's Reading' published by Sheffield City Libraries in 1938 demonstrates why this was not so.[8] The survey looked at the reading of children aged seven and upwards. It is clear that Sheffield Libraries' focus was on the needs of children who had become independent readers and not on providing early readers or picture books that might prepare children to become readers. For the last fifty years the parents of young children in Sheffield have enjoyed the opportunity of spending a weekday hour with their young child alongside the library's boxes, dipping in and out of lavishly produced picture books. This was not an experience any of our readers could possibly have shared. 'For administrative reasons', junior libraries and sections were only open when schools were closed.[9]

So, unless young children had books in the home in the first half of the twentieth century, they were unlikely to enter school with any kind of familiarity with books. The only memory of a young child borrowing 'picture books' from the library is from James Green, born in 1936, so this is a wartime memory. Somehow Attercliffe Library, without a separate

---

7 Hazel, born 1929, interviewed by Mary Grover, 9 May 2012.

8 Sheffield City Libraries, 'A Survey into Children's Reading', 1938, Local Pamphlets Collection 47 042 SST.

9 'A Survey into Children's Reading', 4.

children's library and in the heart of an area that was flattened during James's early childhood, provided some early reading material.

> I remember vividly going with my mum and dad to local library, and coming back with picture books... And even though I couldn't really read at that stage, we used to sit on a Saturday night, in particular when my dad was at home – they'd be reading books and I'd be pretending to be reading.[10]

James's memory is not of being guided through the books but of using them to mimic an adult occupation that was obviously valued by his parents. The vividness of that memory is not of a particular book but of the closeness of the family, which nurtured in the boy a sense that the activity was associated with pleasure, warmth and companionship. Our readers share few such memories. Most parents would not have been read to themselves, and in the 1930s, 1940s and 1950s lacked the books and the time to foster a love of reading in their children.

Special books

Even in otherwise bookless homes, there was often a single, treasured volume: unread but revered. Handed down through generations, its entry into the home often a mystery, an unread book could become unobtrusive evidence that the family was dignified by a history. Such books were dug out for our benefit, rare survivals from a family past that was otherwise unrecorded. Ted, an engineer and son of a plumber, felt we might be interested in a volume inherited from his family, 'a reading book, a story' printed in 1750, but we never saw it – it was buried too deep and Ted was unable to move far enough to dig it out. He remembered its date but not its title. All his life he had preserved the book as an object but was dismissive about its content. He only had time for books with a 'subject', books he 'could learn from'.[11] Art books came into that category.

Elsie Brownlee, unlike Ted, was able to produce, and produce with pride, the family heirloom, *A Compilation of Journals*, dated 1849. Beautifully leatherbound and containing 'A Ladies' Cabinet of Fashion, Music and Romances', it had belonged to her aunt, an unmarried dressmaker who gave it to Elsie's mother. Elsie had other books which she read and reread, but the contents of this volume were unfamiliar to

10 James Green, born 1936, interviewed by Jean Gilmour, 12 October 2011.
11 Ted, born 1919, interviewed by Mary Grover, 19 February 2013.

her. It was treasured because of its genealogy and its potential financial value.[12] Though the content of these heirlooms may have been of no personal interest to Elsie and Ted, the books as objects were of personal value. They were to be preserved respectfully, perhaps in a cupboard or drawer, but not necessarily presented in public. Though it might be hoped that the exotic quality of such a book might make it saleable, it was clear that its chief function was as a private and perhaps the only marker of a family's heritage.

The books that were a presence in Jean's childhood home belonged to her father and were kept on a small oak book-rest. Jean A was born in 1930 when the economic depression that forced many small steel firms out of business caused her father to leave the long-established family firm and move to the agricultural plains of Lincolnshire. There he spent four years trying to make a living as a farmer. He failed, as had the ancestors of so many of Sheffield's miners and steelworkers. Throughout the eighteenth and nineteenth centuries men had abandoned farm work in Sheffield's neighbouring countryside to seek what seemed less precarious employment in the city's foundries and mines. The series of books treasured by Jean's father were A.G. Street's semi-fictionalised accounts of the author's struggles to make farming pay in the 1930s, when many city dwellers were moving back to the rural areas populated by their ancestors. Street's descriptions of the harshness of rural life found a wide readership among the men and women who, across Britain, dreamed that a small farm might somehow be a refuge from the economic forces that were destroying the livelihoods of those in manufacturing and office work. The presence of the books on the oak book-rest was witness both to Jean's father's affluent past and his insecure present.

> We used to come up to Sheffield 'cos this was my father's home town. Used to come up to Sheffield to see his father and all my aunts, and they read to me. They were maiden aunts so they had the time to read to me. I think my father read to me more ... after we left the farm.[13]

Jean's aunts were probably the source of the Milly-Molly-Mandy stories that were favourites for her and for many readers born in the 1930s, 1940s and later decades. These simple but delightful stories were written and illustrated by Elizabeth Lankester Brisley and set in the Sussex countryside where she lived. The author and journalist Lucy Mangan,

12 Elsie Brownlee, born 1925, interviewed by Mary Grover, 21 February 2013.
13 Jean A, born 1930, interviewed by Loveday Herridge, 22 April 2013.

born in 1974, describes her delight in them: 'crafted by a mind that understood the importance and the comfort of detail to young readers without ever letting it overwhelm the story'.[14] Milly-Molly-Mandy's thatched cottage was in sharp contrast to the grim reality of the Lincolnshire farm on which Jean was growing up.

A book never offered to Jean as a child was her father's copy of *The Secret Garden*: '1911 it's got in it. He was given it by one of the maiden aunts. I read it to my children. I always loved that book. I can reread that.' Though Jean saw *The Secret Garden* on display as a child and it was written for children, she didn't in fact read it until she was 19. Before then it stood unopened on the little oak book-rest, valued not as a source of pleasure but as an heirloom, its existence commemorating times when the family firm of Samuel Peace and son, founded in 1850, was a cutlery manufacturer employing hundreds of skilled workers.

'Sue' was the heir of a manufacturer whose fortunes were more stable. Born in 1924, she showed me, when she was 97, a book she had possessed as a child and that had been in the family since 1828: *Dame Wiggins from Lee and her Five Wonderful Cats*. This comic poem whose title page declares that it is written 'principally by a lady of ninety' is about the benevolent Dame Wiggins (who has a nose like Mr Punch) and her resourceful cats. It was first published in 1823 and was actively treasured by members of Sue's family throughout the nineteenth and twentieth centuries. The sequence of inscriptions, much like the inscriptions in a family Bible, demonstrates the value set on books by succeeding generations of this manufacturing family. Sue had tried to interest her great-grandchild in its lively verse and cartoon-like illustrations, but matter-of-factly concluded that its appeal seems now to have disappeared. Its failure to please the next generation in no way diminished her own delight in the pleasure it still gives her.[15]

Another inheritance of great value to its owner is Betty Newman's copy of *A Peep Behind the Scenes* by Mrs Walton, published by the Religious Tract Society in 1877. Betty was born in the mid-1930s. Her father was an administrator, working in the offices of a transport company. It does not seem to have been a particularly bookish home, but Betty owed her early literacy to this book which her grandmother had won as a Sunday School prize in the late nineteenth century. Betty

14 Lucy Mangan, *Bookworm: A Memoir of Childhood Reading*, London: Square Peg, 2018, 81.
15 'Sue' in conversation with Mary Grover, 6 September 2021.

longed to be able to read and this text would be her primer. She read and reread it, arriving at elementary school a fluent reader. *A Peep Behind the Scenes* was witness to her resourcefulness, so when the original copy disappeared after her grandmother's death, she purchased a replacement. As Betty looked down at her present copy of this Victorian tale of the grim reality of the life of an orphaned girl in a travelling theatre troupe and her unlikely rescue by a long-lost relative, she reflected, 'I'm quite amazed but it's true that I could read that before I went to school. That was the first book I ever read.'[16] Betty treasured it not in affectionate memory of a personal relationship with her grandmother, not as witness to a family reading culture and not as an heirloom. Her reacquisition of the volume is a tribute to her own unlikely achievement of learning to read before she got to school. She could not afford to overlook any text that would enable her to learn.

Florence, born in 1923, showed us a special book that she read as a child: *Little Folks*, a compendium of poems and stories that had been her grandmother's. Like Betty's ancient volume mentioned above, this nineteenth-century book played an active part in Florence's development as a reader, but in this case her family fostered her reading. Unlike the heirloom that was positioned as off-limits for a child, either wrapped and placed in a cupboard for safekeeping or set out on display, *Little Folks* was shared with Florence. Her grandfather in Huddersfield and her aunt had both been teachers. Her grandfather opened an account for her at a Sheffield bookshop in the 1930s so that when she went to grammar school in 1934 she was always able to afford her school books. She had many books by her side when she was interviewed, but *Little Folks* was the treasure, as much part of her grandmother's childhood as it had been of hers. It was full of

> school stories, adventure stories, little poems, letters from children who were stationed in India, letters to the editor, you know. It was quite interesting… I was always passionate about reading. In fact, if I was ever naughty and I was sent to my room, my mother always made sure I hadn't got a book because she knew it was no punishment if I had a book.[17]

Florence was sent to a little private school. Her father was 'an engineer in the motor-trade', with relatives who contributed to the costs of her grammar school and commercial college. They endowed her with books

16 Betty Newman, born 1935, interviewed by Ros Witten, 13 October 2011.
17 Florence, born 1923, interviewed by Susan Roe, 24 November 2011.

that they had read and loved and that she in her turn made her own. As she grew older, she would pick up the books her mother had read in childhood: '*Little Women* and *Good Wives*, yes. That was my mother's book. I haven't got it now because I lent it to someone and they never gave it back.'

The book that has been lost or disappeared imprints itself in the memory because of a sense of absence. John Y, born to a highly literate family in 1929, had a whole case full of books of his own.

But all I can ever remember in those books, I must admit, there was a set of war encyclopaedias... I always remember these *War Illustrated* and I don't know what happened to them, but I wish we'd still got them.[18]

Sunday School prizes

Many of the single volumes handed down through the generations were Sunday School prizes. During the nineteenth century religious tracts became a cheap and plentiful source of text, poured into industrial cities by organisations such as the Religious Tract Society, the British and Foreign Bible Society, the Society for Promoting Christian Knowledge and the Sunday School Union, all of which had depots in Sheffield.[19] From the eighteenth century onwards, nonconformist chapels across Britain had sought to promote Christianity and literacy by forming Sunday Schools. However, some men of influence, including various Anglican clerics, feared that the newly literate members of the working class might not confine their reading to the Bible. In 1800 the Bishop of Rochester denounced Methodist Sunday Schools, in particular, as 'Schools of Atheism and Disloyalty'.[20] The years between 1870 and 1900 are usually held to be the zenith of the Sunday School movement, across all denominations. This is the period during which nearly all the prizes we were shown were awarded. Nearly all were fiction. The stories, usually

18 John Y, born 1929.
19 Malcolm Mercer, *Schooling the Poorer Child: Elementary Education in Sheffield 1560–1902*, Sheffield: Sheffield Academic Press, 1996, 91. This history is invaluable. Malcolm was one of our interviewees and was head teacher at Parson Cross primary school in Sheffield, 1968–83.
20 The Bishop of Rochester, 'The Charge of Samuel Lord Bishop of Rochester to the Clergy of his Diocese, delivered at his second General Visitation in the Year 1800', quoted in a critical response to his attitudes by a reviewer in *The Monthly Review*, September 1801, 32–3.

relentlessly uplifting and melodramatic, were rooted in lives as precarious as those of many of the children who were given them.

Winnie Lincoln, born in 1923, ten years earlier than Betty and from a poorer background, still keeps, among the collection of serious history books that are her current reading, her mother's prizes from the 'Salvation Army Slum Corps' [Infirmary Rd]: 'Mum's *The Thorny Path* and *Jessica's First Prayer*', both by Hesba Stretton. These prized possessions, like Betty's *A Peep Behind the Scenes*, reflect the influence that nineteenth-century religious societies had on the reading of families who would otherwise have never possessed books at all. Hesba Stretton was the pen name of the bestselling author Sarah Smith (1832–1911). Her role in helping found the National Society for the Prevention of Cruelty to Children and her work in the Popular Book Club for working-class readers in Richmond-on-Thames are testimony to her practical engagement with the children whose vulnerability she dramatises.

Books such as the hugely popular *Jessica's First Prayer* (1866)[21] cannot be dismissed as mere sentimental and pious melodrama. They were rare reflections of the lives of children such as Winnie's mother, who found, at the end of the nineteenth century, what literary nurture there was available in the rooms of the 'Slums Corps' and within the covers of her Sunday School prize. Three of the books awarded to Winnie's mother, Hannah Stacey, have been preserved by Winnie and her daughter Kathryn. Alongside the two novels by Hesba Stretton are a copy of the King James Bible, presented 'for B.O.L. Attendance at Salvation Army, May 31st, 1898'. Hannah's good character was also recognised by the Sheffield School Board in 1899. For 'punctual attendance', she was rewarded with a copy of William James Rolfe's *Shakespeare the Boy: With Sketches of the Home and School Life, the Games and Sports, the Manners, Customs and Folk-lore of the Time* (1897).[22]

Though the Sunday School prizes treasured by our readers were inheritances from the nineteenth century or early twentieth century, we discovered a slightly different pattern of ownership in the small industrial town of Stocksbridge to the north of Sheffield. With its own

---

21 Sarah Smith's obituary notes that *Jessica's First Prayer* sold one and half million copies worldwide: 'Hesba Stretton', *The Times*, 10 October 1911. It was translated into nearly every European language, contributed to the growth of 'street Arab literature' and inspired social reform. See Brian Alderson, 'Tracts, Rewards and Fairies: The Victorian Contribution to Children's Literature', in *Essays in the History of Publishing*, ed. Asa Briggs, London: Longman, 1974, 245–82.

22 Winnie Lincoln, born 1923, interviewed by Mary Grover, 8 May 2013.

enormous steelworks ('Sammy Fox's') in the steep-sided valley of the Little Don, the population of Stocksbridge had a higher concentration of nonconformist chapels than its mighty neighbour five miles down the valley. The pattern of the main street in the 1940s was described to us as 'pub, chapel, pub, chapel' right along two miles.[23] The Bible featured frequently in the memory of Stocksbridge residents, and the Sunday School prizes they described were their own, not their parents' or grandparents', for example *Lorna Doone*, won for 'Endeavour'. These Sunday School libraries and small commercial libraries had to serve the community's needs until the opening of Stocksbridge Municipal Library in the 1960s.

'We had books in the house! We had books in the house. We had a bookcase!'[24]

Alma, who began her interview by suggesting that she was not read to because '[w]e were a working class family and my father was an engine driver', almost shouted with delight as, later in the course of her recollection, the image of her parents' bookcase suddenly presented itself to her, its significance in her 1930s childhood home inspiring a sense of pride and celebration.

Special places for books not only enshrined a family's reading culture, but their images could frame a memory of a particular book or a particular kind of book, the visual memory of the bookcase unlocking a flood of further memories of its contents. Though Adele was, as we have heard, discouraged by her father from reading, there were, in fact, books in the home, not on display, and many of them his.

> Well, there was a set of Wonderland of Knowledge books which we used to get down and look at those, I can remember looking at those. There was a bound copy of Shakespeare's plays which I remember had sort of vellum covers, we looked at that. A book I did love, it was called *A Century of Humour*[25] and that was full of short stories, short humorous stories, I remember reading that, I do remember that. Dad had a lot of political

---

23 Quoted in 'A Short Story of Readers in Stocksbridge', a pamphlet prepared for the members of 'The Venue' at Stocksbridge following a visit by Susan Roe and Mary Grover in May 2019.

24 Alma, born 1928, interviewed by Liz Hawkins, 8 November 2011.

25 Possibly *A Century of Humour* (1934), edited by P.G. Wodehouse. Adele would have probably read it after she started in school in the late 1930s.

books they were all bound with brown paper they were... We didn't touch his books. [laughs][26]

Just as recall of text can be prompted by physical memories of where a passage is upon a page, so the title and appearance of a book was often imprinted on the memory because of the furniture that housed it and the location of that furniture. Some books were memorable because of their absence from public view; the mysterious brown wrappers of the political books belonging to Adele's father signalled the potency of the texts withheld.

From a family of modest means but economically secure, Shirley Ellins, born in 1936, grew up in a home where the small collection of books was differentiated by the types of furniture in which they were housed. Her father was one of the growing number of workers involved in civic administration in the mid to late 1930s. Shirley was an only child. She was unlike most of our interviewees in that her parents were keen that she should be educated to a high level, and could see from their own experience that high reading skills could be marketable. With her interviewer, Loveday, who in many ways shared her class background, Shirley mapped the physical provision for books in her family home: not just a single set of shelves but different kinds of bookcase for different kinds of books.

> S: There was a little bookshelf which stood on the floor. I can see it now in my mind's eye ... which had the books in from the library, largely taken up by my mother... A little bookcase, a little bookshelf on the floor. Just like that.
>
> L: Now that is a (I've got one exactly the same) – it's a little oak ...
>
> S: – wooden –
>
> L: – about 15 inches wide, and the books sort of lie back [S: yeah] in the cradle of the shelf, with the spines on the outside.[27]

Whereas Loveday's mother used the shelf to cradle precious box sets of novels by Jane Austen and the Brontës, revered and to be returned to, Shirley's mother used hers as a staging-post for books on the move, a few of Warwick Deeping's 68 novels, borrowed from the library, the recollection of which made Shirley laugh.[28] She didn't share her mother's

---

26 Adele, born 1942, interviewed by Liz Hawkins, 19 July 2012.
27 Shirley Ellins, born 1936, interviewed by Loveday Herridge, 22 November 2011.
28 Warwick Deeping was a bestselling author throughout the 1920s, 1930s and 1940s,

taste for these agonised fictions, nor for her favourite author, the more restrained O. Douglas (sister of the more widely known John Buchan).

Far less prolific than Deeping, O. Douglas's short and lightly fiction-alised sketches of life in the villages and small towns of the Scottish borders were published by Nelson in a form that invited cherishing; the editions would ornament any room. In the 1930s they were for sale at 3/–, just affordable for a family with a small amount of disposable income. They were pocket-sized and wrapped in jackets evoking the good taste and wholesome conduct of the women whose lives Douglas chronicled. Shirley didn't laugh at Douglas but never read the novels until her mother's death, when she had to dispose of them. The books had been kept in the bookcase in the 'other room', to be lovingly returned to by Shirley's mother, but not for everyday consumption.

Unlike children with no guidance, Shirley did not seem to engage with the tastes of an older generation; her own tastes were too well catered for. Whereas the cradle in Loveday's home displayed books that she might aspire to read, Shirley defined her tastes against the popular fiction lined up in the oak book-rest by her mother. She laughed affectionately when she recalled the titles her mother delighted in. The fact that she found her mother's taste for Warwick Deeping funny was a measure of the educational value her parents had put on her reading. As a child Shirley was taken to the junior sections of the city libraries and also had books bought for her, books that she could reread and treasure as her own. Her memories of childhood reading are bound up with books and shelves, objects associated with pleasure and intimacy. Their survival in her memory evokes the tenderness of Shirley's relationship with her mother.

> One of the very earliest memories I have, and certainly a really pleasant one, compared with some others that were less pleasant: I was sitting in my little chair, which was really a miniature adult chair, by her knee while she read

---

whose works were translated into 17 languages. His novel about single parenthood, *Sorrell and Son* (1935), resonated with many readers who had been orphaned. The daughter of a German who was the illegitimate son of a domestic servant remembers her father's reverential 'Das ist ein buch'. The critical establishment in Britain was less enthusiastic, and Deeping came to represent, among others, what Q.D. Leavis called the 'faux bon': an author valued by those who knew no better. See my discussion of the way his value was contested in *The Ordeal of Warwick Deeping: Middlebrow Authorship and Cultural Embarrassment*, Madison, NJ: Fairleigh Dickinson University Press, 2009.

The House at Pooh Corner, which I still love. And we laughed, both of us, so much and I was helpless and rolled on to the floor with laughter.

Novels were transient, to be borrowed from the library. Except for the O. Douglas collection, the books on her parents' bookshelves were to be reused: 'their tune books for the Methodist Church – they possessed their own tune books': Arthur Mee's *1000 Heroes* and her father's book, 'a biography, Southey's Life of Nelson'.[29] Shirley's parents shared a bookcase of three shelves that contained reference books and classics, which Shirley accessed at an age her parents judged appropriate. The only book from these shelves she remembers reading as a child was *The Water Babies*. Then, when she was old enough, Shirley must have been judged fit to lay her hands on the volume most treasured by her mother: 'the famous Shakespeare that mother won as a child when she was 14 from Crookesmoor School (for Progress) – complete works, actors and actresses. Which is my pride and joy.' This heirloom is still actively read. When Shirley spoke at one of the first 'Reading Sheffield' gatherings, she held it in her hand, her pride in it and in her mother's achievement evident. Her mother's narrative was part of her own and the book treasured both because of its content and because of what it demonstrated about the intelligence of Shirley's mother when she was 14 years old. She had won it years before a girl of her class could have gone on to receive the education that her daughter was to receive with the increase in grammar school places in the late 1940s. Given Shirley's association of fiction with a degree of frivolity it is perhaps not surprising that she became a history rather than a literature teacher.

David Flather, from a far more affluent family, was an ardent reader of popular fiction. His mother died when he was two, in 1933. His two successive stepmothers had little interest in him or his reading and his father was consumed by the demands of running a steel factory in volatile times. As he wandered through the empty rooms of his relatives' houses, David would come across whole bookshelves of clearly categorised books. His grandfather had a wall of Masonic books, as unappealing to the small boy as her mother's Warwick Deepings had

---

29 Arthur Mee's *1000 Heroes*, subtitled *Immortal Men and Women from Every Age and Every Land* (2 vols, 1935), presented profiles of men and women whose moral superiority and illustrious achievements would inspire the reader. Robert Southey's *Life of Nelson* (1813) was republished throughout the nineteenth and twentieth centuries. The Everyman edition (Dent, 1951) was readily available and affordable in the 1950s.

been to Shirley. Neither child, in spite of the value set on books by their families, recalls a shelf of children's books. David's path to becoming a reader was probably as solitary as many readers from bookless homes.

Rare survivors

Several of our readers, including Elsie Brownlee, kept adult books that had been significant to them as children, but she is the only one of two readers to have shown us children's books that she had owned and loved in her infancy. Elsie grew up in the 1930s in a home where reading was not highly prized. Her father was the company secretary of a small engineering works, with enough disposable income in the early 1930s to own or hire a motorbike and sidecar in which he took his family on holiday to Anglesey one summer. He also paid for the 5-year-old Elsie to attend 'Miss Brittain's' on Springvale Road, and at age 7 to move on 'to this school on Commonside run by Mrs Taylor'. She 'loathed' both schools. Mrs Taylor was constantly setting terrifying exams, and had nothing to do with Elsie's future love of reading.

Elsie's family lived in the modest but desirable smoke-free terraces on the western hills above the industrial valleys a couple of miles from the city centre. But Elsie's mother was given money neither for bus fares to the library nor for books from a bookshop. In fact, the library had been out of bounds until a lodger, training to be a nurse, dispelled the Brownlees' belief, shared by many other families, that library books were full of germs. Elsie remembers two books. She treasured a book given to her when she was six by an unmarried aunt and a widowed grandmother. *Tick, Tack and Tock* is inscribed by them both, 'Christmas 1931'. This book must have been expensive to buy. The 16 coloured illustrations in it are advertised on the front cover, an exceptional number for such a tiny book at that period. Elsie read it 'time and time again'. The only other book she can remember possessing was *Scrubby Bear's Adventures*; 'I think I had that in my stocking.'[30]

Scrubby Bear's charm was that he was continually getting the wrong end of the stick. As Elsie recalls the story her voice takes on the tones of an adult reading to a child. The intimacy she shared with her mother, before the dreadful day when she was walked to Miss Brittain's infant school, was commemorated by these two little books. These possessions gave Elsie an opportunity to reread, setting her on her path as a reader

30 Elsie Brownlee, born 1925, interviewed by Mary Grover, 21 February 2013.

despite what became a detestation of formal education. 'Oh, I hated school, I hated it, I really did.' It cannot have helped Elsie that her father took the view that girls were just going to get married, so the education which he paid for was 'a waste of time and effort'. Though privately educated, Elsie left school at 14, as did all our state-school-educated readers born in the 1920s except for those able to take up free places in a selective school on the basis of their scholarship examinations, taken at the age of 11.[31]

Aunts and grandparents

Most of the books owned by poorer families were not purchased by parents. A striking number of the many annuals and the few childhood books shown to us were inscribed by an aunt or grandmother. Though the principal wage-earners in nearly all our readers' families were men, for Jean A and for many other readers, the books they owned were often given to them by women, chiefly aunts. The generosity of these childless women, in terms of both money and time, was significant, particularly as men's wages and job security were badly hit by the Depression. Between 1922 and 1939, 47,000 people left Sheffield to escape the insecurities of a city so dependent on manufacturing, 5,700 people in 1933 alone.[32]

An educated aunt could transform a child's life. Alma's father was an engine driver. Alma, who was born in 1928, has no memory of books in the home or of being read to, but she was named after her 'lovely Aunty Alma' who valued reading. She bought her niece a copy of *Peter Pan*.

---

31 Although the Education Act of 1936 raised the school leaving age to 15, this was not implemented until 1948. Until then, state-educated children attended an elementary school. They could sit a scholarship examination at 11 to access funding which would enable them to attend one of the very few grammar schools in Sheffield or to gain a bursary for a selective private school such as Sheffield Girls' High School, attended by two of our interviewees in the 1940s. The Butler Education Act of 1944 required Local Education Authorities to create three categories of secondary school: grammar, secondary modern and technical. Children were allocated on the basis of the examination which came to be known as the '11-plus'.

32 Sidney Pollard, 'Labour', in *The History of the City of Sheffield 1843–1993, Volume 2: Society*, ed. Clyde Binfield, Roger Harper, David Hey, Richard Childs, David Martin and Geoffrey Tweedale, Sheffield: Sheffield Academic Press, 1993, 260–78.

[It] had a picture and tissue paper ... and I wanted to read it and I just read it! And I can remember loving that book because of the tissue paper pictures. So that was my very first book.

The love expressed by Alma's namesake translated into the child's love for the book, delight in the delicate tissue pages that protected the lavish illustrations bound up with her love for her aunt.

Julia Banks, born in 1931, a generation later than the readers introduced so far, was brought up in the 1940s by a single mother who kept her family on her wages as a corsetiere. 'My mum's sister always read to me as a bed time story – that sort of thing.' This was possibly Aunt Lil, the aunt who, when Julia passed her 11-plus after the Second World War, enabled her to get on with her history essays by buying her the set texts. 'I've still got Black's Elizabeth that she gave me that I used to queue for at school or use from the reference library.'[33]

Dorothy Latham, also born in 1931, was the daughter of a colliery electrician. Dorothy, like Julia, became a reader because of the nurturing of her female relatives in the early 1930s. Their encouragement of the child's reading had a soundtrack:

even my grandma, who lived in Tinsley. I mean I know it was a totally different education – but she'd been a teacher, my grandma, and ... my Aunty Mary was the same, a beautiful organist and my mother was very musical. So in a strange way I was brought up in a ordinary household but somehow I got the best.[34]

Though the families of our working-class readers had to 'count the coppers' of parental time, parental attention could also be in short supply in more affluent families. Peter Mason's father was a mining engineer. His parents did read to him, but it was his married aunt, trained as a teacher, who encouraged him to read:

My parents were rather dubious about my ability to spell correctly and read, and so my aunt, my Aunt Margaret, introduced me, believe it or not, at a very tender age, to crosswords, and from then onwards I had no trouble in spelling.[35]

He grew up an avid reader and, in his teens, also explored the romances that his Aunt Margaret passed his way: James Hilton's *Lost Horizon* and

33 J.B. Black, *The Reign of Elizabeth 1558–1603*, Oxford: Oxford University Press, 1936. Julia Banks, born 1939, interviewed by Liz Hawkins, 15 February 2012.
34 Dorothy Latham, born 1931, interviewed by Clare Keen, 17 October 2011.
35 Peter Mason, born 1929, interviewed by Susan Roe, 28 September 2011.

Random Harvest.[36] The boy then used his reading skills to read to Aunt Margaret's husband, who was blind.

If a grandparent lived in the home, which was often the case, they could play a role in reading to a child or in escorting them to the library. In the early 1950s the grandfather of Margaret H not only walked her to the library from her bookless home but took her to the cinema; there was one round every corner in the centre of Sheffield where her parents kept a pub. 'I can remember going two or three times a week because that was another way of getting out of the house. I loved the cinema and I still do.' Margaret remembers with pleasure, not children's films, but her grandad's favourites: cowboys and detectives.[37]

The power of a grandparent to remove a child to a space where imaginative exploration could take place is illustrated by Meg Young's memories of learning to read during the war.

> My granddad had an allotment down at Rivelin Valley where we used to escape to and it was nice and calm and peaceful, and he used to take me down there, and my brother, and even the seed packets – I learnt names of lettuces, radishes and the flowers, everything my granddad asked me to read.[38]

Judith, an infant during the Second World War, has no memory of her parents reading to her; she concludes that her mother would have been too busy. She would bathe her four children 'in this big tin tub one after the other. Poor mum, how she coped with four I do not know. It took all me time to cope with two, in a modern age!' Judith's grandmother, a difficult woman, arrived to live with them when Judith was three. 'It made it a bit crowded, but that's what happened in those days.' The older woman did impress on Judith the value of books. 'She was always on about books and that – she'd been well educated, grandmother.'[39]

In the early 1940s when James Green reached school age, he graduated from the picture books he had pretended to read in his parents' company to an omnibus given to him by someone he cannot remember, but most

---

36 Both novels are by James Hilton. His bestselling novel *Lost Horizon* came out in 1933. It was the first soft-cover book to be published by Pocket Books, in 1939. Frank Capra's film of the novel made spectacular use of its Tibetan setting. *Random Harvest* (1941), about memory loss caused by shell-shock, was also a bestseller and also made into a film.

37 Margaret H, born 1945, interviewed by Susan Roe and Mary Grover, 10 May 2018.

38 Meg Young, born 1936, interviewed by Mary Grover, 6 June 2013.

39 Judith G, born 1939, interviewed by Loveday Herridge, 14 February 2013.

probably a relative. In it were three books: *Robinson Crusoe*, *Little Women* and *Gulliver's Travels*. The stories were a bit beyond him but the volume is one he will never forget.

> It was my own book, probably the first book I'd really owned, you could go through it and you could go through it again, and so it was with me for quite a long time. And at that stage, I probably wasn't all that good at reading, so it'd take me a long time, and it was quite a hefty book.

Possession of that book gave him the precious opportunity to reread, each reading coloured by the shifting stages of his maturity.

Sometimes a friend took on the role of a relative and nurtured a child's reading. Dorothy Norbury struggled to read throughout her life but she always wanted to. She was born in 1933 and her parents ran a newsagent's.

> They were always very busy and they never did read to me. But I was a very poor reader. I had a girlfriend that lived next door and we were born four days between each other. We grew up like sisters and we used to have sleepovers, and one of my greatest joys was to lay in bed with her while she read to me.[40]

At the first of our annual gatherings of our interviewees in 2013 we invited Shirley Ellins to describe the rich reading life she had shared with her mother, their mutual absorption in the book in hand. When Shirley ended by raising, with love, the prize that her mother had bequeathed to her, the complete and illustrated plays of Shakespeare, Dorothy was visibly moved. She explained that Shirley's account had brought home her sorrow that the books she had craved all her life were never made her own, because she had recently discovered she was dyslexic, so the trick of deciphering them was never to be hers.

'Treasure troves of all sorts of wonderful things'

There was, of course, a minority of children growing up before and during the Second World War who, before they became independent readers, experienced the nurture of being read to and having accessible books around them. Frank Burgin and Norman Adsetts did not grow up in affluent families but, different though their family backgrounds were, they were both able to build up stashes of books which were all their own; both had a strong sense that their reading was valued.

40 Dorothy Norbury, born 1934, interviewed by Susan Roe, 22 September 2011.

As a child in the 1940s, Frank Burgin was made aware by his father, a Conservative-voting miner, of the precariousness of mining as a way of making a living. They were one of a few sets of parents to see reading as a way for their son to get on:

> Oh, I used to get all the time [from his father] – 'look, lad, you've got to have some book larnin else you'll get nowhere'. He didn't know what I'd got to learn – he knew that I'd got to be learning it from books.[41]

Even though Frank's mother was not educated beyond elementary level, she had seen, as a housemaid, that books furnished the houses of the wealthy and successful. Nationally, the chief source for female employment in the first decades of the twentieth century was domestic service, in which 32 per cent of Sheffield women were employed in 1918.[42] Mary Walton, historian and librarian, was 'surprised' to note how many of the users of Sheffield's first public library, opened in 1856, were servant girls.[43] Frank's mother and Jessie Robinson, a 'tweenie' in a vicarage to the east of Sheffield, confirm the link between domestic service and an awareness of the value of books; however, as the historian Tania McIntosh points out, 'this opening was smaller in Sheffield than in some other cities due to the relative paucity of the servant employing class'.[44]

Both of Frank's parents associated reading with economic success and read to him. From the age of three Frank can remember being given books for Christmas. 'I always saw books as an absolute treasure trove of all sorts of wonderful things.' Both his parents had papers and

---

41 Frank Burgin, born 1938, interviewed by Loveday Herridge, 21 August 2012.
42 Sylvia Dunkley, in conversation with Mary Grover, 28 May 2020. 'At the end of the First World War the benefit system was skewed to get women back into domestic service but a lot liked it because they had their own bedroom.'
43 Mary Walton, *A History of the Parish of Sharrow*, Sheffield, 1968, 38, n. 10.
44 Tania McIntosh, '"A Price Must Be Paid For Motherhood": The Experience of Maternity in Sheffield, 1879–1939', PhD thesis, Department of History, University of Sheffield, 1997, 49. McIntosh does not make an exact comparison of Sheffield numbers in domestic service with other cities, but Sidney Pollard's analysis of Sheffield's class distribution bears out her suggestion that in Sheffield the proportion of working-class to professional or managerial class contrasted significantly with the national average. It was a pattern that persisted. In his chapter entitled 'Labour' in *The History of the City of Sheffield*, Pollard points out that the 1951 census for Sheffield reveals a 'severe shortfall' of people in Classes I and II (14.2 per cent) as opposed to the national average of 17.8 per cent. This class distribution makes it unsurprising that domestic service was less available to Sheffield women than to women elsewhere.

magazines delivered to the house, including *Woman's Weekly* and the *Daily Mail*. Frank is unusual in being so certain that he was read to and having the value of books so explicitly imprinted on him. He benefited, as did many of our readers, from having no brothers and sisters to share resources. Roughly a third of our readers were either only children or felt as though they were, because separated by a large age gap from much older or younger siblings.

The confidence Frank has in his recollection of being read to by both his parents owes a great deal to the narrative constructed by his parents about his development as a child, and the connection they made between his reading and his future employment. Families who have managed to acquire and then retain shelves full of children's books have built a timeline of stepping stones across the period of childhood oblivion. These memories are lost if a child has been brought up without physical markers of the past or without adults with the time or inclination to revisit, retell or recreate that past. Since he was an only child, Frank's family had not only enough money for books and comics, but also the time to read and talk to him, to help him recall early childhood experiences and point him forward into a future for which reading might prepare him. In fact, Frank left school at 14 to become an engineering apprentice, but it was perhaps the sense that 'book learning' was valuable that contributed to his steady exploration of education throughout his life. He was the only one of our readers to have gained a doctorate.

Homes with books

As you would expect, affluent homes had more books. Affluent parents did not, however, necessarily support or encourage their children's reading. Erica, born in 1937, came from a family that was well off, but her access to books was restricted by her father, despite, or perhaps because of, his intellectual interests. The owner of a factory dealing in pearl goods, Erica's father had been to Cambridge. He was an admirer of the alternative educational ideals of Rudolf Steiner associated with anthroposophy.[45] The progressive primary school in Derbyshire that he

---

45 Anthroposophism had a strong influence on educationalists in Europe between the two world wars, including, as we will see, in Sheffield. A humanist spirituality developed by Rudolf Steiner (1861–1925), it had its roots in German mysticism and Theosophy. Steiner emphasised the importance of developing the ways a child apprehended the world through the senses before introducing the more abstract

chose for his children was not influenced by anthroposophy, but similarly focused on connecting sensory and intellectual development. Erica was sent a PNEU (Parents' National Educational Union) school, inspired by the teachings of Charlotte Mason, who believed that children shouldn't read until they had learned to respond to the environment through all their senses.[46] So, like poorer children, Erica did not encounter children's books in her infancy. Like Irene, whose collection of annuals are still precious to her, Erica treasures the book she could first call her own, a book of folk stories called *Granny's Wonderful Chair*, given to her by a maid who had come from Northumberland. 'I've got the copy because she gave it to me, and that ... which sounds ridiculous, [is] the first book that I read.'[47]

David Flather's father owned a much more extensive manufacturing business than Erica's, but neither child was surrounded by picture books or early readers. We will never know whether the orphaned two-year-old was read to by a maid or nurse when his mother died. His stepmothers took little interest in him. David was heir to both intellectual and manufacturing dynasties in Sheffield, but despite that, and the presence of shelves of books in the homes of all the relatives who cared for him, his only memory of reading with a parent is of standing at the knee of his father while both pored over the cricket pages of *The Times*. This was probably during his holidays from the prep school to which he was sent at the age of four. David was invited to join the adult world of print, but no one seems to have suggested that he could explore books that were all his own.

Doreen Gill was also orphaned and found herself with a step-parent uninterested in her or her reading tastes. 'If I picked a book up to read, she'd say, "Put that down and come and help me do so-and-so. You're wasting your time and my time." You know. So she'd always find me a job to do.'[48] For both stepchildren, reading was a way of escaping the control of an adult uninterested in their development or the value of their internal life.

---

medium of print. Engagement with natural science and with spirituality should lead to an increase in self-knowledge, hence the term 'anthroposophy'.

46 Charlotte Mason (1842–1923) was the founder of the PNEU movement, still highly influential in the home-schooling movement. Her works can be read online. *Parents and Children* (1897) contains the stirring line: 'It's up to you, parents of small children, to be the saviours of the next thousand generations of children.' https://amblesideonline.org/CMM/M2complete.html.

47 Erica, born 1937, interviewed by Mary Grover, 9 February 2012.

48 Doreen Gill, born 1934, interviewed by Mary Grover, 18 May 2012.

David, like the much less wealthy Irene, was a solitary reader. Both treasured the books they read throughout their lives. David produced a meticulous list for us when we interviewed him. He was attentive to the reading of his own children in the 1950s and 1960s. But because his wife, Sally, was often ill, his daughter, Ruth, was most often read to by the 'help' and by her grandmother. Ruth still has a picture that her maternal grandmother painted of the chair in which she read to her. It is a nursing chair without arms, and sits in the sunny bay of an Edwardian country living room, perfect for cradling a book and a child.[49]

Jocelyn, born in 1926, was a member of a long-established Sheffield manufacturing dynasty and the daughter of a successful steel manufacturer and Master Cutler, who valued his daughter's education. She was fortunate in being read to both by her parents and a by 'very dear nanny who was into reading herself'. But as Jocelyn points out, the supply of new children's books was not great even to those who could afford them.

> It's difficult for people nowadays to realise how few books came out and they were rare beasts and you waited for your birthday to get a copy. Now there's so much; you go to a bookshop and I'm overwhelmed. I can hardly ever choose anything 'cos there's too much to choose from.[50]

If books were 'rare', so were spaces in which one could read. Few of our readers, whatever their economic background, would have had the warmth, peace and privacy to sit still with a book for any length of time. In the 1930s, however affluent the family, bedrooms would have been unheated, and the front room in a terraced house was heated only for guests or at Christmas. Shirley Ellins's experience in the 1940s was typical of all our readers.

> They were fairly strict, fairly strict. Bedrooms were for sleeping, lights off. Not door closed, but just ajar. And I went to bed fairly early … the activities were downstairs, including the reading.

Those of our readers who, like Shirley, grew up in families equipped with books and with adults with the time, interest and space to help their children explore them, had images of those books and memories of parental insistence on the value of reading them. These images and echoes led them to conclude, like Carolyn W, that they were 'probably' read to even though no memory persists.

49 Ruth Potts, born 1960, interviewed by Mary Grover, 25 February 2019, about the influence of her father, David Flather, on her childhood reading in the 1960s.

50 Jocelyn, born 1926, interviewed by Mary Grover, 17 October 2011.

Betty R, born in the 1920s, cannot fail to remember the pleasure of reading and of sharing books with others. Books were central to family life. Her father, as a colliery electrician, was more highly paid than a miner, and he married a woman who had been a teacher in a private school. Betty's mother came to the marriage not only with books but with connections with friends who sent the family parcels of books, a boon to the family, who lived near the colliery, a considerable distance to the south-east of Sheffield city centre and far from a library. Her mother's love of music and reading was shared not only with Betty but with her cousin, Keith, and the neighbouring children. In the late 1920s the house in the mining village of North Staveley would be full of children gathering around the ex-teacher asking her to 'sing the song that makes us cry' ('Danny Boy') or to read to them (*The Water Babies* – another story of loss). Distressingly the visitors used to tug at her mother's clothes to be near her, but Betty learned to share her mother, a precious resource to the community, with other children, just as Frank Burgin learned to share the volumes of his *Children's Encyclopaedia* with the children of other mining families in his pit village four miles north of Staveley.

Though she can recall none of the stories, Betty can remember being shown the pictures in her mother's copy of Aesop's Fables, because Aesop is such a 'funny word'. The Bible stories made much more impression because she and her cousin acted them out, fishing Betty's young sister out of the 'big pram, big wheels, lovely she was' and putting her in the iris leaves for bulrushes until Pharaoh's daughter found her. Her cousin Keith took his cue from his aunt, taking on the role of teacher in a session of a favourite game: 'Now Betty went to school'.

> He used to teach me the letters. He could write and do As Bs and Cs … and he'd teach me. I used to do an A with the curl, just like that using a curl. You know and on the Ds a curl.[51]

Betty's mother created a playroom like no other described to us. The children learned that they could get down any book from the low shelves as long as they put it back in the place they found it. No wonder that, when Betty got to school, she soon learned to read. Then, once she could read herself, Betty would read to her little sisters: 'just read little stories, you know, little fairy tales and made things up, or tell a little

---

51 Barbara 'Betty' R, born 1925, interviewed by Loveday Herridge, 26 September 2011.

bit of poetry to them'. With her cultural and economic resources (the family could afford someone who walked the children to school) Betty's mother created a maternal narrative for her daughter, recalling for her the children she played with and the stories they acted out together, until Betty's memories became a collection of directly remembered and narrated memories.

Although Mary Robertson, whose holiday on Bridlington Sands is pictured at the beginning of this chapter, had books in her home she does not seem to have been read to during the family's Sunday afternoons with their books. Her father used to go to sleep reading the newspaper and her mother would read light romances. Generally, Mary's mother 'seemed to be too busy' to read to her. It was Mary's sister, two and a half years older, who read to Mary when she was 'little': 'mostly when we were in bed at night – night, it would be early evening we would go to bed. Yes, she would always read to me.' Yet the books that were read to Mary are not treasured in the way Elsie passionately treasures *Scrubby Bear's Adventures*, perhaps because the supply was fairly constant and the presence of books habitual. Mary thought hard and concluded that her parents 'must have' bought her books, 'mostly annuals', but they have little significance for her now. Whereas Irene has kept all the annuals she was ever given, Mary retains only one and struggles to recall the title of a favourite book. 'Mabel Lucy Atwell's, those were the kind of books we had', she recalled.

References to a 'kind of', 'sort of' book are common among middle-class children who, like Mary, were conscious that there were different 'kinds' of books. Peter B, one of our readers, described the books in his home as 'the usual child books'.[52] This kind of observation was only made by children from homes with a range of books to hand both for adults and children. In a home with no designated places for adults' or children's books, every book was as much a children's as an adult's book. Each book in a home such as Irene's was unusual. And such was the value put on these precious objects that the adult Elsie, for example, still celebrates them. Not only does Elsie read aloud, with pride and satisfaction, the inscriptions in the children's books given her by her aunt and grandmother, but she also reads snatches of the tales themselves in the voices she assigned to these fictional animals. She re-enters the world of her childhood as an adult, and the way she does so blurs our sense of what belongs to infancy and what to adulthood.

52 Peter B, born 1930, interviewed by Susan Roe, 29 May 2012.

Although Elsie Brownlee was less affluent than her contemporary, Mary Robertson, both children were cut off from a plentiful supply of books precisely because they were middle class. Access to libraries was dependent for such children on the supervision of an available adult. By contrast, working-class children were often able to visit the municipal libraries on their own. In my next chapter I describe the difference these libraries made to the lives of children able to access them. The orphaned John D, like Mary and Elsie a child of the 1920s, took himself off on a solitary trek to a municipal library when he was still at primary school.[53] But Mary, Elsie, Frank and Betty only had access to books owned by the family. Frank and Betty, growing up in pit villages, were geographically removed from municipal libraries; Mary was socially removed from them. Mary and her siblings 'didn't go to libraries when we were little because we weren't allowed out of the end of the road you know'. The library adventures described in my next chapter were not for Mary. Her sister was her reading companion and the warmth of that companionship rather than the books they read is the source of great pleasure still – and guilt. Eighty-five years later Mary could not quite forgive herself that when her sister withheld her precious attention because she was so caught up in a book of her own, Mary would stand right in front of the older girl taunting her with the insult 'Reader, reader, reader'. She reflected, 'I must have been a horrible child!'[54]

Kath was born in 1928 and was the daughter of a core maker, a highly skilled steelworker.[55] Like Mary, she had an older sister who read to her. For rather different reasons she also recalls her response with embarrassment.

> [My sister] used to tell me stories out of William books and things like that ... she used to read to me these stories and I used to then tell the kids at school the stories that I made up about the characters. [laughs] William stories I knew off by heart so I could juggle all the – you know – silly things he got up to in all the stories and – just stand there – and tell the rest of the class. And when I think about it now, I shudder. You know, I must have been a provocative little girl![56]

53 John D, born 1927, interviewed by Mary Grover, 7 June 2013.
54 Mary Robertson, born 1923, interviewed by Susan Roe, 7 March 2013.
55 Core makers are responsible for making sand or wax moulds, or cores, that are used in foundries for the production of metal castings.
56 Kath, born 1928, interviewed by Clare Keen, 16 November 2011.

'Reader, I built it!' Children's bookcases

By whatever means, our readers laid their hands on books and made reading their own. When they became habitual and compulsive readers, they often changed the shape of the home in which they had grown up and developed a new kind of relationship with a parent because of their love of reading. Three of our readers recall having a bookcase of their own when they were children, two of them in a home with no other bookcases.

Alan was a slow starter as a reader. He was born in 1944. He remembers being read to by his aunt and his sister but not his parents. His father was a steelworker with some disposable income. His parents cared enough about their son's education to buy him Arthur Mee's *Encyclopaedia* which sat in a bookcase alongside his mother's collection of novels by Mazo de la Roche. But buying the encyclopaedia was the first and only step in his parents' engagement with his reading. Alan very rarely consulted the encyclopaedia because 'it wasn't until years later that I discovered there was an index! It was tucked somewhere in the middle so I didn't find it until years after I got it.'[57] In contrast to the old-fashioned *Little Folks* compilation which Florence's parents helped her negotiate, the full riches of the gift his parents gave Alan were in fact withheld because they could not teach him how to use it. So his reading stalled for some time. His Rupert Bear annuals and then the *Dandy*, *Beano* and occasional *Rover* kept Alan going, but when he got to his secondary modern in the mid-1950s,

> I seemed to have this sort of explosion, you know, I'd sort of discovered reading and I'd got a lot of time to make up and everything. I was probably, looking back, I probably didn't understand them at all.

It was then that he built up his own book collection made up of books he bought with his own pocket money and gifts from a family friend who was head of the local education committee: 'if I ever mentioned a book in his presence he would get it for me'. Alan would often use the front room (only heated at Christmas) as his private reading space. Eventually his book collection began to get out of hand so Alan built himself his own bookcase.

John Y, born fifteen years earlier than Alan in 1929, was also the son of a steelworker. Asked if his father read, he replied, 'No, because he

57 Alan, born 1944, interviewed by Susan Roe, 2 May 2012.

was a big chap, you know ... he worked on heavy machinery.'[58] Yet John's father had a positive attitude towards reading. In the early 1930s his father moved the family to one of the newly built council houses in Hollins End to the south-east of the city, the high rents only affordable to skilled workers. John was given a small room of his own with just enough space for the bed and a bookcase: 'And the bookcase was floor to ceiling at the bottom of the bed, so that you were sat in bed and there the books were.' John was interviewed with his wife, Meg, from an eminent Methodist family. When he recalled his bookcase, he looked guiltily at Meg as he recalled 'the other thing about the bookcase'. It was

> one I probably shouldn't admit to, because I know how Meg is, that I used to create a secret cupboard in here, in amongst the books. And I made a door and pasted the ends of books, the title pages, just to hide it and confuse you. Desecration I suppose it was, of a book...

Desecration, but it created a sanctuary at a time and in a community where private space of any kind was a luxury.

Lastly, Adele: 'I think I had one bookcase in my bedroom. I can see it now and I can see that the shelves were just full of books eventually. But only that bookcase.'[59] The existence of that bookcase is remarkable given that Adele had never seen a book in the hands of either of her parents, and her father mocked her love of reading when she was reading 'one of those "William" books by Richmal Crompton'. 'And I loved them and even though he was right out of my milieu – as a middle-class boy – I didn't really realise this till later of course. I absolutely adored them.' Yet, unabashed by this initial discouragement, Adele insisted: 'I wanted to be bought books.'

Her account of her family's ownership of books is interestingly confusing. On the one hand, she had the only bookcase. On the other hand, her father did in fact own books which were very important to him. These were political books, covered in brown paper covers: 'we didn't touch those'. Adele's book collection was on display; her father's was not. At last, Adele's commitment to reading elicited a supportive response from her father:

> Eventually my father started recommending books to me, which was a big surprise to me, having never seen him with a book in his hand. So, I assume

58 John Y, born 1929, interviewed by Mary Grover, 6 June 2013.
59 Adele, born 1942, interviewed by Liz Hawkins, 19 July 2012.

that he had read a lot when he was living on his own. And he recommended people like P.G. Wodehouse.

Adele's teachers were baffled at this strange taste in a teenage girl in Sheffield, but Wodehouse was only one of several authors that her father began to point her towards. 'He recommended authors – "Have you tried reading …" this, that and the other, you know.'

> And he recommended *Sorrell and Son* by Warwick Deeping, which I've since come to realise had a very great impression on him, because his mother died when he was very young – and this is what the basis of the story is – and I hadn't realised that.

Adele's delayed engagement with her father through books is not unlike the experience of Jean, whose childhood on a failing farm in Lincolnshire was described earlier. Both Jean and Adele's fathers lost the habit of reading. After moving out to Lincolnshire, away from a family of recently prosperous industrialists for whom books were part of the fabric of life, Jean's father no longer had time or a suitable environment for reading. Adele's father stopped reading while chasing work as a painter and decorator in the period of austerity that followed the Second World War. Adele's responsiveness to her father's late engagement with her own reading gradually unlocked tastes and memories in a man who had suppressed them or put them aside while he made a living and helped raise a family. His daughter's persistence in reading and her absorption in books helped her father reconnect, in later life, with the books that had been part of his own youth. Once children sought out books independently of the home, they themselves had the power to transform their home environment. They made a reading habit normal and sometimes opened reading opportunities to parents who, for whatever reason, had been unable to create them for their own children.

CHAPTER TWO

Running up Eyre Street

Independent Young Readers and the Public Libraries

Judith G lived close to the central branch of the commercial 'tuppenny' Red Circle library, and accompanied her mother in her search for romantic novels. Judith herself raced up to the public Central Library as soon as her mother had enrolled her as an independent reader. In that magnificent new building, built in 1934, she found all she wanted: books appropriate for her at every age, the Reference Library and the Graves Art Gallery. Among the endless shelves of books and the riches of early British twentieth-century art, Judith found a refuge from a cold and crowded home. Unable to take up the grammar school place she had won, Judith, like the wealthier Mary Robertson, left school without higher qualifications. Throughout their lives she and her mother continued to share their reading habit with books borrowed from the nearest municipal library.[1]

1 Judith G, born 1939, interviewed by Loveday Herridge, 14 February 2013.

We used to go down the backwacks to it from Shiregreen 'cos it was ever such a long ... I was only a young kid ... we used to walk all through Concord Park and down all the backwacks there.

Kath M[2]

The 'backwacks' or urban footpaths led Kath and her family to the public library, the main source of books for elementary school children growing up in the 1930s. Sheffield and Kath's library couldn't be described as local. The Saturday expedition was a long hike: four and a half miles in total. Although there was a box of municipal library books in the local school, the new Firth Park Library, opened in 1930, inspired Kath and her family to spend half a precious Saturday walking there and back. A child's pathway to a source of reading matter outside the home was rarely a well-trodden one in the 1930s. Most parents had no habits of navigation to share. Kath is unusual in describing family outings to the library. Most of our readers describe their visits to the library alone, when they were established readers, perhaps at the age of seven or eight.

The accounts of how newly independent readers steered their course through unfamiliar territories in order to satisfy their appetite to read contrast with the few who, by virtue of their relatively privileged class, had their reading choices mapped for them. The determination and the independence of these working-class, would-be readers reflect the close link between the practice of reading and the confidence to forge identities not simply determined by social expectations and economic necessity. By setting off across the city, often alone, these children engaged with unfamiliar networks (social, municipal and cultural), with few navigational aids to reach their goal: a building full of books.

'A brawny building': Sheffield Central Library

In nearly every case, these independent quests eventually led to a public library. Unquestionably, the best-stocked was the impressive art deco Central Library, built in 1934. It would not have been built, during this era of economic depression, without the generosity of a wealthy Sheffield businessman and art collector. John George Graves was an apprentice watchmaker from Lincolnshire who made a fortune running a mail order business in Sheffield, eventually employing 3,000 people. The philanthropist insisted on the provision of the Graves Art Gallery on

2 Kath, born 1928, interviewed by Clare Keen, 16 November 2011.

the top storey of the three-storey building. The 700 artworks were free to all. Among them were Graves's fine collection of twentieth-century British paintings, a collection developed by its gifted first curator, John Rothenstein, later director of the Tate. The paintings and the building itself were a lure to some of our readers.

Ted, an engineer with a strong leaning towards art, won a part-time place at Sheffield Art School as a young teenager in the 1930s – just over the road from the building-site that was to house the art gallery treasured by him in later life.

> Thursday and Friday I used to go to an art school. And when we used to go out in the afternoon we used to watch them building the new library ... we used to watch the cranes, the big stones. Very interesting that was. I was with that library right from the beginning.[3]

Ted's connection is unique among our readers. The room in which we interviewed Ted is full of his art books; his response to the Central Library was aesthetic rather than literary.

Another young reader was impressed by the appearance and scale of the building. Whereas Ted had watched its construction in the mid-1930s, Judith G discovered it in the 1940s, rising miraculously intact from the rubble of the city centre following the Blitz of 1941. Her first visit, with her mother, filled her with awe: 'It was quite daunting because it's a really brawny old building isn't it? I think it's a lovely building.' But Judith's chief passion was for the wealth of reading matter the building contained and the peace its spaces offered, almost a mile from the crowded terraced house that she shared with her extended family in the 1940s and 1950s. Saturday afternoon was her time to make the Central Library her own and to keep warm.

> You could sit there with any book you liked, encyclopaedias, because at home it was, you know, hustle and bustle, we didn't have much because we had no money and there weren't a television in those days, this is the fifties, coming up to the fifties, and I just used to go to the library for a bit of peace on my own. Because there was four of us and my grandmother and father and mother all rattling round one house, we didn't have much by the way of comforts, shall we say, there was no central heating... Right up till I was about 16, you used to find me in the library reading all the books because it was nice and it was warm and you could stay there until they closed at five o'clock. I used to read and read.

3 Ted, born 1919, interviewed by Mary Grover, 9 February 2013.

'All the books' was probably quite literally true, as she simply worked her way along the shelves. Under 'M' she found Augustus Muir's *Joey and the Green Wings*. Judith can still recite the poem at the heart of the book. Like so many self-directed readers, her chance encounters were rarely with what are now considered classics. Though this children's novel seems to have left no trace in children's book history it sounds original, combining aliens from outer space with a little lost chick 'who went cheep in in the night', consoled by the moon which 'stretched her arms out so shiny and bright'. At 14 Judith went on to the adult library, where she worked her way down whole shelves full of the historical novels of Jeffrey Farnol and Georgette Heyer.

I call this chapter 'Running up Eyre Street' in tribute to the proselytising Judith. She was first enrolled in the library by her mother, whose own needs were catered for by the commercial 'tuppenny' or 'circulating' library round the corner. Once Judith was a member of the Central Library, she used it independently of the family. She made the journey regularly, her route longer than it would be now because, in the late 1940s, the direct route, a major thoroughfare confusingly called the Moor, was still a bomb-site. To skirt the rubble Judith made her way down the parallel Eyre Street. She soon decided that she should share the joy of library membership. At 10 years old in 1948 she took advantage of her mother's Saturday afternoon nap to run up Eyre Street with Sheila Thompson so she could join the library.

> They gave you a little round ticket which you kept and slotted the book's name in that, God, I remember that... I must have been eight or nine... and my mother played pop with me [gave her a telling-off] because she didn't know where we were.

The Central Library was, for Judith, a place of physical and imaginative escape and an arena in which she felt she was in control.

The creation of Sheffield's municipal library service

The library that Judith ran towards was the flagship of what became one of Europe's finest municipal library services, celebrated in the delightful short film *Books in Hand* (1956).[4] The quality of these free municipal

---

4 *Books in Hand*, 1956, Sheffield City Council Libraries Committee, https://www. yfanefa.com/record/2585.

libraries enshrined our readers' love of books and validated their passion for reading. They were key to developing the reading habit.

Sheffield had been the first town in Yorkshire to respond to the 1850 Public Libraries Act which allowed a library rate to be levied. Based on the stock of the Mechanics' Library, Sheffield's first municipal library attracted at least a third of the adult population to register when it opened in 1858; after three years, of the roughly 4,000 who renewed their tickets, over 2,000 were artisans.[5] Yet despite that early enthusiasm, at the start of the twentieth century the libraries were badly run and poorly funded, and the quality of the buildings and stock had declined. By 1920 the services were in a poor state, but in the 1920s and 1930s they were remarkably transformed by two professionally trained librarians: Richard Gordon and Joseph Lamb. It was thanks to them and to increased support from a Labour council in 1926 that our readers were able to access books independently, regardless of their social or economic circumstances.

From the other side of the Pennines, where he was chief librarian of Rochdale, Richard Gordon was recruited in 1921 to overhaul the Sheffield libraries service: 'when he was in charge libraries became marvellously alive'.[6] He and his deputy, J.P. Lamb, worked to replace 'inbred' staff who had been 'almost exclusively recruited from Sheffield' and who had been 'actively discouraged from attempting to qualify in their profession'.[7]

Gordon was not just a competent manager. He was an eloquent advocate for the library service whose political and personal skills helped overturn fifty years of scepticism among ratepayers about the value of libraries. He believed libraries were 'community schools where all may increase and supplement their education', but in his dealings with Sheffield's fiscally cautious councillors he successfully argued that the council should pay for massively increased stock and extended library provision throughout the city in the interests of its own prosperity. Gordon pointed out in a 1927 BBC broadcast that Sheffield spent just over 11d per head of the population, in contrast to Bradford's 1/8d and

5 J.P. Lamb, *The City Libraries of Sheffield 1856–1956*, Sheffield: Sheffield Libraries, Art Galleries and Museums Committee, 1956, 11.

6 J.P. Lamb, 'Obituary of Richard Gordon', *Library Association Record*, November 1966, 418.

7 Lamb, *The City of Libraries of Sheffield*, 29.

Manchester's 2/0.[8] Against the odds, Gordon and Lamb succeeded in providing the city with a purpose-built, modern central library, nearly eighty years after the library service started.

Gordon was succeeded by his deputy, Joseph Lamb, in 1927. In 1956, looking back on their work, Lamb identified the need for improved understanding of the wider purposes of a good library service among Sheffield's civic and industrial leaders.

> The value of books had never been properly understood in Sheffield, and the years of library neglect, though they had been vaguely felt by the public as a loss, had accustomed people of influence to the idea that life could go on pretty well without them.[9]

During his time as chief librarian Lamb increased the value of the library service to key 'people of influence' and demonstrated to Sheffield's manufacturers that their businesses would benefit from the research skills of trained librarians working within a well-run library service. In the 1930s he established SINTO, the Sheffield Interchange Organisation, to exchange information about steel and related subjects between local businesses and research and academic organisations. Civic leaders began to appreciate that librarians could be trained to exercise research skills that might increase the quality of manufacturing and marketing. And librarians, often with no post-elementary education, began to feel of value to the community, taking pride in their command of the printed word and their ability to master new fields of knowledge. The increase in prestige felt by librarians assigned to SINTO and throughout the Science, Commercial and Technical departments of the library can be heard in the words of librarians interviewed by us and others. Alysoun Bagguley ran SINTO in the 1960s. Sometimes representatives from the metal industries would ask to 'see the gaffer' and be surprised to discover a woman. 'I've got this steel...' was a common preface to a highly technical enquiry. Baggueley went on to run the World Metal Index – 'a joy, an absolute joy'.[10] The mostly female librarians who were of such service to the metal industries in the 1940s and 1950s had not, of course, had access to the scientific knowledge that their male contemporaries had been able to acquire in their better-funded grammar schools. Borrowing from the

---

8 R.J. Gordon, 'Sheffield Public Libraries', *BBC*, broadcast 27 January 1927, transcript, 5, held in Sheffield Local Studies Library, MP 1587M.
9 Lamb, *The City Libraries of Sheffield*, 32.
10 Alysoun Bagguley in conversation with Mary Grover, 19 May 2015.

public library, often associated with the female reader of light fiction, was now publicly linked to the masculinised world of manufacturing, science and making money. Lamb argued at a librarians' conference in Oxford that the book was 'the most important tool of industry', and his speech was reported in the *Yorkshire Post* in 1932.[11]

During the Second World War, Lamb established the worth of the library service to Sheffield ratepayers in many other ways. The Central Library, which was the emotional centre of Judith's life outside the family during the 1940s, also served as a centre for public information and assistance services for the whole city after the air-raids of the Sheffield Blitz in December 1940, because it was one of the few city-centre buildings remaining unscathed. The efficiency and effectiveness of the libraries in this crisis further enhanced the awareness of the practical and social value of librarians' skills and the printed matter with which they dealt.

The kind of books Lamb sought to provide for the general reader in Sheffield had much to do with the fact that he was self-educated, and like so many of our readers robbed of post-elementary education by the early death of a parent.[12] He came from a large and loving working-class family in St Helens in Lancashire. He was surrounded by books and encouraged to read: Rudyard Kipling, Walter Scott, Harrison Ainsworth and the school stories of Talbot Baines Reed.

On the death of his father Lamb had to leave his grammar school. 'Chance or fate' placed him in a public library, 'a dull, dreary place with great stacks of dirty books, screened from the profane public gaze by a long Chivers's Indicator'.[13] The Chivers's Indicator was a great wall of numbers that divided the reader both from the librarian and the library stock. Once a catalogue had been consulted and the number of the desired book had been identified, the reader looked upwards to discover whether there was an 'ivorine' indicator against the number of the book sought.[14] If there was, the librarian could be summoned from his sanctuary and asked to fetch the book required. Lamb's horror at

---

11 J.P. Lamb, 'Library Aids to Industry', *The Yorkshire Post*, 26 September 1932, 8.

12 We owe a great deal of our understanding of his contribution to Sheffield cultural life to the research of Val Hewson, whose discussions of the context and significance of this libraries pioneer can be found in her research posts on the Reading Sheffield website.

13 J.P. Lamb, 'Librarian when Young: Part 2', *The Librarian and Book World*, 45.2 (February 1956), 34.

14 Discussed in Elizabeth Melrose, 'J.P. Lamb, M.A., F.L.A', in *The Provision and*

this system made him, with Gordon, a passionate advocate of shelves where nearly all books were available on open access. Sheffield children were encouraged to hunt for books in ways that seemed untrammelled, either by the Chivers's Indicator or by the missionary zeal of a newly trained librarian. Though Lamb's obituary recalled that he 'never let it be forgotten that it was he who was in command',[15] he fostered a sense among readers that they were in charge of the process of selection. Not for him the children's sections where 'a trained librarian, bursting with good intentions, attempts to lead the defenceless creatures to "worthwhile" books'. He declared that Sheffield libraries would 'be free from attempts to direct children's reading or [from attempts] to force the child, either by recommendation or book selection, to the kind of books adults think he ought to read.'[16]

His policies bore fruit. Numerous Sheffield librarians remember the opening of the new Firth Park branch library in 1930, with its magnificent children's room. Jack Walker, one of its first librarians, describes the pandemonium of opening day: 'when the children came out of school, there were hundreds waiting. The doors opened outwards and I had to force my way out of the main door.'[17] The police had to be called in to control the crowds.

The policies of Lamb and Gordon and the work of their library teams served the city well. Book issues rose throughout the decades when our readers were beginning to use the libraries: 365,000 in 1925–6, 3,640,000 in 1932–3, and 3,750,000 in 1945–6.[18] Joseph Lamb was guardian of Sheffield libraries from 1927 to 1956, key decades in the lives of our readers. Without him many of them would never have developed the reading habit to the extent they did.

Use of Library and Documentation Service: Some Contributions from the University of Sheffield Postgraduate School of Librarianship, Oxford: Pergamon Press, 1966.

15 J.G. Ollé, 'J. P. Lamb: The Last of the Patriarchs', *Library Review*, 24.7 (1974), 295–300, https://doi.org/10.1108/eb012607.

16 J.P. Lamb, 'Librarian when Young: Part 1', *The Librarian and Book World*, 45.1 (1956), 4.

17 Jack Walker, quoted in James R. Kelly, 'An Oral History of Sheffield Public Libraries, 1926–1974', MA thesis, University of Sheffield, April 1983, 31.

18 Val Hewson, '"Even Edgar Wallace may be discovered...": The Fiction Policy of an English Public Library in the 1930s', unpublished paper given at 'The Auden Generation and After' conference, Sheffield Hallam University, 17 June 2016.

The library as interchange

Ted and Judith regarded the Central as their local library, but most children who used it did so because it stood near the bus interchange between the worlds of the working-class terraces where they lived and the selective schools in more middle-class parts of town. Neither Ted nor Judith went to a grammar school. Though Judith passed the 11-plus to a prestigious girls' grammar school her family were unable to afford the uniform. The disappointment is still with her today. Most of the children who wandered with her round the shelves of the Central Library in the late 1940s had not missed that opportunity. The selective schools which many of them attended were surrounded by Edwardian villas rising on the western and north-western slopes of the city. The working-class terraces of the nineteenth century were built on the slopes above the noxious valleys to the east of the city centre where the large steelworks stretched towards Rotherham along the valley of the Don. The transition between one part of town and the other was marked by the civic buildings in the centre of town, eclipsed in scale by the mills to the east. Most buildings in the centre were blackened by industrial smog in the 1930s and 1940s, but not the Central Library, so recently built. Faced in white stone, elegant and not as grandiose as the neighbouring Town Hall, its open spaces and literary riches made it a welcome haven for grammar school boys and girls as they changed buses on the way home from school.

Mavis accessed the Central Library's treasures because she passed the scholarship exam to the Sheffield High School for Girls, which took only the very top scoring scholarship girls alongside fee-paying pupils. In the 1930s and 1940s pupils were awarded scholarships at selective secondary schools on the basis of their ranking in the scholarship examination or the later 11-plus, not because a school was local. Of the 19 of our readers who listed Central as among the libraries they used, 13 were grammar school pupils travelling across town to the school to which they were allocated, and three were privately educated children.

Mavis was unusual because she was used to solitary travel. She had grown up in an isolated but industrial environment because the colliery weigh station managed by her father was deliberately set apart from both the colliery and the residential community to discourage corruption. She walked two miles to her elementary school, sometimes getting a lift with the milkman and sometimes with a coal lorry, lining her seat with a piece of newspaper to protect her from the coal dust on the passenger seat. Once she started to attend the prestigious Girls' High School, Mavis found it more convenient to use the Central in between bus journeys than to visit her 'local' Attercliffe Library, a long and solitary walk away.

The Central was in some respects a social sanctuary. The distinctive grammar school uniform could make children vulnerable in the streets near home, marking them out from elementary classmates who had failed. James passed the scholarship but declined his place because he could not face 'the solo run' out of the area in which he lived to the grammar school across the city.[19] An anonymous contributor to a local history website in Sheffield describes going into the Central on Saturday mornings, if he had the bus fare, because he couldn't face going to the local library: 'it wasn't the thing for a young lad to do in our neighbourhood'.[20] Such pressures on young working-class people to conform to neighbourhood norms are mentioned by men among our interviewees but not women.

Once they got there, the Central Library offered bookish children from neighbourhoods where reading was regarded as odd or risible the safety of anonymity. On Saturdays it must have been full of grammar school pupils who barely knew anyone else there. Two girls speak eloquently of the freedom that these independent journeys and independent choices conferred. In Florence Cowood's description of her exploration of the newly opened library in the mid-1930s we get a sense of the rewards won by going solo.

> I think I was rather a solitary child, in that your parents are busy working. And I used, on a Saturday morning, I used to go have a little trot around the Moor [the road between the Red Circle and Central libraries], by meself, you see. And I used to go to Central Library, get my library books, go up to the gallery. I used to like to go up there to look at the pictures. And then I used to go down to the reading room. You could read all sorts of magazines down there, and I used to spend [the whole day], you know, really, and then come home on the tram ... and read my library books ... I had loads of friends, but in those days, when you went to a grammar school people came from all over the city. So my best friend lived in Pitsmoor, and another out at Grindleford.[21]

19 James Green, born 1936, in conversation with Susan Roe and Mary Grover, 27 July 2017.
20 Anon., posted on Sheffield Forum website, https://www.sheffieldforum.co.uk/, 15 February 2015.
21 Florence, born 1923, interviewed by Susan Roe, 24 November 2011.

The solitariness of Florence's Saturdays, in part because grammar school attendance isolated her from the children in her neighbourhood, meant that she was alone with books while children at local schools were playing out. But Florence's reading would have knit her more firmly into a widespread friendship group based on her grammar school. Florence lived on the relatively affluent side of town where her father was a reasonably paid mechanic in the burgeoning motor trade. She lived near Abbeydale Girls' Grammar, but her school friend in Pitsmoor breathed the polluted air of the terraced housing which served the workers in the city's major steelworks, and her best friend lived out in the country, probably travelling to Abbeydale by train. Florence borrowed novels by Daphne du Maurier, Mary Webb and Elizabeth Goudge, going on to buy and reread Goudge's *Green Dolphin County* and du Maurier's *The King's General*. In the late 1930s, on the threshold of adulthood, Florence consumed *Gone with the Wind*. Such tastes in popular fiction would have been shared by grammar school girls across pre-war Britain, creating a national community of readers who would have recognised each other's tastes if they were to meet in teacher training colleges or universities. Florence never went on to higher education. She became an accomplished artist, another beneficiary of Lamb's acceptance of the Graves bequest.

The hubbub of the local library

Compared to the hush that settled on the group of disparate strangers in the Central Library, the local library could be a noisy social space. On their Saturday visits to Maureen B's grandmother and aunt in the late 1940s and early 1950s, Maureen and her mother took in Burngreave Library, just up the road from the working-class terraces of Pitsmoor, but a little higher up the hill, with more spacious houses and less polluted. Once there, Maureen milled about with her friends, creating quite a rumpus. 'We would stay till the books would come in that we wanted.'[22] The librarian 'had a bell and then we had to be quiet and then the noise level would rise again'. They were usually waiting for the new Enid Blyton, the Famous Five novels being Maureen's favourites.

In the 1960s Blyton's apparent saturation of the children's market caused anxiety among literary mentors, parents, teachers and librarians, especially as alternatives emerged. Children's literature with a less narrow class base

22 Maureen B, born 1945, in conversation with Mary Grover, 17 July 2016.

and more linguistic inventiveness began to be available. In 1942 the Puffin edition of Eve Garnett's *Family from One End Street* was published. This was the first of Garnett's novels about the family of a London dustman. They delighted the working-class Jude Warrender in the 1950s; 'they were charming, quite charming'.[23] She now sees that despite the middle-class standpoint of the author, it was 'a kind of breakthrough'. Yet none of our other readers mention her. It would be interesting to know if her books were categorised as fiction about 'waifs': a category found by the 1938 Sheffield Library children's reading survey to be unpopular. The representations of childhood that Sheffield children devoured in the 1930s and 1940s were overwhelmingly middle-class: the boarding school stories of Angela Brazil, Elinor Brent Dyer's Chalet School series, Dorita Fairlie Bruce's Dimsie novels and the many varieties of 'an Enid Blyton'.

The increasingly prolific Blyton generated a range of different kinds of stories. Like the enormously successful contemporary publishing enterprises of Penguin, she created a brand but never stopped creating sub-genres of that brand. Noddy, her series for very young readers, was published from 1949 onwards, too late for most of our readers. By 1950 there were eight Famous Five novels with far more to follow, and a total of eight 'Adventure' novels. Both delivered the same kind of pleasure. The part these books for older children played in helping our readers develop the reading habit cannot be overemphasised; nearly all the girls who attended grammar schools mention reading yards of them.

Maureen L, like Maureen B, found her Enid Blytons in her local library. Maureen L, who grew up on the large council estate of Southey Green in the north of Sheffield, describes a regular girls' night out in the 1940s:

> There were about four of us who used to go to the library, that's what we did on a Monday night … there were two children who lived across the road for a time, they went – Ann and Caroline Barr, I think their names were – and another friend, so there were three or four of us at least who used to go to the library on a Monday night – … I used to borrow the maximum, probably about three books, and I would have read them ready for the next Monday.[24]

The reading choices of both Maureens were based on leads given by friends and the long runs of particular authors that were readily

---

23 Jude Warrender, born 1950, interviewed 8 February 2013 by Sheffield Hallam University English student Rebecca Fisher.
24 Maureen L, born 1941, interviewed by Mary Grover, 30 April 2012.

available. Family members do not seem to have been part of the process of choosing books. Nor were librarians. Indeed, as we have seen, chief librarian Joseph Lamb discouraged too much direction of children's reading. The librarians on Monday nights might have had enough to do just keeping the girls quiet.

Another author almost as popular as Blyton, with an appeal to both boys and girls, was Richmal Crompton. The readership of the Just William books was neither gender- nor age-specific. Peter B, the son of an engineer who had also been a musician in a colliery band, read them when he was at junior school, but is apologetic about his enjoyment. 'It sounds dreadful now but … they were reasonably well written and grammatical.' Perhaps it was his contemporaries at Oxford who led him to be ashamed of his childhood tastes.[25] Or perhaps a librarian had radiated disapproval at an early age. Julie Howard had *Just William* whisked from her by a rogue librarian at the Manor Library in the 1950s.[26] It was judged unsuitable for a junior school child, and Julie is still not sure why.

None of Crompton's other fans were troubled by her cultural status. For many of them *Just William* is associated in their memory with the adventures of Biggles by Captain W.E. Johns. Crompton and Johns both provided that valuable material that keeps a teenager reading until they are able to access and enjoy authors categorised as 'adult'. The difference between Johns and Crompton in our readers' lives is that the joy of William's subversive behaviour seems to have outlived the thrills of Biggles. The 90-year-old Ted, who watched the building of the Central Library in 1934, says affectionately, 'I still read the Just William books. I've got some in my house', and interviewees smile as they recall the pleasure given. Madeleine comments 'of course I heard them on the radio'. The BBC Light Service featured two of the books in 1947, both sets of episodes scheduled for 7.15 p.m., an acknowledgement of the adult appeal of the stories. Blyton was never dramatised by BBC radio and the 1949 production of a Biggles adventure on the Light Service appeared at midday in the programme 'Hullo Children', so firmly categorised as juvenile. The William books were stocked by the commercial tuppenny libraries as well as by the municipal libraries, so their readership had a wide class, gender and age base.

25 Peter Baker, born 26 March 1930, interviewed by Susan Roe, 29 May 2012.
26 Julie Howard, blogpost, 18 August 2019, https://www.readingsheffield.co.uk/?s=julie+howard (accessed 13 June 2020).

Fat books

If the distance between home and library was long, the size of the book borrowed was an important consideration. John D, who, like Kath, had been born in the late 1920s, was an only child and had never known his father. When he could read, John made the solitary journey to his 'local' library, Attercliffe, 'several miles' there and back. The very length of the journey determined the kind of book that John needed. On one of his earliest trips he was attracted by a book with alluring line drawings of animals and their guardian, a doctor with a bowler hat and an improbably round nose.

> I had borrowed this book, it was, I think ... a Dr Dolittle book ... I got home and I'd read it in an hour of course so I took it back to the library and they told me 'Go home, you can't have any more books, you can only have one borrowing a day, you can't go back.' I think at that time I only had one ticket anyway so it meant that although I'd walked several miles to the library, there and back, it meant that I was frustrated because I couldn't borrow a book that I wanted.[27]

So the next day it was to be a fat book, without too many illustrations. The wealth of slight, slippery and funny books that now surround children in infant school libraries, if not at home, was not available for any of those we interviewed. They all became habitual readers and they needed regular supplies of continuous text. Richly illustrated texts such as Hugh Lofting's Dr Dolittle stories were lacking in this respect. Indeed, John is the only reader to mention a Dr Dolittle. They would have been expensive for a library to purchase and a poor investment for the child who walked a mile to collect the single book to last the week. In 1935 the 10-year-old Ken made weight his main criterion for choosing the first book he borrowed from Firth Park Library.

> The very first one I got was the thickest one I could find, called *The Great Aeroplane Mystery* by Percy F. Westerman. Absolute rubbish, of course, but it was a thick book so ... you could only borrow one book a week then.[28]

27 John D, born 1927, interviewed by Mary Grover, 7 June 2013.
28 Ken, born 1925, interviewed by Clare Keen, 16 November 2011. Westerman's many adventure stories do not include this title.

'Freedom of choice in an atmosphere of Beauty'[29]

Ken's wife Kath homed in on Firth Park Library at the same time as her future husband, but from a different direction. It was no accident that this library attracted both children, one from down and the other from up the hill. It was one of the first three libraries in Sheffield to have a special Junior Section. The first was in Walkley in 1924, followed by a specially built annexe to Hillsborough Library in 1929. The library had two wings extending from an imposing but welcoming lobby. From the library windows readers looked out on to woodland. The newly built library was stocked with 20,000 books in 1930 at a time when city finances were eroded by the need to offer relief to those hit by the intensifying economic depression. In his meticulous oversight of Sheffield's children's libraries Joseph Lamb sought to provide books in ways that would enable children to feel that they were making independent choices. He looked back with excitement on his own untutored explorations and did not want to rob Sheffield's children of that sense of serendipity that is the privilege of the autodidact. Unusually for a man with a sense of mission, he was not prescriptive. As a fellow librarian comments, 'He preferred to entice children to read without attempting to give an air of formal education or classify books in age groups. This to Lamb was an obnoxious habit common in many American libraries.'[30]

In a personal memoir written on his retirement in 1956 when he had established Sheffield Library Services as an international model of excellence, Lamb quoted the mantra of another great librarian, Louis Stanley Jast, who declared that in a library there should be 'Freedom of choice in an atmosphere of Beauty'. Lamb was delighted both by the practical virtues and aesthetic qualities of his new junior library in Hillsborough, opened in 1929. A year later he lyrically evoked its 'reference reading slopes', tables round and square, 'with a central base instead of inconvenient legs at the edges', all designed in 'a modernist tendency', the woodwork oak, 'with egg-shell polish', the 'walls decorated in gold'.[31] He would have relished the apparent aimlessness of Anne's

---

29 Louis Stanley Jast, quoted in Lamb, 'Librarian when Young: Part 1', 1.

30 Melrose, 'J.P. Lamb, M.A., F.L.A.'.

31 J.P. Lamb, 'Some Notes on Library Planning I: Sheffield', *The Library World Supplement*, 33.5 (1 October 1930), 150.

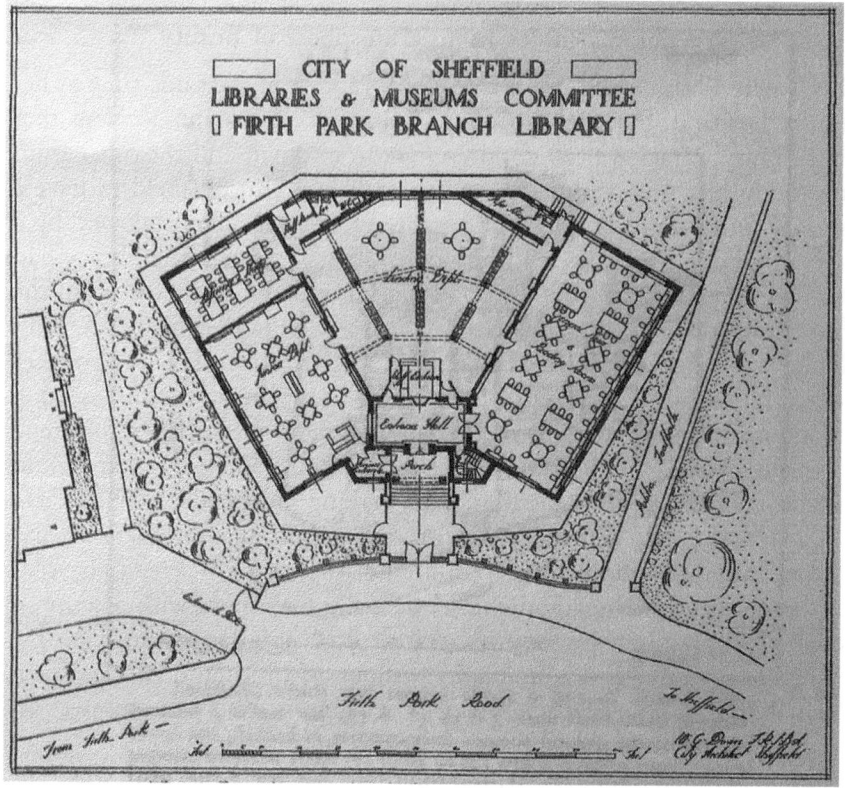

5 The floor plan of the new Firth Park Library, from J.P. Lamb, 'Some Notes on Library Planning: Part I, Sheffield', *The Library World*, 33.5 (1 October 1930), 157

perambulation around that same library in the 1950s and beyond. She declares, 'My attitude then and now is always to wander round.'[32]

In 1956 Lamb described the children's libraries he helped create in Sheffield:

> In them, there is beauty in furniture, decoration and ornaments; a range of good, attractive books; many activities to interest the few with outstanding gifts: suggestive book displays, talks, cinema shows, a literary magazine for the creative, plays, story hour talks, dramatic recitals – but only for those who *want* to take part in them. No advice, unless asked for, no pressure for any particular books; above all, no odour of formal education. The children

32 Anne, born in 1944, interviewed by Susan Roe, 5 April 2012.

who come to the library should be free from tuition or pressure of any kind; they should be left to find their own ways among books.[33]

Just as Lamb himself had done.

Once established, junior sections in Firth Park, Hillsborough, Central, Walkley, Woodseats and Park libraries attracted visits from neighbouring elementary schools in the 1930s. The children were treated to storytelling by newly qualified young librarians and were taught how they could become independent library members. Many of our readers owe their love of books to the culture of those early junior libraries.

Jean Mercer used Park Library (built in 1904 with adjacent swimming bath) from 1927 to her death in 2019. In the 1930s it was still holding its own despite the grandeur of its near neighbour, the newly built Central. The daughter of a fruiterer, Jean had been taken to the library by her family from an early age, but it was on a school library visit to Park that she encountered the inspirational Miss Heywood.

> She was absolutely wonderful at telling stories. She would sit on the counter and tell these stories, and especially about Epaminondas. He was a little black boy and he was lovely. He never did anything right but Epaminondas was lovely.[34]

In 1911 the American Sara Cone Bryant published a popular retelling of the stories of the wayward Epaminondas, a figure from black American folklore.[35] Though the British author Constance E. Egan wrote a sequence of stories about Epaminondas in the 1950s and 1960s it would have been this American version that Miss Heywood read in the 1930s. These 'noodlehead' stories were clearly entrancing to the white working-class children sitting on the floor of Sheffield's Park Library in the 1930s but, for obvious reasons, are not on our library shelves today.

The library 'lifted' you

Jude Warrender, like Jean, was from a working-class home and her mother encouraged reading. She loved going to Firth Park Library in the 1950s, 'because it was a nice place to go' and she longed to wear the

---

33 Lamb, 'Librarian when Young: Part 1', 4–5.

34 Jean Mercer, born 1925, interviewed by Mary Grover, 10 August 2010.

35 For a discussion of the racist context of this 'noodlehead' story, see the post from the John Crow Museum of Racist Memorabilia at Ferris State University, https://www.ferris.edu/HTMLS/news/jimcrow/question/2009/january.htm (accessed 13 June 2020).

6 The Children's Library at Woodhouse, opened in 1931

badge of a library monitor. 'So I used to gaze at other children, I just never had the courage to ask.' Feeling herself unentitled to claim a role in the guardianship of books, Jude instead imported the library, the magic of its systems and its culture into her own private imaginative world.

> I used to play at libraries at home. And I had a little chest of drawers, which I shall show you a picture of, it was a tiny spice chest, about this sort of size, at home which a neighbour had given me with tiny drawers with the spice names on. And I used to cut out little cards for the few books I had, so they would be in these drawers – I mean the cards only filled one drawer, but I used to play library.

Julia Banks, a grammar school girl like Jude, was brought up in the 1940s by her mother, who was a corsetiere. She loved the children's area of the local Woodhouse Library, the arts and crafts décor enhancing the entrancing qualities of the books within it. Though she and her mother had books in the house, most of the homes on the council estate in which Julia grew up contained no books at all, so 'the library in Woodhouse was a great influence'. To be surrounded by books in the elegant arts and crafts interior of the children's library space was to be 'aware of an outside – not just so concerned with the immediate'.[36]

36 Julia Banks, born 1939, interviewed by Liz Hawkins, 15 February 2012. I discuss

Both Julia and Jude were grammar school girls growing up in post-war Britain when cataclysmic events had made the prospects of change both terrifying and exhilarating. Post-war girls were offered more chances to enter an 'outside' world than girls born fifteen years or so earlier had been. (Jean, for instance, was deprived of the scholarship place she won because of her family's economic circumstances.) Both Julia and Jude became teachers. As Lamb and Jast would have desired, they recalled the library spaces that became their own: physically comfortable and aesthetically stimulating. Most importantly, they recall the provision of an infinite supply of the books they craved and the thrill of seeking and finding them.

Without a compass: 'I didn't know quite where to start'

Once a child had arrived at a library, he or she had then to navigate a space unlike any other they had encountered: an arena of apparently endless choice with categories kept to a minimum. In 1938, when he and his team had created junior libraries across the city, Lamb conducted a survey of children's reading in ten of the city's libraries. The 2,700 responses revealed that a book as popular of *Anne of Green Gables* was much more likely to owe its popularity to the recommendation of a friend than that of an adult librarian, teacher or parent. Neither the radio nor films influenced children's choices at this period. Apart from the informal recommendations of friends, children entered the library with few ideas about what they were aiming to select. Lamb concluded that 'It is ... clear that "purposive" reading is not common among children, and it is perhaps as well that this should be so.'[37]

The survey revealed that from the ages of 8 to 10, children's appetite for reading of all sorts increased rapidly, but that after 10 it diminished. Girls read more than boys, and both girls and boys read more fiction than non-fiction. Overwhelmingly, the most popular genre was the fairy story. Grimm's and Hans Andersen's collections were the most commonly borrowed. Aesop's Fables came third, followed by *Robinson Crusoe, Alice in Wonderland* and *Treasure Island*. These choices perhaps owed something to the books that were read in junior school. *Treasure Island* was mentioned by seven of our readers, five of them boys.

the ways in which Woodhouse library shaped her perception of class identities in Chapter 8.
37 'A Survey of Children's Reading', 1938, Sheffield City Libraries, 9.

Their encounter with *Treasure Island* was regarded as significant in part because it seemed to mark a graduation from child to adult. As Bob W put it, *Treasure Island* was 'the first adult book I ever read'.[38] Frank Burgin considers that he 'graduated into the classics' by means of *Treasure Island*, which he probably got from one of two 'great big book boxes' in his junior school classroom when he was about eight.[39] Christine was the only girl who recalls the book; she had it read to her in school in the late 1940s.[40]

So, once you found your way to a library independently, how did you know where to begin? Malcolm Mercer, born in 1925 on the hill behind the Central Railway Station, was guided by his intention of succeeding in life despite his failure to pass his scholarship examination for a grammar school place. In 1939, at the age of 14, Malcolm left elementary school to work in a shop. By the time he compiled the little notebook of books he had read between the ages of 15 and 17, just the age when a grammar school boy would have been preparing for his school certificate, his reading had become far more directed, though it is not clear by whom. Malcolm set himself all sorts of goals that reflect the richness of his life and the strength of his determination to educate himself. His notebook records, alphabetically under the name of each author, the books borrowed from Park Library. Novelists include John Buchan, Rider Haggard and Charles Dickens. Under 'A' he lists Antonius Marcus Aurelius' *Meditations*, Harrison W. Ainsworth's Victorian thrillers, *Boscobel* and *The Tower of London*, and then, in 1942, just before he was called up, Hans Christian Andersen's fairy tales. These works of fiction belonged to his father's generation, but the works of non-fiction were very much up-to-date. They reflect the boy's seriousness of purpose, which led him to become a teacher, the head of a successful primary school, to obtain an MPhil from Sheffield University and, in his spare time, to write a model work of social history: *Schooling the Poorer Child: Elementary Education in Sheffield 1560–1902* (1996). The non-fiction choices were chiefly vocational: works on how to dress a shop window, scouting manuals or guides to self-improvement. He also sought out books by illustrious men who could offer him proven roadmaps to some as yet unidentified success.[41]

38 Bob W, born 1940, interviewed by Trisha Cooper, 19 February 2012.
39 Frank Burgin, born 1938, interviewed by Loveday Herridge, 21 August 2012.
40 Christine, born 1940, interviewed by Peter Watson, 12 March 2013.
41 Malcolm Mercer, born 1925, interviewed by Mary Grover, 10 August 2010.

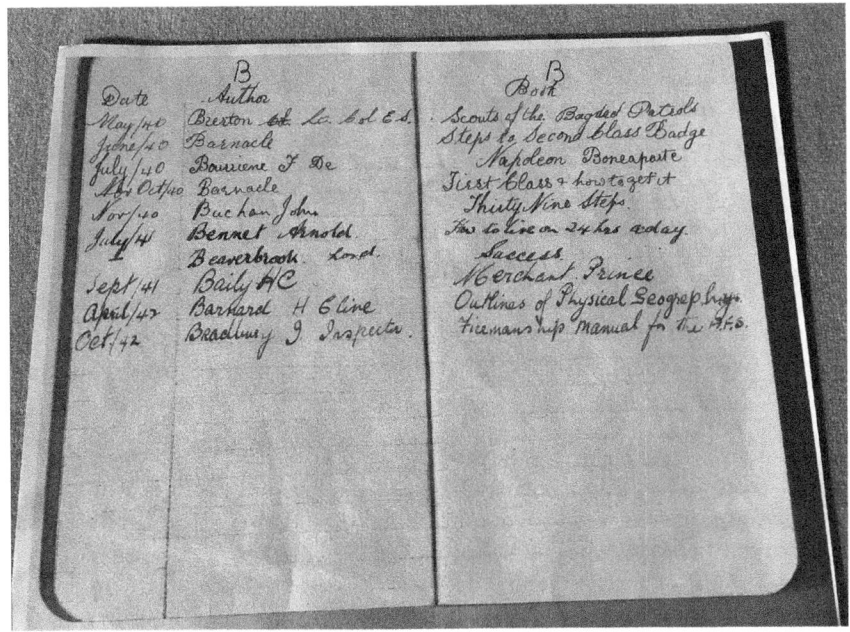

7 Malcolm Mercer's book diary: letter B

Born ten years later than Malcolm and with more educational advantages, Shirley Ellins and Mavis were both beneficiaries of the 1944 Education Act. They passed their 11-plus examinations and were able to attend selective schools where they were taught by specialist English teachers. Yet their exploration of the library was largely unguided. They both relied heavily on the alphabet method. Shirley remembers

> looking across the Os, at Baroness Orczy, and there was this person called 'Ouida' – O, U, I, – of whom I'd never heard! And there were rows of them. Because they were old fashioned, nobody took them out you know, and I was searching for Orczy, so that I could get a Scarlet Pimpernel book.[42]

Over and over again, such readers were attracted by the long runs of Orczy, Edgar Wallace or Mazo de la Roche. Just like the appetite for the 'hefty', a long run promised yards of precious text.

Mavis, also with a top 11-plus pass, must have wandered round the adult fiction shelves of the Central Library at the same time as Shirley, in the late 1940s.

42 Shirley Ellins, born 1936, interviewed by Loveday Herridge, 22 November 2011.

> As I walked in – didn't know quite know where to start – and started at the Ws. I found Hugh Walpole, Leo Walmsley and I don't quite know … I think accidentally someone had filed Warwick Deeping in the Ws and I read him and I just read others by those authors.[43]

Mavis's confidence in following a lead owed much to her habit of independent exploration but also to the interest of an uncle who selected books for her and encouraged her to develop her literary preferences. Fifteen years older than Mavis's father (the manager of a colliery weigh station), he had taken on a parental role to his younger brother who was eleven years old when their father died. In the holidays, when both Mavis's parents were working, the girl would visit her uncle who was head teacher of a school near Doncaster. He would lead his niece into the school hall' from a very early age', where the school library was all hers.

> And there were picture books, children's books. And he used to buy me books, often books which were much older than the age I was, and because I thought he knew what he was doing, if he bought it me and I found it hard, it must be my fault and I better make sure I could read it [laughing] because he would ask me about it when I saw him again and funnily enough he did manage to lead me on... His was the one book which triggered off lots of others. He bought me, when I was about seven, he bought me a book of Greek myths.

Most children lacked a mentor 'to lead them on'. Trusting in her uncle's direction, the 8-year-old was able to use her junior school trips to the local library profitably and she read her way through the Greek and Roman section. Then a few years later her uncle bought her *The Mill on the Floss*. Because of her trust in him, she persisted with it despite finding it a struggle.

> And that got me into reading George Eliot because if I liked that, which I did, and when I'd read it about three times I thought 'Mmm, she's written some more', and that kept me going for another few weeks. So, he sort of sparked me off when I first went to the library.

She considers that *The Mill on the Floss* and other novels by George Eliot

> moved me on because they weren't in the children's section. I was allowed to use my junior ticket and then they gave me an adult ticket which meant I could get not three books, I could get five books – I kept my junior ones as well – and I think that launched me into the senior library. So indirectly

43 Mavis, born 1937, interviewed by Mary Grover, 12 March 2012.

my uncle was very influential. He probably had no idea. He was the most influential person in my reading.

Her uncle provided his niece not only with books but also with a source of cultural authority. Her trust in his judgement gave Mavis the confidence to tackle difficult texts that would have daunted many. He enabled her to explore out of curiosity and without fear. This cultural confidence contributed to her success in the scholarship examination. Mavis gained the highest pass among her cohort of female candidates in winning a place at the prestigious Sheffield Girls' High School. She herself makes the point that, despite her grammar school education, her reading as a young teenager remained an eclectic mix of the childish and adult, the pulp and the classic. She read 'them all at once'.

> I was reading lots of other things. It would be George Eliot one week, it would be *The Island of Adventure* the next, or *The Adventures of Scamp*. I'm not sure if it was the Pullein-Thompson the horse stories – I had a horse phase, like all little girls, but I was reading quite a lot of adult fiction at the same time. Especially as the stuff that I got led on to was always available. You didn't get a big queue for the next George Eliot whereas you did for the Enid Blytons.

So, *Adam Bede* might have been a stop-gap until the latest Famous Five reappeared on the shelves.

Our readers' histories of independent voyages of discovery have a particular immediacy. The pleasure our readers took in recalling the physical nature of their book hunts reflects their delight in their own ingenuity, persistence and good luck – in living near a library, in finding a reading companion or in having a relative, like Mavis's uncle, who could open up whole cupboards full of books. The ways such aspiring readers mapped, retrospectively, the routes they devised to satisfy their craving to read show that by becoming readers, these children not only widened their imaginative and intellectual horizons, but also acquired a power to navigate their physical and social environments to suit their own purposes. Their growing confidence in their ability to find books helped them develop their reading tastes with a habit of expectancy and openness that persisted into adulthood. For many, and perhaps unexpectedly, roads less travelled were more likely to open up in the absence of a clear route map.

CHAPTER THREE

Hefty Books and Tuppenny Weeklies

Frank Burgin was born in 1938 in Mosborough, a pit village to the south-east of Sheffield. His mother was a local girl who had been in service and his father was a miner, from a family of miners. 'It's all I wanted to do when I was a little lad. I used to dig holes all over the garden.'

Frank was an only child. Both parents read to him, usually his mother. 'There was always someone to read to me … a sort of evening thing.' The house was full of books, mostly his parents' Sunday School prizes. Magazines and comics were delivered by the newsagent himself: *Woman's Weekly* for his mother, the *Daily Mail* for his father and *Film Fun* for Frank. He preferred the *Dandy* and the *Beano* but *Film Fun* was the approved comic because 'there were actual stories in there full of text'.

There was no local library. Most of the books Frank read were from the elementary school book box or from the books on his parents' shelves. His parents wanted him to do well at school, which he didn't.

Frank left his elementary school at 14 to take up an engineering apprenticeship in Sheffield. He has always read and continued his education in evening classes. He was the only one of our readers to gain a PhD.[1]

1 Frank Burgin, born 1938, interviewed by Loveday Herridge, 21 August 2012.

Many families, like Frank's, helped their children become independent readers by buying weekly comics, subscribing to a set of encyclopaedias or, in the 1950s, to a set of classic novels. Though the habit of buying individual books was beyond the means of most, the compendiums of fiction and poetry, the reference books or the surprisingly durable and shareable comics had the power to create small reading communities and to point children to worlds of print that would otherwise have been completely inaccessible. The way these resources were used was shaped by the way they were paid for, the way they were shared and the physical nature of the textual object itself.

If they had the financial resources, a family might buy their child an encyclopaedia. The very word conferred reliability – a library on one shelf, its authority unquestionable. These encyclopaedias could be bought volume by volume by subscription, but often appeared as a complete set on a child's birthday. Only one reader from a working-class family describes reading one at home between the wars. Winnie, whose father worked with railway horses and who came from a family of blacksmiths, still treasures, at 95, a beautifully produced single volume from a set of *The Southern Encyclopaedia of Knowledge*, the front part missing. The family could only afford one volume.[2] Frank Burgin's father bought his only child a full set in the 1940s. Alan B, as we have seen, was bought a set in the 1950s by his father, a steelmaker. Most children who possessed a full set (Arthur Mee's *Children's Encyclopaedia* was a favourite) had a father in middle management or highly skilled manual work: a motor engineer in the burgeoning automobile market, a master printer, a colliery electrician. The fathers of both Dorothy Latham and Betty Roberts were colliery electricians, highly skilled, well paid and married to women with bookish tastes. We have met Betty's mother and the nursery full of books, some of them sent to the family by friends of her mother. Dorothy owed her access to an encyclopaedia to a friend of her mother. It became a community resource in the colliery village just as Frank's did.

> I think somebody mum knew sent mum the money and we got these encyclopaedias. Twelve. All sorts of information you could find, and I can remember everybody from the village used to be coming up – 'can we look in your encyclopaedias?'[3]

2 Winnie Lincoln, born 1923, interviewed by Mary Grover, 8 May 2012.
3 Dorothy Latham, born 1931, interviewed by Clare Keen, 17 October 2011.

In 1920s Leeds, the impoverished Richard Hoggart, who grew up to be a cultural commentator, remembers what he owed to the owners of similar treasure troves, men with 'a couple of small shelves of books with a one-volume encyclopaedia prominent'. Such informal librarians would also help their neighbours with their correspondence.[4]

Ken's father was a company secretary. Though he could afford to buy his son a set of encyclopaedias in the 1930s, the contrast between Ken's immediate surroundings and the communities imagined by the authors of the encyclopaedia amused the boy.

> I used to gobble those up because they had things in each volume (which must have been that thick I should think) things to make and do. 'Things every boy can make' ... And none of them I could! Cos it used to say things like, 'Go to your friendly optician and ask for two lenses, a concave and a convex one. And make your own telescope out of them with cardboard tubes.' 'Go to your grocer, your friendly grocer' ... and I used to think 'local'? 'Friendly'? They must live in a friendly place! [laughter] And I used to know Mr Salt, the optician, but I daren't have asked him for any lenses to make a telescope.[5]

At Christmas in 1930 the 7-year-old Mary Robertson and her older sister were given all twelve volumes of the prestigious Encyclopaedia Britannica. Though surrounded by books of every kind, the daughters of the well-paid analytic chemist found this one 'our greatest source of delight'. Mary's father did not send her to an academic school, such as the Girls' High School. Her parents' chief aspiration for her was that she should care for them in their old age. So it was from these volumes that she and her sister 'learned everything we knew', reading them together on the sitting-room carpet.

Meg's relationship with the family encyclopaedias fostered a particularly intimate engagement with their contents. She, like Shirley and Mavis, was a grammar school girl in the 1940s. Her father, like theirs, was engaged in managerial or regulatory activities. He was an engineer and inspector for the General Post Office and came from a family of active Methodists. The family, though not affluent, were familiar with texts from which they sought information or inspiration. Meg turned to their encyclopaedias during the Second World War.

---

4 Richard Hoggart, *A Local Habitation: Life and Times, Volume 1: 1918–1940*, Oxford: Oxford University Press, 1989 [1988], 153.
5 Ken, born 1925, interviewed by Clare Keen, 16 November 2011.

In the encyclopaedias there was a section on Arabic, writing the alphabet and so on, which I thought might come in useful with my father being out in Egypt and the Middle East. Of course, I didn't see him from the age of four until he came back in 1946. And I can remember trying to teach myself to write Arabic. I guess I would have only been about eight or nine, I think.[6]

Twenty years later in the 1960s Meg and her husband bought their two small sons a set of second-hand Encyclopaedia Britannicas, on weekly subscription. Their son, now fifty, 'still has these Britannicas, proud place in his home, in his own library at home'.

The authority of an encyclopaedia is peculiarly vulnerable to the passage of time. Yet its power to enshrine a moment in a childhood when a particular horizon was opened up, often with a cherished family member, means that we found that many of our readers still kept their childhood encyclopaedias, perhaps, like Meg's son, appreciating the sacrifices made by his parents to supply him with knowledge and opportunity.

Wonder books: 'Brimful of joyous entertainment'

In addition to the truncated, single volume of the *Southern Encyclopaedia*, Winnie Lincoln did have her own encapsulated library. Born in 1923, Winnie had little chance of gaining a place at one of the few girls' grammar schools of the early 1930s and left school at 14. Though her father had not been educated beyond elementary school, both he and Winnie's mother encouraged her reading, and they both read: her father Westerns from the local tuppenny library (a small commercial library) and her mother the Bible, from which she quoted confidently. Winnie herself owned *The Children's Golden Treasure Book*, a compilation first published by Odhams in 1935. When her interviewer read aloud the subtitle on the front cover, 'Brimful of joyous entertainment', Winnie nodded emphatically 'And it was!'. The book was brimful of poems by 'Mrs Ewing', Christina Rossetti and Mary Lamb, but chiefly lengthy extracts from classics, the full versions of which Winnie was never to explore: 'Maggie and the Gypsies' from *The Mill on the Floss* and 'Surprise for Katy' from *What Katy Did*. It is not surprising that the sources of these extracts were to remain hidden because the novels from which they were taken were not cited. Winnie thinks her parents acquired the volume with the help of coupons from the paper; she is not sure

6 Meg Young, born 1936, interviewed by Mary Grover, 6 June 2013.

which one.[7] Though such compilations may not always have led children to the classics that they mined, they were, like the encyclopaedias, personal possessions. Such compilations of fiction, made in the 1930s but reprinted well into the 1950s, were popular with publishers because much of the material was free from the constraints of copyright. These bulky compilations of extracts from classic novels offered the precious opportunity to reread. The sense that the contents 'belonged' to the reader accounts for the vast affection in which these volumes were held.

Carolyn, born in 1944, remembers a big book, 'one like the annuals but it was all old stories, not sort of the comic strip things and the quizzy things'.[8] A family with few resources and uncertain of the merits of the fiction on offer had confidence in the mighty omnibus. Such a volume is the first book that James Green can remember. It was given to the 7-year-old in 1942, a rich gift for such a bleak Christmas. It contained, among others, *Robinson Crusoe*, *Little Women*, *Gulliver's Travels* and two others unremembered. Asked why he remembers that particular book above all others, Jim was emphatic.

> Because it was my own book, probably the first book I'd really owned, you could go through it and you could go through it again, and so it was with me for quite a long time. And at that stage, I probably wasn't all that good at reading, so it'd take me a long time, and it was quite a hefty book.[9]

That omnibus was the text that transformed the boy who knew how to read into one who could read anything that was put in front of him, and who felt compelled to extend the range of what he read. In some part that resource would have compensated for the fact that the secondary modern in which Jim found himself when he turned down his grammar school place had nothing like the library resources he would have found at a grammar school.

Buying reading matter

Annuals and encyclopaedias were more often bought than novels. As post-war austerity began to ease and paperback books proliferated, more affluent families began to contribute to pocket money or to buy novels, but even in the 1950s they are nearly always recorded as gifts. In the

---

7 Winnie Lincoln, born 1923, interviewed by Mary Grover, 8 May 2012.
8 Carolyn W, born 1944, interviewed by Trisha Cooper, 19 February 2012.
9 James Green, born 1936, interviewed by Jean Gilmour, 12 October 2011.

late 1940s Bob W, the son of a steelworker, bought his first book. There 'used to be the very slim books you could go down to the newsagents and buy them. And it was ... oh God, gosh ... Sexton Blake.'[10] These short detective adventures thrilled boys from 1893 till 1978, 4,000 stories by nearly 200 different authors, its hero admirable less for his deductive powers than for his ability to escape from traps set for him by evil brotherhoods and foreign megalomaniacs.[11]

Frank Burgin discovered them in the box of books that passed for a library in his elementary school in the 1940s. The addictive quality of such stories, and their relative affordability to a boy earning enough to have a few pennies to spare, is illustrated by the image of Rupert, the fruiterer's delivery boy 'freewheeling' through the pages of a 1934 detective thriller for adults, Alan Melville's *Weekend at Thrackley*. Before embarking on his battle with a criminal mastermind, the book's hero narrowly escapes being run over by this boy cyclist 'with a fourpenny novelette in one hand and a quarter-stone of potatoes, half a dozen leeks and a few similar items dangling from his handlebars'.[12]

Whereas in the interwar period the purchase of books for a child was a rare treat, even for an affluent family, in the 1950s children's classics became more affordable and the use of book tokens, launched in 1932, became more widespread. In 1952 Regent Classics brought out 'the world's best-loved and most famous stories, presented in an easily read type and an attractive format, giving an opportunity of building up a fine library of masterpieces at a moderate price'. Each volume was 2/6, the paper coarse and the texts sometimes abridged (*Moby Dick* is shrunk to 248 pages), but they were hardback and the covers striking – a great resource.

Reading as 'blotting out'

Kath was born in 1928, the daughter of a core maker with seven children.[13] Her parents were both readers but there would have been no money to buy books and no space into which she could retreat to explore

---

10 Bob W, born 1940, interviewed by Trisha Cooper, 19 February 2012.
11 See E.S. Turner, *Boys Will Be Boys: The Story of Sweeney Todd, Deadwood Dick, Sexton Blake, Billy Bunter, Dick Barton et al.*, Harmondsworth: Penguin, 1975 [1948].
12 Alan Melville, *Weekend at Thrackley*, London: British Library, 2018 [1934], 36.
13 A core maker made sand cores for foundry moulds.

them except the library. Kath's older sister was a great resource before Kath herself learned to read, telling and reading her stories. When she became a reader Kath weaned herself off her sister's constant supply of Just William narratives and would 'curl up on a chair or something and read and blot out the other people'.[14]

In an equally crowded home, with four generations all gravitating towards the kitchen where her mother provided constant support, Judith's absorption in her book would be penetrated by the voice of her Aunty Marjorie, haranguing her mother: 'Doesn't that child do anything? She's always got her nose in a book.'[15] Irene's mother sometimes shouted at her daughter because 'I'd got my face in a book – instead of doing other things', but none of these girls were particularly daunted.[16] Neither was Doreen, the only reader who was actively discouraged from reading because it was a 'waste of time'.[17]

Doreen had become an habitual reader at the orphanage in Ripon where she was sent in 1942 at the age of eight. Her mother had died while her father was abroad in the army. When the war was over her father collected his children from the orphanages to which they had been distributed and fetched them back to the rubble-filled streets of Attercliffe, where so many workers in the steelworks lived. He then introduced them to their Belgian stepmother. The interior world of books to which Doreen was in the habit of retreating was perceived by her stepmother as a realm where her writ had no sway, a real threat to the woman trying to assert some authority over three young strangers. Doreen was a rare example of a working-class girl who found a private space and a source of light by which to read. She stood at her bedroom window until the sun went down.

The book that Doreen read repeatedly was *Anne of Green Gables*. Nearly every one of its readers treasured L.M. Montgomery's story about the adopted daughter of a Canadian farmer who succeeds in getting an education, but Doreen found that it spoke to her directly. When asked why it was such a favourite she replied 'You realise that there's more than you orphaned'. It was a book that went some way to reconciling her to loss and displacement. She took it out time and time again from the nearby Attercliffe Library.

14 Kath, born 1928, interviewed by Clare Keen, 16 November 2011.
15 Judith G, born 1939, interviewed by Loveday Herridge, 14 February 2013.
16 Irene Hailstone, born 1921, interviewed by Susan Roe, 28 February 2012.
17 Doreen Gill, born 1934, interviewed by Mary Grover, 18 May 2012.

Many books marked a transition between childhood and adulthood: *Anne of Green Gables*, *Daddy-Long-Legs*, *What Katy Did* or *The Girl of the Limber Lost*, for example. They tended to celebrate the heroine's success in integrating herself into society either by marriage or by acquiring an education, but other coming-of-age novels celebrated the power of the heroine to set herself apart from these social roles. Born fourteen years later than Doreen, Josie Hall was an adolescent in the 1950s, part of a loving family which, nevertheless, she took pleasure in keeping at bay. Josie identified with Jane Eyre.

> I can see Jane sat in the window seat hiding from her cousin, reading the book and I presume maybe I was a bit like that. I never thought about it before. Hiding away, reading a book. Not wanting anybody to find you.[18]

The desire to read set Josie apart from her family, temporarily removing her to a 'hidden' space. That private space of intellectual and imaginative freedom can, of course, deliver educational and professional competence which removes the reader to a different place and social class. Such social displacement can lead to a painful loss of connection with home. None of our readers mentioned this. Few of our female readers would have been able to capitalise on their reading skills by gaining the educational qualifications that would have delivered such rupture. Those who went back late to education did so when they had raised their children.

The books that surround Josie in her present house did not remove her from her childhood family nor deliver a disruptive shift in social class, but they were an inheritance deeply valued and capitalised on by her own children. Amused, but rueful, Josie recalled how books came between her and her own daughter.

> I remember Caroline, and I'm sure she'd left home by this [time] and come back in her teens for Christmas day, and I thought, 'it's a mistake this buying them books', because you never see them, all day Christmas Day lying on their bed reading, just appearing for meals.

Both Caroline and her mother hid away from the family with their chosen book, but Caroline was let be, never hunted down.

18 Josie Hall, born 1942, interviewed by Mary Grover, 4 May 2012.

Father and child

Most of our readers who graduated from childhood reading to what might be described as mature adult material did so under their own steam. Long working hours and a father's role in the family as wage-earner rather than nurturer meant that a father's tastes would not often be communicated to a child. Companionable journeys in search of books from local libraries or street stalls were far more likely to have been taken with mother, although, as we have seen, a mother's taste was sometimes gently mocked. When Gillian was asked which books first made her 'feel grown up' she mentioned 'the light romances' that her mother borrowed.[19] When the 17-year-old Mary Robertson read her mother's tuppenny library romances she 'always felt guilty because, you know, you didn't read those kind of things then'. It is difficult to know from where such shame arose, as she was taught by nuns who didn't sound very censorious. 'Bless 'em, they were lovely, it was a lovely school but I don't think I learned a lot.'[20]

Though girls such as Gillian Applegate and Mary Robertson tended to disassociate themselves from their mother's tastes, girls nearly always had respect for a father's tastes even if they did not follow his lead. In the 1950s both of Christine's parents had high educational aspirations for their grammar school daughter. Her mother wanted her to be top of the class, but made no connection between educational achievement and the kind of books she should read. Her father was an insurance agent and musician who tried to guide her reading habits, pushing her from an early age 'towards these classics that were in the bookcase: the Wilkie Collins and that type of thing, which probably was a little bit old for my age group'. Though Christine responded to her father's guidance, she herself preferred the Chalet School stories.

Pat Cymbal, on the other hand, shared her father's literary tastes. He was a Lithuanian furrier who in the 1920s gave up his profession to live in Sheffield because it was his wife's home town. There is no doubt who was the cultural authority in Pat's life. She affectionately dismissed her mother's taste for fairy stories but describes her father telling his children 'stories of the Greek heroes, etc., which eventually led onto the Iliad and the Odyssey, you know'. He was also 'a great fan of the Idylls of the King, Tennyson'.

19 Gillian Applegate, born 1941, interviewed by Mary Grover, 3 May 2012.
20 Mary Robertson, born 1923, interviewed by Susan Roe, 7 March 2013.

And we loved those stories, and he would read them over and over. [laughing] And I remember, when I went to grammar school, we started to do Tennyson and I could recite whole gobs of it off by heart, you know, before we started. I still can to this very day.[21]

Far from solemnly directing his daughter to improving works, Pat's father's delight in well-written and diverting fiction simply became hers, as she shared his taste not just for the 'classics' but for Edgar Wallace, P.G. Wodehouse, Jerome K. Jerome and Rider Haggard. In addition to British popular fiction, Pat relished Damon Runyon's tales of 'hoodlums on Broadway': 'he writes about them all as though they're just ordinary people, you know and they're all villains and murderers, but it's very funny'. After twenty years as a buyer in a large fashion house, Pat did a degree in literature and taught English at Sheffield Girls' High School in the late 1940s. Like Christine's father, though perhaps less purposefully, Pat's father had prepared his daughter for a grammar school education. And significantly it was Mr Cymbal, one of the few foreign migrants to Sheffield, who connected his child with a sophisticated and contemporary literary culture. Most of our readers in the late 1930s had a much more limited awareness of literary scenes beyond the genre fiction of tuppenny libraries, Edwardian popular fiction and a narrow selection of classics.

Newspaper reading

One potential window on to the world beyond Sheffield was the newspaper. Yet it was never, apart from *The Children's Newspaper*, described in the hands of a mother. The paper often defined an exclusive space claimed by the man of the house, acting as a barrier between father and family. Raised against the hubbub in the kitchen living room, it sheltered the returning wage-earner in the evening. Many working-class children in homes without books describe the newspaper as their father's only reading matter: the *Daily Mirror*, the *Daily Express* or the local paper. When Judith's father raised his paper in the evening it signalled that the living space was now his solitary domain: 'he used to have the kitchen to himself, kind of thing'. Given that this was usually the only room in the house with a fire, this meant that the family lacked a warm place to sit and read themselves.

The Second World War often prompted a change in a child's access to the newspaper. A child often shared with a male relative an urgent

21 Pat Cymbal, born 1926, interviewed by Liz Hawkins, 14 September 2011.

curiosity about the events of the world beyond Sheffield. While Meg's father was fighting in the desert, she and her mother went to live with her grandfather.

> And he took the *Daily Express* and I was encouraged to read all the headlines to do with the war, you know, the advance of the Eighth Army and so on. Yes, at a young age I knew more names of towns in Egypt than in this country! ... And we always looked for photographs and so on in the paper, to see if we could recognise him.

Towards the end of the war the teenage Peter Mason was scouring the pages of the newspaper with his father for news of his brother, who had disappeared in the Burmese jungle. Peter's father always encouraged his remaining son to read the newspapers.[22] Loss and anxiety spurred these parental figures to engage a child in the family with the outside world through the medium of the newspaper. Newspapers were one of the first sources of print read by Noel, born in 1939. Before he went to school, he remembers that he 'started reading newspapers and I probably was inquiring about the War.'[23] The war initiated every child's sense that the adult world might at any moment break in upon and destroy the familiar. James Green, born in 1936, read the front page of his father's *Daily Express* when he was eight years old. He, like Noel, was anxious to learn about the progress of the war.[24]

A few children from fairly affluent and aspirational families were bought *The Children's Newspaper*, produced by Arthur Mee, editor of *The Children's Encyclopaedia*. It reflected his serious moral and religious purposes. It also aimed to increase general knowledge and awareness of current affairs. Two of the three readers who mentioned it remember the puzzles and competitions. Christine's father was keen that she should enter the short story competition in the late 1940s, which she did, gaining 'an honourable mention'.[25] Betty, whose mother had been a teacher and assigned a dedicated 'playroom' to the education and entertainment of her children and their friends, provided her with a weekly copy in the 1930s. Betty's description is lukewarm:

> All sorts of things were in it. Things that were happening in Australia or New Zealand and you'd get maps of them and get the animals and things

---

22 Peter Mason, born in 1928, interviewed by Susan Roe, 28 September 2011.
23 Noel, born 1939, interviewed by Loveday Herridge, 1 August 2012.
24 James Green, born 1936, interviewed by Jean Gilmour, 12 October 2011.
25 Christine, born 1940, interviewed by Peter Watson, 12 March 2013.

they had there. You'd have little crosswords to do and writing a little story. It had various kinds of little poems that we'd never really heard of. Quite strange – a little story went on each month.[26]

The Children's Newspaper was published until 1965. In the 1950s Edna bought it for her son who, like Betty, was unimpressed. Given his lack of curiosity Edna was surprised that he had been congratulated on his general knowledge by his teacher. "'Well," I said, "it's not because he reads". I bought that *Children's Newspaper* and I got the articles out of it, not him.' But, as her son pointed out, she passed on what she learned from it to him.[27]

'I ate comics': comics, magazines and reading communities

Perhaps Edna's son would have preferred a comic. Josie, who read everything that came to hand, spent Christmas Days in the 1950s with her favourite presents, the latest *Dandy* and *Beano* annuals. Launched in 1938, the *Beano*, with its cast of irrepressible scamps, seems, in the 1940s and the 1950s, to have been read by children across the social classes and to have appealed equally to male and female readers despite being aimed at boys.

At the beginning of the twentieth century childhood weeklies were nearly all gender- and class-specific. Girls were not as well served as boys. In the late nineteenth century, anxiety about the decadent effect that the lurid adventures in the 'penny dreadfuls' might have on British manhood prompted the creation of a number of weekly magazines designed to tempt boys away from mere sensation and to educate and entertain our future leaders. As a young man in the early 1920s, Sheffield's illustrious chief librarian, Joseph Lamb, contributed to this mission by gaining a small income by writing for one such magazine, *Young England* (1880–1937). The leading weekly in this field was the *Boys' Own Paper*. Launched by the Religious Tract Society in 1879, it was published in weekly issues which were bound in a bumper annual to be bought at Christmas. So successful was the formula that competing magazines such as *Chums* (1892–1941) emerged, with much the same kind of content: public school sporting stories and adventures of derring-do in the colonies interspersed with well-researched and absorbing biographies, accounts of exotic travel and

26 Barbara 'Betty' R, born 1925, interviewed by Loveday Herridge, 26 September 2011.
27 Edna, born 1928, interviewed by Ros Witten, 25 July 2012.

instructions on how to build useful items such as canoes. Detective and spy stories later became popular. These earnest but thrilling publications were not mentioned by our working-class or middle-class male readers. Sales were declining in the 1930s and 1940s when most of our readers were growing up. *Chums*, like other magazines, went under in the Second World War because of the paper shortage.

Lamb moved on to writing for *Young England* by way of his taste for pre-war tuppenny weeklies such as *Boy's Friend* and the *Boy's Herald*: not as shocking as the 'penny dreadfuls' but not as improving as *Boys' Own*. Lamb described his boyhood expeditions with his brother across Lancashire in search of them. '[We] were so keyed up during the week awaiting the next instalments of our favourites that we walked a couple of miles the evening before publication to obtain advance copies from an obliging newsagent.'[28] Though it was not the job of the library to stock magazines and comics, Lamb never despised them.

In the introduction to his essay on boys' weeklies, George Orwell described how in 'any poor quarter in any poor town' in the 1930s you were never far from a small newsagent, with its 'poky little window with sweet-bottles and packets of Players, and a dark interior smelling of liquorice all-sorts'.[29] Dorothy, who attended a talk I gave to a Sheffield community group, described such a room as 'a paradise'. Her local newsagent, in the late 1920s, allowed her to 'pore over' comics that had not been sold by closing time as long as she 'didn't crease them'. Jean remembers a friendly newsagent in the 1930s as a source of great bounty.

> I can remember getting *Chick's Own – Rainbow* as well. She was a huge lady. She would sit on the table and it was covered with papers and comics and things. You had to pay for them of course. Oh Mrs Dabbs![30]

Not only was the newsagent's a Mecca to which children took themselves off, but the comics bought enabled them to read others swapped with friends and family members. A.C. Jenkinson's survey of childhood reading from the late 1930s suggests that 'hand-to-hand trading of comics amongst boys' meant that 'the number read must be far greater than the number sold'.[31]

28 J.P. Lamb, 'Librarian when Young: Part 1', *The Librarian and Book World*, 45.1 (1956), 3.

29 George Orwell, 'Boys' Weeklies', *Horizon*, 3 (1940); reprinted in *Inside the Whale and Other Essays*, Harmondsworth: Penguin, 1957, 175.

30 Jean H, born in 1926, interviewed by Mary Grover, 8 May 2012.

31 A.J. Jenkinson, *What Children Read*, London: Methuen, 1940, 66. It is difficult

Jenkinson also discovered the strong appeal of boys' comics to girls, especially the *Wizard* and the *Rover*. The only one of our readers who recalls with pleasure the *Magnet*, one of the boys' weeklies that troubled George Orwell, was the highly literate Mary Soar. As Orwell notes, both the *Gem* and the *Magnet* were 'much read by girls'.[32] Before the failure of Mary's father's printing business in the mid-1930s, money was found to have the tuppenny *Magnet* delivered to the door. It introduced the girl to the world of Billy Bunter and the Famous Five of Greyfriars. Although Jenkinson did not find that boys had the same interest in girls' comics, Bob W, a child in the late 1940s, does describe exploring the women's magazines he picked up at home: 'There were good stories in the *Woman's Weekly*'.[33]

In 1940 the *Magnet* was found by Jenkinson to be much less popular than the more recent leaders in the field of school stories, *Hotspur* and the *Rover*, but none of our readers mentioned these newer publications. Orwell points out that the public school ethos of the more recent magazines did not differ much from their older rivals. All such publications, set in boys' public schools and modelling the ethos of 'fair play', were deplored by Orwell on ideological grounds. Writing in the left-wing *Horizon* in 1940, he described the conservative, misogynist and imperialist ethos underpinning such stories, a world where

> major problems of our time do not exist, that there is nothing wrong with laissez-faire capitalism, that foreigners are un-important comics and that the British Empire is a sort of charity-concern which will last for ever.[34]

to use Jenkinson's pioneering survey as the basis of comparison between Sheffield and reading nationally, as Jenkinson does not specify the location of the schools from which he drew his respondents. The pupils surveyed were all of the more able. The 2,900 questionnaires were completed by girls and boys from A streams: 57 per cent from what would now be called grammar schools and 43 per cent from 'senior' schools, predecessors of the post-1944 'secondary moderns'. Some of the information given was edited out, as I mention in my Introduction.

32 Orwell, 'Boys' Weeklies', 183.

33 In addition to Jenkinson's survey, other useful sources of readers' responses to comics include Mass Observation, File report 1332, July 1942, 'Books and the public' and material in the Reading Experience Database, http://www.open. ac.uk/Arts/RED/index.html. James Chapman's *British Comics: A Cultural History*, London: Reaktion, 2011, provides invaluable context.

34 Orwell, 'Boys' Weeklies', 200.

Jonathan Rose suggests that these worlds, remote from most of their readers, did not represent something that was admired, something to aspire to or even something real. Rather, they were a revelation that home was not all that there was. He discusses the apparent absurdity of the journalist Chaim Bermant, as a child newly arrived in Glasgow from Belarus in the 1930s, trying to assimilate into the culture of Glasgow by adopting the slang of Lord Snooty from the pages of the *Beano*. But Bermant found that the *Beano* served its turn. The boy not only came to share with his new neighbours an argot almost as remote to them as it was to him but also a sense that every child could simply spend twopence to escape a familiar and possibly oppressive environment. The remoteness of the worlds depicted in the tuppenny weeklies was the whole point – and the basis of their allure.[35]

It is impossible to gauge the effect of such comics on their readers' values, but whereas the earlier and equally conservative *Boys' Own* and *Chums* had been launched as improving, their less earnest successors in the 1940s could be dismissed by parents not for their politics but because they appeared to lack any educational value. Shirley Ellins's Methodist parents disapproved of comics and magazines for their frivolity: 'I guess, they thought they were trivial. And not educational. And perhaps wouldn't stretch me. They never censored other reading. And money was tight!' They may only have cost a few pennies, but even Mr Ellins, a man in secure employment at the Town Hall, would need to justify such a regular outgoing.

Recalling their reading of comics before and after the Second World War, our interviewees mention the Christmas annual, paid for by subscription throughout the year, much more frequently than they mention weekly comics. As we have seen, the only books owned by the daughter of a steelworker, young Irene Hailstone in the 1930s, were annuals such as *Pip, Squeak and Wilfred*, gifts from relatives rather than her parents, and treasured possessions.

Between the wars, weekly comics or magazines were a rare treat rather than ubiquitous trash for most of our readers. Even after the Second World War, comics were still a luxury out of the reach of most working-class children. When Josie Hall's father returned from grim years in the

---

35 Jonathan Rose, *The Intellectual Life of the British Working Classes*, New Haven, CT: Yale University Press, 2001, 333–4, discussing Chaim Bermant's *Coming Home* (1976).

Far East to work in the steelworks, he did what he could to nurture his 5-year-old daughter's intelligence.

> It was just after the war, and working-class people, they just didn't have books in the house. I remember being … I must have been a very young child but I was like really fond of newspapers and I think, yeah, because there was probably nothing else to read. And sometimes my father used to come home from work with a big pile of second-hand comics, and it was like manna from heaven: I just used to fall on them.

It was a comic that revealed to the author Alan Garner that he had got the knack of reading. A poorly child in the 1930s and 1940s, Garner's mother told him fairy tales and read him nursery rhymes, but the moment when he realised he had the power to read himself came in isolation hospital: 'I was looking at "Stonehenge Kit, the Ancient Brit" in the *Knockout*, the best of all the comics. And then I took off.'[36] The educational content may have been difficult for Shirley's parents to discern but the power of comics to help a child 'take off' and to associate reading with pleasure was obvious in our interviews. The avidity, the appetite and the autonomy of children on the hunt for comics illustrate the role comics played in making reading fun.

Frank Burgin, the only child of aspirational parents in a mining village south of Sheffield, remembers from the late 1940s not his parents' preferred publication, *Film Fun*, with its high proportion of text to pictures, but the *Dandy* and the *Beano*. 'I ate comics', he recalls with relish. Frank was contemporary with David Flather, the son of one of Sheffield's major industrialists: both boys revelled in the antics of the Bash Street Kids whose wild ways were as remote to Frank, who was brought up with strict rules of conduct, as they were to David, orphaned, wealthy but kept apart from local children. Josie reflected on the 'manna' such publications represented: 'it wasn't particularly because it was the comics. It was the written word, I suppose … looking back, with hindsight.' And perhaps the companionship of these anarchic creations.

The children who were bought comics either came from homes where the father was in well-paid employment or where there was only one child. Maureen L, like Frank Burgin, had no brothers and sisters. She too became a fluent reader just after the war with the help of the *Beano* and *Dandy*. Her father was a 'labourer' at the steel and engineering

---

36 Alan Garner in conversation with Andrew Tate, https://highprofiles.info/interview/ alan-garner/ (accessed 27 December 2021).

toolmaker's Samuel Osborn. Maureen's mother did all she could to support her child's reading habit, despite not being an habitual reader herself. Both of Maureen's parents bought her comics, not books. As Jenkinson found, many boys, including those going to selective secondary schools, referred to comics as 'books'.[37]

Throughout the first half of the twentieth century, comics could introduce children to a world where reading was a source of pure pleasure and, often, a social activity. They created shared fictional and comic gags and they established a commonwealth of letters where the possession of one comic might enable a reader to lay their hands on another.

Girls' weeklies

Maureen's father worked 12-hour shifts at the steelmaker and engineering tool manufacturer Samuel Osborn, and her mother had a part-time job so, even in those bleak post-war years, they had still enough disposable income to buy prodigious numbers of comics, five a week while Maureen was at primary school: *Bunty, School Friend*, the *Dandy*, the *Beano* and another 'boy's comic' (is it possible that Maureen's father was fulfilling his own childhood dreams?)

A few girls read the hugely popular *Sunny Stories*, which under the guidance of Enid Blyton became a favourite with young girls from the late 1930s. Judith G remembers it in the 1940s.

> [I]t had cartoons in it, and all about Princess Margaret and The Queen, you know – what was that governess that got told off for writing about her? I don't know. She used to write little stories about that. I remember they used to buy us that every week, so I think that's what started us reading.

By far the most frequently mentioned publication aimed at girls was the *Girls' Crystal*, published from 1935 to 1963. When the magazine was launched it was a novelty. Dorothy H, born in 1929, makes the point that she didn't have girls' comics in the 1930s. '*Girls' Crystal*? … I can't remember any girls' comics at that time. They didn't come out till a bit later.'[38] Its appeal must have been great for it to weather the paper shortage during the war, when many comics went under.

All but one of the women who mentioned their delight in the *Girls' Crystal* went to a grammar school, in the late 1930s and the 1940s.

---

37 Jenkinson, *What Children Read*, 66.
38 Dorothy H, born 1929, interviewed by Susan Roe, 7 May 2013.

Curiously, it appears to have had most currency in the kind of school where English teachers might be expected to be censorious. It was when Shirley got to High Storrs grammar school that she made a friend who lent her copies in the 1940s. Jean Wolfendale, a near contemporary of Shirley's at the same grammar school, had the good fortune to have the weekly delivered to her home. She felt it was 'quite a decent comic but you couldn't possibly have mentioned that in school because that wasn't the done thing as it were'.[39]

The stories in this stirring magazine were mostly written by men using female pseudonyms. Horace Boyten renamed himself Enid Boyten in an attempt to identify himself with a more famous children's author (and was forced to change the pseudonym). The authors who wrote under the names of Jean Vernon ('The Mad-cap Form Mistress'), Audrey Nichols ('Nurse Rosemary'), Diana Martin ('She Was a Fugitive'), Stella Knight, Pearl Fairland and Gail Western ('Tony the Speed Girl') were all male.[40] It was a magazine rather than a comic until 1953, and its launch coincided with a period when girls were beginning to be offered greater educational and occupational opportunities. Many of its stories were set in girls' boarding schools, some were historical adventures and a few were set in foreign parts. In the 1945 annual, racism is far less overt than it was in the boys' magazines that troubled Orwell in 1940. The annuals of the late 1940s contain a mixed cast of characters. Boyfriends appear but are not central to the plot. Boys appear far more frequently than girls did in boys' story magazines of the 1930s. Foreigners feature, such as 'the brave little Chinese girl' who befriends the plucky Delia (dropped behind Japanese lines in the Second World War). It is the Chinese girl, not Delia, who has the last word in the account of their adventure.[41]

The girls were certainly sold short in the craft work proposed for their entertainment. The weighty Boys' Own annual in 1930 instructed boys on how to build their own 'B.O.P. Metropolitan' wireless receiver and the later Eagle (in its first incarnation 1950–69) was full of features on science and technology. In the late 1940s the Fleet Street journalists responsible for producing the content of the Girls' Crystal were still encouraging their female readers who had grown up through the war to engage in

39 Jean Wolfendale, born 1935, interviewed by Sahra Ajiba, 14 October 2011.

40 http://www.collectingbooksandmagazines.com/crystal.html (accessed 21 August 2019). This account references 'A Look at the Crystal', by Esmond Cadish, in the 1984 Collectors Digest Annual.

41 Janet McKibben, 'The Girl from the Sky', in The Girls' Crystal Annual, London: Fleetway House, 1945, 95–108.

traditional maidenly pursuits: making the utilitarian ornamental, often by the addition of pom-poms. In the 1949 *Girls' Crystal* annual girls are invited to create a 'dusting brush' adorned with a pom-pom so colourful that it 'makes housework almost a pleasure'.[42]

This domestic role is very much at odds with the conduct of the heroines of the stories in the pages of *Girls' Crystal*. Whether in school, the African jungle or on occasional forays into the Far East, the heroine's goal is to have her voice heard. Her quest is for justice rather than romance. Hers is often a lone voice of principle, in contrast to the merry crew of comrades that dominate the narrative of boys' school stories, such as the Famous Five of Greyfriars in the *Magnet*. The heroine's moral independence is often asserted against the culture of the dominant group or against the bad judgement of the adults to whom she has been entrusted.

These weekly magazines and the annuals were read by girls of all ages: from Madeleine, struggling to read at the age of five in 1945 (she had asked a generous relative if she could have a *Girls' Crystal* annual rather than a doll),[43] to the teenage Dorothy Norbury (for whom the magazine marked the beginning of adulthood: 'The comic that I read that made me feel grown up was the *Girls' Crystal*').[44] Romance is sometimes suggested, but the girl at the typewriter looking out from the contents page of the 1945 *Girls' Crystal* annual looks less like the secretary of the local doctor, who, if she is lucky, might propose to her, and more like the author of the stories listed beside her. [45]

Dorothy Norbury, the only non-grammar school fan of the *Girls' Crystal*, was the daughter of a newsagent. The comics he stocked helped develop her reading despite her dyslexia. Less fortunate was Mary J, whom I met in a retirement home. Mary, like Dorothy, was dyslexic and would have liked to read comics and magazines but her mother banned them because she felt they were common. Later in her life Mary's mother apologised to her daughter for her prohibition, saying she felt that if Mary had had her way, she would have become a reader.[46]

---

42 *The Girls' Crystal Annual*, London: Fleetway House, 1949, 121.

43 Madeleine Doherty, born 1940, interviewed by Trisha Cooper, 29 October 2011.

44 Dorothy Norbury, born 1934, interviewed by Susan Roe, 22 September 2011.

45 *The Girls' Crystal Annual*, London: Fleetway House, 1945, 2.

46 Mary J, in conversation with Mary Grover in Blenheim Court Residential Home, Sheffield 2017.

9 The *Girls' Crystal Annual*, 1945

The ways in which both boys' and girls' comics and magazines were circulated demonstrate the ways in which reading tastes could be shared and thereby create social groups: but the more public, the more socially divisive. The ways in which reading was associated with social status was rarely mentioned by our interviewees, but it was clearly important to the mother of the grammar-school-educated Edna, born in 1929. Edna discovered her mother's *Woman's Weekly* when she was a teenager in the 1940s. The marriages that concluded the romances in its pages were inverted images of her mother's own. Whereas the young women in *Woman's Weekly* were likely to enjoy a romance that offered social elevation, Edna's mother had, in her own opinion, married beneath herself. Her family had been prosperous builders – 'half of Woodhouse was owned by their family' – but Edna's father was a steelmaker and his mother was illiterate. Edna's mother looked down on the tastes of her in-laws: 'they read these trashy magazines and me mother said "Don't be reading those." Now *Woman's Weekly* and *Woman's Illustrated* were a little bit more posh.'

The way Edna describes her mother's literary and social snobbishness suggests that she distanced herself from her mother's values. Despite taking a 'posher' magazine, Edna judged her mother's family to have merely a 'smattering of culture I'd say'. Edna's own educational aspirations had at first been fostered by both her parents, but these ambitions were dashed when she was not allowed to apply for the scholarship that would have allowed her to stay on at grammar school beyond the age of 16. Their assumptions of cultural superiority had not been translated into sustained support for Edna's education.

Gradually, children who read became aware that the size, context and organisational structure of the texts they read influenced what they chose and how they read. Some also became aware that the way texts were packaged or accessed influenced the attitudes of others to the reading material in their hands. Edna was unusually aware of the ways in which apparently private reading tastes expose a reader to social categorisation on the basis of those tastes, her awareness prompted by the contrast in her parents' social backgrounds. Most readers made such connections between private pleasure and social identity a little later than Edna.

Classes tended to be geographically segregated in 1930s and 1940s Sheffield, so exposure to unfamiliar social worlds and new kinds of reading came late: perhaps in the workplace, a marriage, the army or in institutions of higher education. Some families, as we shall see, were linked with social networks that did extend reading opportunities, but, as always, it was the municipal libraries that provided books to the widest range of social classes.

CHAPTER FOUR

Reading Scenes

Social Networks and Reading

David Flather's father owned the long-established firm of W.T. Flather, which manufactured specialist steels. David's mother was a skilled pianist, descended from a notable non-industrial family: the Leaders.

David identified his mother's family as 'the bookish part of my life ... although my mother took no part in my upbringing'. David's mother died when he was an infant. His father was the main influence on his early reading. They pored over the newspapers for the cricket scores and, in 1937, when David was six, for accounts of the coronation. Like many other of our readers, David visited libraries on behalf of the adults in his family: 'the book carrier'.

From the age of five David attended boarding schools and then Cambridge, to study engineering. Maps were his constant companions and a great love, unlike his father's copies of P.G. Wodehouse.

> He'd got whole rows of these, but they were 1920s and I just couldn't get into them. They weren't our scene in the sort of late thirties, early forties.[1]

David trained as an engineer but was a skilled technical writer. He never shared his passion for reading with his colleagues, but he and his wife Sally were constant reading companions.

---

1 David Flather, born 1931, interviewed by Mary Grover, 31 May 2012.

David was unusual in feeling that, as a young man, he was part of a social 'scene' in which books were currency and literary tastes discussed. His parents were both part of particular literary scenes – but very different ones. The Leaders on his mother's side were journalists, historians and Liberal politicians, while the bookshelves of industrialists on his father's side of the family enshrined their Masonic values and their love of Victorian and Edwardian popular fiction. David's paternal grandfather 'wrote Masonic books'. Diverse though these literary cultures were, they all (except the Masonic literature) fascinated the young boy, often left alone in the homes of relatives scattered across South Yorkshire. David himself became an adept technical writer for the steelmaking firm of Edgar Allen.

David and his father clearly enjoyed the same kind of recreational reading before David formed a social group outside the home. At home and in the libraries of his boarding schools he was able to explore the adventure stories of Ian Hay, Rider Haggard and John Buchan, authors to be found beside his father's armchair and on the shelves of commercial and public libraries. But David's choice of comics, the *Beano* and the *Dandy*, was shared with boys and girls from very different class backgrounds: Frank Burgin for example who, as we have seen, bought them himself in preference to his parents' choice: *Film Fun*. David, unlike Frank, doesn't recall any sense that his reading might have been monitored by his father. David's complex social inheritance did not confer much sense that there were books or magazines that were not for people of his sort, until he became a young man, mixing with other youngsters who wanted to seem up-to-date.

At Oundle, the public school that David attended in the 1940s, the boy was, perhaps, more likely than any of our other readers to have encountered members of the idle and moneyed classes who are the object of Wodehouse's gentle mockery, but it is he who most explicitly distanced himself from the world depicted, placing that world in the past as 'old hat', a scene he recognised perhaps but did not want to be identified with. By contrast, Adele's painter and decorator father recommended Wodehouse to his daughter, and the communist and grammar-school-educated Ken (born six years earlier than David in 1935) said that 'of course' P.G. Wodehouse was a favourite source of entertainment. For Ken and Adele, Wodehouse was a source of pleasure, relatively private and unashamed. Never having encountered the kind of society that Wodehouse satirised, they had no need to distance themselves from the world depicted. David rejected Wodehouse publicly, perhaps because that world was not entirely unfamiliar. When he was a young man, his assertion of literary distaste was a way of consolidating his membership of a group that was up-to-the-minute. By contrast, most of our readers exhibited little sense of desiring to be a member of a group in which shared literary tastes were socially significant.

The two readers who most explicitly showed awareness of what is up-to-date and 'old hat' were from homes with books, David Flather and Shirley Ellins. Shirley's father was, by virtue of his permanent job as a council administrator, part of a group of men and women at ease with printed matter, with access to the Town Hall library of newspapers and magazines. His colleagues would probably have had a similar educational background and shared a similar frame of cultural reference. Shirley laughed affectionately at what she perceived as her father's rather stuffy tastes and her mother's enjoyment of Warwick Deeping and O. Douglas. It was only when her mother died that she read all her books.[2] In the cases of both David and Shirley, familial or social reading cultures encouraged not only confidence in forming reading tastes but a pressure to define themselves against the tastes of an older generation with which they were reluctant to be identified. Children from bookless homes were unlikely to be censorious of the reading tastes of others or abashed by their own. They were untroubled that they might be classified by what they read.

Both David and Shirley became avid borrowers from Sheffield's municipal libraries, which attracted readers from a wide range of backgrounds. The users of municipal libraries were so numerous and so diverse that it is difficult to imagine that membership of the municipal library conferred a sense of communal identity, unless, like Elsie Brownlee's parents, you defined yourself against them in the belief they were hosts to infectious diseases.

Private libraries, by contrast, were each associated with a particular kind of social group. These libraries and their users were remembered vividly by our readers even though they were chiefly used by older relatives. The investment of time and money in hunting down books in a neighbourhood tuppenny library or in the more costly Boots Book-lovers' Library in a town centre not only demonstrated that a parent valued books but also introduced our readers to a space where books were business. The profits made by these commercial libraries were built on creating unofficial reading communities: the queues outside the

2 Shirley Ellins, born 1936, interviewed by Loveday Herridge, 22 November 2011.

local tuppenny library or the scattering of genteel women among the palms of the Boots Book-lovers' libraries.

Boots Book-lovers' Library: 'It worked a dream'

When in the film *Brief Encounter*, made in 1945, Laura is shown exchanging her library book at a branch of Boots Book-lovers' Library, we are meant to conclude that she is a woman of a certain class and cultural refinement. It is one of the markers of the social world to which Laura belongs, which intensifies the viewer's sense of all that would be at risk were she to indulge her intense desire for the stranger she meets in the tea-room at the station where she changes trains. Few of our Sheffield readers would have recognised the significance of Laura's habitual encounter with this particular sort of library, because all but three of them were unaware that Sheffield even had a branch, right at its centre, on the High Street.

These libraries were founded in 1898 by Florence, the wife of Jesse Boot, whose hugely successful chain of pharmacies still dominates high streets today. The libraries were usually sited on the same premises as the pharmacies and were in use until 1966. Yet Maureen L spent her Saturdays in the 1950s in shops either side of Sheffield's branch of Boots and never knew there was a library above it. Although it was only round the corner from their school it made no mark on the memory of our readers who were pupils at the Central Grammar. John D only discovered it in the mid-1930s because he was interested in photography and the specialist equipment he longed for was displayed on the upper floor of Boots, where the library was housed. Membership of the library, like the latest lens, became a dream that could never be realised. Brought up without a father, John said of his family, 'we weren't rich enough' to borrow copies of his favourite author, Edgar Wallace, from the neighbouring cheaper commercial library in Darnall where they were to be found in plenty. He added, 'but if I'd wanted to borrow them privately rather than municipal, I would have gone to Boots in town'.[3] So, to be conscious of the existence of the Boots library it was necessary to be part of a social network that mapped its significance or, like John, to discover it by chance.

The décor of the interwar Boots libraries was usually designed to enhance a sense of exclusivity. In Beeston, one of Nottingham's suburbs,

3 John D, born 1927, interviewed by Mary Grover, 7 June 2013.

11 Boots library, Sheffield, 1933

the Boots library was in a tasteful mock-Tudor building mimicking the more affluent villas in the surrounding streets. In historic Bury St Edmunds the façade of the Boots store was ornamented by statues of Anglo-Saxon kings. Though the Boots library in Sheffield was not signalled memorably from the outside, it was in a lofty room, its art deco interior not much different from that of the nearby Central Library. It was, however, relatively cramped and plainly furnished; the contrast with the elegant interior of the Brighton branch suggests a low level of investment on furnishings and décor.

Across the country the system for borrowing was the same, three types of subscription reflecting different levels of service. In 1937 Boots *Bargain*

12 Boots library, Brighton, 1929

Books magazine had an advertisement for subscriptions to the regular library. A 'B subscriber' could borrow one book a week for an annual subscription of 7/6, the books being over a year old; an 'A subscriber' could borrow six volumes a week for an annual subscription of 17/6 (just under a week's wages for a steelworker). The 42/- subscription enabled a member to request one volume a week 'on demand', a list of desired titles having been lodged at the library. Such members would not have explored the open shelves but sat at the counter with their own assistant, who had already assembled an array of books selected from the personal notebook.[4] Although this superior level of membership meant that reading choices could be discussed with an experienced librarian, the system denied such a borrower the serendipitous discoveries of readers, such as Mavis, who started her first exploration of the adult books in the nearby municipal library by reading every author whose surname began with the letter 'W'.

During the Second World War Boots was buying one and a quarter million books a year and had a million subscribers, so its purchasing

4 Jackie Winter, *Lipsticks and Library Books: The Story of Boots Booklovers Library*, Dorset: Chantries Press, 2016.

policies had a distinct influence on publishers if not a direct influence on our Sheffield readers. A fairly wide selection of fiction and non-fiction was available on open shelves, by both classic and contemporary authors.

If a novel had a dubious reputation, it received a Red Label and was kept behind the counter and only issued on explicit request.[5] In *Brief Encounter* Laura has reserved the 'latest Kate O'Brien'. O'Brien was a feminist and literary prize winner, two of whose novels about women's sexual experience had been banned in Ireland in the six years before the making of the film in 1945. Laura's choice not only signals her sexual desirability but also a sense of cultural sophistication and social exclusivity. The librarian had kept the Kate O'Brien for her 'hidden under the counter for two days', so it probably bore the Red Label. By keeping such titles off the open shelves but available on request, Boots was able to maintain its reputation for good taste while giving customers a sense of privileged access to literature that was unsafe in the hands of less sophisticated readers.[6]

Boots stocked many of the same kinds of novels that lined the shelves of the cheaper commercial libraries, but its copies were hardbacks and in better condition. The lowest level of membership was equivalent to the price of a Christmas *Girls' Crystal* annual for which a working-class family would have had to save throughout the year. Popular genre fiction sat alongside more literary works that might have figured in the recent review columns of the London papers or in literary magazines.

Mavis, whose mother worked in the offices of Coles, the big department store across the road from the central Sheffield Boots, used Boots library illicitly while filling in the time between the end of school and the hour when her mother finished work, probably using her alphabetical method of book discovery. 'When I was eight or nine, I went and cluttered up my mother's office, "helping", and then, when someone important came I went and cluttered Boots up.'[7] She found a notice at the library's

5 Judith Wright, Senior Archivist at Boots UK, comments that it is impossible to retrieve information about titles with a Red Label because so few Boots library catalogues survive, and none of the borrowing records. Email to Mary Grover, 23 March 2021.

6 Nicola Wilson discusses the way that Boots and other circulating libraries dealt with their borrowers' interest in books with a questionable reputation in 'Boots Book-lovers' Library and the Novel: The Impact of a Circulating Library Market on Twentieth-Century Fiction', *Information and Culture: A Journal of History*, 49.4 (2014), 427–49.

7 Mavis, born in 1937, in conversation with Mary Grover, 28 November 2015.

entrance instructing her that she could only join as an 'adjunct' to her parents' membership:

> so I had to go and look up the word 'adjunct'. I thought it sounded military, like adjutant and of course I wasn't entirely wrong. But when I discovered what it meant, I used it anyway, going in, in the school holidays when my mother was working at Coles. It must have been in late junior school because I could stay at home on my own after nine. I didn't go to the children's section in Boots because it was too near the assistants. So, I explored the adult section, never spending more than 10 and 15 [minutes] mind. Nobody could stop you sneaking in and reading the books off the shelves.[8]

David Flather and Sheila Edwards were the only two of our readers who recalled family use of a Boots library, and they linked its use to their parents' generation. Sheila, whose father was a weights and measures inspector, used her mother's subscription in her teenage years until 1952, but she never renewed it on her own behalf.[9]

David Flather's father remarried when the boy was in his teens. The family lived between 1939 and 1949 in the comely market town of Retford to the east of Sheffield. David's stepmother had a taste for romantic novels and, when he was a young teenager, she regularly sent him to the Boots Book-lovers' Library to collect them. Being one of the 'On Demand subscribers' she was able to lodge with the library her own list of desired books, based presumably on her reading of book columns in magazines, newspapers and journals or on conversations with friends. She must have had reading networks; she was very much in charge of what she borrowed. She had two library assistants: her stepson, David, and a senior member of the Boots library staff. David describes the drill:

> And every time you went in, 'Have you got any books for Mrs Flather?' 'Oh yes, we've got two today' and you'd take them back in and tick them off the list. And then she'd keep adding to the list and it worked a dream. It worked a dream.

Characteristically, Q.D. Leavis dismissed the supposed passivity of the majority of Boots library users who opted for the lower priced

---

8 Val Hewson, in Gateshead in the early 1960s, also remembers gaining access to books in the adult library. 'When I was about 11 or 12, I bullied my mum and dad into joining the adult library so I could have their tickets. I used to choose books, but always with my "cover story" of getting their books ready. But no-one ever checked, and I guess the staff knew perfectly well.' Personal communication with Mary Grover, 25 March 2022.

9 Sheila Edwards, born 1937, interviewed by Alice Seed, 16 January 2013.

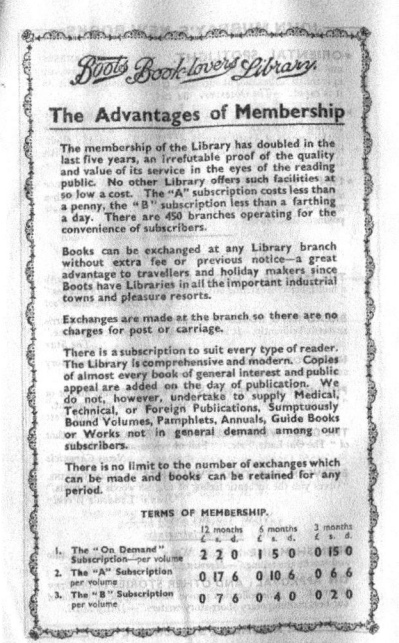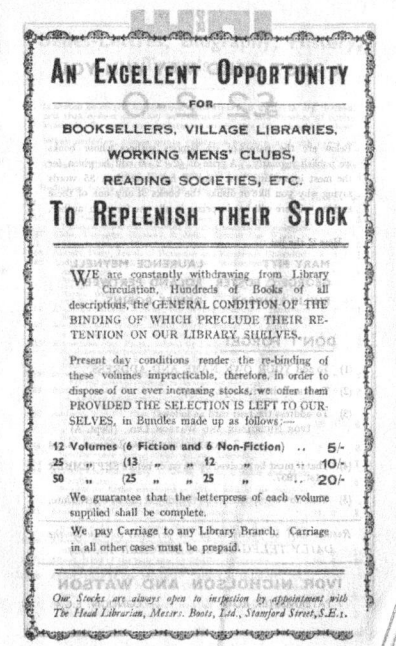

13 Boots 'Book Bargains' No. 1, 1937

membership, their books being chosen for them by the librarian. Leavis contrasted such borrowers with the more 'enterprising' 'On Demand' borrowers (overlooking the fact that it is easier to be enterprising if you are affluent and can afford magazines which might guide your taste). David does not discuss what his stepmother 'demanded', but he was clear why she directed him to Boots rather than Retford's municipal library.

> The other thing that you have to remember in those days, that the public library, they weren't exactly banned but they weren't the places that you went... Certainly, there was a public library in Retford. I think I went to it once in ten years because it wasn't really in our net, for no other reason than that.

The second Mrs Flather might have shared the upper middle-class prejudices satirised by John Betjeman in his poetic monologue 'In Westminster Abbey'. As the resident of a superior dwelling in London's Cadogan Square half-listens to choral evensong from the Abbey she muses, patriotically,

Think of all our nation stands for
Books from Boots and country lanes,
Free speech, free passes, class distinction,
Democracy and proper drains.[10]

Sheffield was not a fertile breeding ground for such views. When David went to live with relatives on the west of Sheffield in the early 1950s the attitude of those 'in his net' to public libraries was quite different.

> I mean, conversely, when I moved to Sheffield, we were only a few doors from Ecclesall Library, as it was there, and we became very frequent visitors. It became a major source of books and it always has been.

David must have been one of the first users of Ecclesall Library. It was established in 1949, in a large Victorian villa called Weetwood House. In this newly stocked library, the young engineering student, home from Cambridge University, could find in the early 1950s all the John Buchan and Rider Haggard he could wish for – and it was all free. For most of their lives the source of the wide range of fiction read by David and his wife Sally was their local municipal library. They were completely untroubled by any sense that possession of a municipal library ticket might compromise membership of a particular social world.

Though only two of our readers mention borrowing from Boots, the stock of its libraries contributed to the reading lives of many more Sheffielders than one might imagine. Whereas the cheap editions, often paperback, stocked by the less prestigious tuppenny libraries probably fell to bits given their rapid turnover, we regularly saw old copies of Boots' library books in the possession of our Sheffield readers, their dull hardback covers still unbattered and the Boots shield logo cancelled with a red cross. Sheffield Boots bargain basement (two floors beneath the library itself) sold discarded library stock and produced sale catalogues of books withdrawn from the library. In the absence of any extant catalogues of Boots libraries stock, these lists of books for sale are our best resource for knowing what titles were available on the library shelves. Judith Wright, Senior Archivist at Boots UK, records that 'around 800,000 books and magazines were disposed of annually, with a large number being sold to public libraries or supplied to prisons and institutes'.[11]

10 John Betjeman, 'In Westminster Abbey' (1940), in *The Best of Betjeman*, selected by John Guest, Harmondsworth: Penguin, 1978.
11 Judith Wright, summary of the history of Boots Book-lovers' Library, sent to Mary Grover, 11 March 2019.

Judging by the catalogue of books for sale in 1939 the majority of the fiction stock was made up of romances and detective novels, which would have pleased Elsie Brownlee. 1939 was the year she started uncongenial office work and found solace in romantic fiction. In Boots bargain basement she found tired copies of novels by those queens of romance, Mary Burchell, Ruby M. Ayres, Ethel M. Dell and Betty Trask, and hundreds of books with the word 'honeymoon', 'kiss' or 'love' in their titles by authors whose identity may be beyond recall. The non-fiction shelves would have been hunting grounds for the young and enterprising John D, who remembers buying reference books, 'damaged', for one penny.

> I do remember one, and I'm a little bit miffed about that because it was an old Atlas of the World, New Zealand at that time was still Van Diemen's Land or whatever. I took this home and thoroughly digested it.

Though the bargain basement was a significant source of books, the libraries themselves do not seem to have presented serious competition to the well-stocked municipal libraries, even for those who could afford them. The scant mention of Boots libraries by our interviewees suggests the relative absence in Sheffield of readers who might have marked their social superiority by the kind of library they used.

Tuppenny libraries: 'Reading, your cheapest pleasure'

Just as the Boots library, which was the source of these second-hand books, was off the map for most of the readers who purchased them, equally beyond 'the net' of young David and his family were the cheaper circulating or subscription libraries. These varied in type and size. Some were a few shelves in a newsagent's, some filled a whole shop unit and some were part of small chains, the Red Circle being the most often mentioned. It cost two pennies to borrow a single book so no subscription was needed. During the 1930s and 1940s, such small-scale 'tuppenny libraries' were visited both by adults and by children entrusted to collect books on their parents' behalf. Ken was one of two of our readers to have been a member on his own account. In the 1930s he was a proud member both of the newly opened municipal library opposite Firth Park (opened in 1930) and the tuppenny library down the road at Firvale shops: 'that had a huge selection of stuff and of course that's where you read all the humorous books'.[12]

12 Ken, born 1925, interviewed by Clare Keen, 16 November 2011.

The child couriers sent to collect their parents' tuppenny choices had to concentrate. While the youthful David was engaged in a formal and efficient transaction with Retford's Boots Book-lovers' Library on behalf of his stepmother, the children who visited tuppenny libraries on behalf of their fathers carried their reading histories in their head. Long working hours made men dependent on their children to make their choices. In the 1940s Jean Wolfendale would be sent to choose Westerns and detective novels for her father. In the 1930s Winnie Lincoln was her father's ambassador.

> He were interested in sport, or mostly horse racing and things like that, and Westerns of course – anything on horse racing. He was a bit of a gambler – I'd be in trouble if I brought back what he'd already read![13]

The books were paperbacks but 'they were still passable, you know'. The library used by Winnie (no bigger than just one room, always busy) was a branch of the Red Circle franchise which dominated the commercial library market in Sheffield from the 1930s to the 1960s when, like Boots Book-lovers' Library, it ceased to flourish. On the shopfront of the branch used by Judith's mother was blazoned the proud promise: 'Reading, your cheapest pleasure.'[14]

The most common reason for visiting these libraries as children was to accompany a mother in her hunt for romances. Our readers mention six branches of the Red Circle library across the city: Darnall well to the east of the city centre, Snig Hill just half a mile to the north of the city centre, Infirmary Road north-west of the city centre, Bellhouse Road yet further north in Firth Park, and two either side of the city centre (the one pictured, behind the Moor, and the other off Angel Street), all in busy shopping areas. There were no branches in the affluent west part of the town. Though the memories of using these are contemporary with the memories of visiting Boots, from the later 1930s to the 1950s the childhood impressions of visiting the Red Circle are much more vivid than the relatively few memories we have of the Boots experience. While Boots covered its books in uniform and sober colours with an ugly little metal-rimmed hole in the spine for the identifying tag, the Red Circle's windows and shelves, at the Moor branch for example, were a mesmerising kaleidoscope of lurid images.

13 Winnie Lincoln, born 1923, interviewed by Mary Grover, 8 May 2012.
14 Judith, born 1939, interviewed by Loveday Herridge, 14 February 2013.

14 The Red Circle library behind the Moor before the Second World War

I can still see it – two glass windows, not very big, just like that, and you went in the door and all the books were lined on the walls ... with their faces ... and they all had covers on, like you look at old books, they're just coloured aren't they – funny what sticks in your mind – in the window they used to have several books. You know, they were advertising them, and I can remember this one and it had a paper cover on and there was a skull and there were pearls rolling down its face – I must have been a macabre child! – and it was called *Devil's Tears* and that's stuck in my mind for sixty-odd years. My mother used to like what they called 'bodice-rippers', romantic novels and stuff.

Judith thinks that her mother took her 'just to get me out of the house and give her a break from four kids and my father'. Though Judith did not share her mother's tastes, she caught her sense of enchantment.

Every week [we] used to go down there and I can still see it with the red circle on the front and it was just like two shop windows with books in. Circulating library they called it, which I think is a lovely name. I always used to think it might revolve!

The sense of Red Circle magic was shared by Maureen B who, like Judith, went to the library with her mother. The couple went into the Snig Hill branch every Saturday on the way back from shopping in the city centre. It provided a lively and informal social scene for lovers of genre fiction. As they got off the bus, Maureen could see the queues snaking out of the library and around the block. On entering, the girl savoured the aroma; the room was filled with 'a smell all of its own'. Snig Hill issued every book in fresh sugar paper; purple and loosely fitting, each with 'Red Circle' printed in black. The bright covers of the enticing novels were covered up as they were handed over to the customer and, when the book was returned, the purple sugar paper was whisked off and dropped on the floor behind the counter. Maureen, only five or six, would be on tiptoe in front of the counter, inhaling the smell of the wrappings and marvelling at the glorious but disturbing waste. In post-war Sheffield paper was still in short supply. 'The ladies just picked up the book so that the sugar paper fell off it, then I watched them pull it straight off and shoot it up in the air.'[15] As the covers fluttered down, the child was filled with a new anxiety – that the ladies returning the books would get into trouble because over every inch of those purple covers were scribbled and imprinted records of the borrower's life during the preceding week: shopping lists, messages, memos and the rings from mugs of tea. 'Very few were pristine.' Maureen's mother never went on to use a municipal library.

Elsie Brownlee not only bought her romances from the Boots bargain basement but is unusual among our readers in that she used a tuppenny library well into the 1960s while most people's memories focus on the 1930s to mid-1950s. She is also unusual in having used it on her own behalf and not for a parent. In the 1950s she worked in a bank by day and as an auxiliary nurse in the evening. After a hysterectomy, with weakened health and soon to be the sole carer for her chronically ill mother, she had to give up her dearly prized second job in the local hospital. She had only discovered her vocation to be a nurse in her thirties, having been pressured by her father to leave school early and become an office worker. She remembers her bitter sense of loss as she listened to the helicopters flying over her house taking patients to the spinal unit attached to the hospital: 'Withdrawal symptoms – "Oh, I wish as I was in there." It was awful really.' The Red Circle library was a comfort.

> I didn't really have a lot of time for reading but what reading I did, I found [it at] this Red Circle library at the top of Angel St. I liked to read Mills and Boon type stories which you couldn't get out of the Central Library – their

15 Maureen B, born 1945, in conversation with Mary Grover, 17 July 2016.

books were far too stuffy for me and so I used to go and get the books from the Red Circle library. Mary Burchell was one of them.[16]

The plots of Burchell's novels are conventional romance plots, but then so are the plots of the operas on which many of her novels are based. 'Mary Burchell' was the pen name of Ida Cook from Sunderland, whose passion for opera was financed by her 110 novels published by Mills and Boon. In the late 1930s she and her sister used their opera trips to Germany to smuggle 29 Jews to safety.[17] The plots of the novels may be less astonishing than Ida Cook's own life but they are interesting, often addressing the dilemmas faced by female musicians or career women whose vocations conflict with their romantic desires. Elsie may well have been directed to Burchell's novels by the librarian at the Red Circle who offered a personal service comparable to that received by 'On Demand' subscribers in a Boots library.

> I got quite friendly with the woman down there because I must have gone in quite frequently because she would say, 'I've got so-in-so in' and put it on one side for me. You know, things like that.

When travelling round readers' groups in Sheffield we constantly heard about other, small private libraries, usually remembered as very busy. They were often referred to as tuppenny 'shops' as they were usually attached to other kinds of retail business. There were hundreds of them and, unlike the Red Circle branches, they were round the corner from most readers, even those on the west of the city.

The kind of conviviality provided by these commercial libraries or 'bookshops' is illustrated by the experience of Norman Adsetts. Norman's father, Ernest, was a skilled salesman and manager. He and his business partner increased the numbers of customers in 'Abbetts', their ice-cream parlour and sweet shop on Derbyshire Lane, by opening a tuppenny library next door. This strategy bore out the value of the guidelines offered by Ronald Batty in his 1938 *How to Run a Tuppenny Library*. Batty stressed the value to a shopkeeper of annexing a library to a shop because the discussion of books helped to establish a personal relationship with customers, which would then lead them to buy goods from the shop when returning books to the library.

16 Elsie Brownlee, born 1925, interviewed by Mary Grover, 21 February 2013.
17 See Louise Carpenter, 'Ida and Louise', *Granta* 98, 2 July 2007, https://granta.com/ida-and-louise/ (accessed 12 January 2022).

It is far easier to get matey over the last book that Mae West has written than two ounces of almond jelly. It is true that you can talk about Mae West even if you haven't got a library, but then you can't charge twopence each time you do it. With books to lend your small talk becomes turnover to the extent of at least sixteen and eight pence a year per customer, providing you have the art of running a two penny library at your finger-tips and a good stock of books behind you.[18]

None of our readers mentioned reading read the novels of Mae West, but by 1938, the date of Batty's book, she had written *Babe Gordon* (1930) and *Diamond Lil Man* (1932), both closely connected with successful plays. Both novels would have introduced readers to sophisticated humour and hard-boiled characters far removed from the heroines of Burchell's romances.

The range of stock in these tuppenny libraries was often governed by large distributors of books. The bookseller W.H. Smith supplied Abbetts and many other such tuppenny libraries, which were named after the 'matey' proprietor rather than the supplier of books. A man with the personal skills of Ernest Adsetts could foster an informal reading circle which gave a solitary reader a sense that her enthusiasm and tastes were valued and of interest to others. To the comfort of social familiarity was added the often consoling nature of the fiction borrowed. Like Elsie Brownlee, Judith mentions the use of such a library in the context of loss. Judith's mother turned to the Red Circle library behind the Moor, not far from where she lived, for the romance that was missing in her second marriage to a much older and reclusive man.

Diane, who participated in our interview with her aunt Wynne, visited a small tuppenny library in the back room of a suburban villa. Despite the riches of the newly opened Ecclesall Library only half a mile up the road, the tuppenny library was still crowded in the early 1950s. Diane remembers the queues spilling out into Rustlings Road beside Endcliffe Park. Like Maureen, David Flather and the young Judith Warrender, Diane was fascinated by the procedures involved in issuing books.

I think he was called Mr Smith and in one back room there was a treasure trove of books and I could pick three books as a young child and my mother picked three books and she also picked three books for her husband, my father. And the fascinating thing was – I can't remember money changing

18 Ronald F. Batty, *How to Run a Tuppenny Library*, London: Gifford, 1938, 11–12.

hands – but we had a little code written in the front of the books and our code was 33S, which I learned later was 33 Stainton Rd. But those three books were so important to me. We could have the books for a fortnight and then when the fortnight was over, obviously, we went back to change the books.[19]

Mr Smith's personal connection and commitment to his customers would have impressed the tuppenny library pundit Ronald Batty. When Diane's family moved to the east side of Sheffield Mr Smith's van appeared, full of books, the family still with the code that tracked all the Enid Blytons that Diane had already read: 33S.

Such small commercial lending libraries did not necessarily require much capital. A contributor to the online 'Sheffield Forum' recalls a very small private library:

> I had an uncle, Reg, who had an industrial accident. With the money he got in the settlement he purchased a mobile library from someone. It consisted of a pile of books and a wooden hand cart. I remember visiting my Aunt in the late 40s and seeing all the books on shelves in the living room.[20]

Growing up in a tuppenny library

Norman was the youngest of our readers to access such a library independently, and he needed no directions to find it. The 4-year-old was allowed to roam freely among the shelves of his father's adult lending library beneath the family's living rooms. 'I just read anything and I didn't exercise any preference or choice. Anything with print on it I would devour; I got a taste for pulp fiction', Edgar Rice Burroughs and the Sexton Blake series being particular favourites.[21] Even though he says that his father was not much of a reader, he was obviously an inspiring storyteller. After his son had devoured the written adventures about the Wild West in the library stock downstairs, Mr Adsetts drew on his memory of silent films to help settle Norman to sleep. He wove new stories from established characters: 'When he was putting me to bed, he pinched characters out of Zane Grey.'[22]

---

19 Diane Haswell, born 1947, in conversation with Jan Chatterton, 18 October 2011.
20 Posted by sweetdexter on Sheffield Forum, https://www.sheffieldforum. co.uk/topic/421169-memories-of-sheffield-libraries/page/2/?tab=comments#c omment-7654792 (accessed 14 February 2016).
21 Norman Adsetts, born 1931, interviewed by Mary Grover, 17 February 2014.
22 Pearl Zane Grey (1872–1939) was an American author whose popular adventure novels were set in the American West. *Riders of the Purple Sage* (1912) was his bestselling book.

Before he went to school, Norman had become a self-tutored reader.

> When I started reading, I taught myself and I would read words that I didn't know how to pronounce but I would gradually work out what they meant. There was a word 'avalanche' which I never, not till five or six years later, knew how to pronounce. In my mind I used to call it 'avahlahis'.

He picked up a copy of *Clansmen*. It had come out in 1936 and was by a favourite author of his mother. Heralded as 'A long new novel by Ethel Boileau', its 448 pages are no sentimental account of the romance of the clan. It spans two centuries, 1743–1936. Although the tale's hero at first appears to be a romantic Scot yearning to fulfil his ambition of being an old-fashioned laird in the 1930s, the real hero is a Jewish financier who affords the young man a partial realisation of his dreams. The book fuelled Norman's curiosity about the current world as much as it fed his appetite for adventure.

Norman managed to retain a few books that still contain the library's frontispiece and he showed us one of these – a volume that survives as a testament to the riches available in the hundreds of small private lending libraries that served the city between the two wars and well into the 1960s. The book has the 'Abbetts' lending record pasted inside the front cover. Norman later sought out and bought early editions of other books that he had read in the library as a child. He pulled out a copy of Philip Gibbs's novel *The Cities of Refuge*, the 'book that had the most impact on me', when he was about eight or nine. The cities of refuge were the cities of Europe to which White Russians fled following the communist revolution.

> I notice from this copy which I bought later that it first came out in 1937 so it must have been one of the first books to be put into the library... And I didn't know from Adam what it was all about but I read it with fascination... It was a very tragic and sad story about these very privileged people ... now homeless and penniless, trying to make their way in the world. That was a grown-up book. It was grown-up in all kinds of ways. There was sex in it, there was murder and killing in it. There was everything in it, most of which I didn't understand but I read it and shared in the sadness of it all.

The reader who had least far to go to satisfy his reading tastes was, perhaps, the reader who travelled furthest. Not only did Norman's unguided explorations lead him to enter the private worlds of fantasy created by Edgar Rice Burroughs's Martian novels, but they prepared him, prematurely perhaps, for the adult world in which he would play a very public part. When he left Oxford University, where he studied Philosophy, Politics and Economics, he followed in his father's footsteps to become a salesman. In 1966 he joined a small firm distributing insulation materials. It had been founded by his father from the proceeds of the library and ice-cream businesses. His father built it up in the 1970s to be the biggest firm of its kind in Europe, and Norman became its director. With the wealth created by this firm, Norman helped establish and endow the vast library or 'learning centre' of the newly created Sheffield Hallam University in 1993. In his retirement Norman has also created another, private library. Around his desk are shelves of early editions of the books that formed his early reading tastes: Gibbs, Boileau, Burroughs and the multiple authors who created Sexton Blake. Their original covers provide the kinds of prompt for memory that Irene Hailstone, whom we met in Chapter 3, found in her treasured copies of her early *Pip Squeak* annuals. Norman's partial recreation of that formative tuppenny library has helped him construct an autobiographical narrative, every physical text an anchor for memories that might otherwise have been lost. Their presence is partly an act of homage to a father who, though not a fluent reader himself, created a world of print which his young son explored without guidance but without check, appropriating whatever he could make some sense of.

The commercial and municipal libraries remembered by our readers established a habit of choice at a time when literacy levels in Britain were high, roughly 98 per cent. Whatever the social group, users of any sort of library had their tastes respected and catered for. We can appreciate the transformational power of any kind of library-based network when we consider the strategies used by literate people, across the world, throughout the ages and from positions in every sort of social class, to exclude those with inferior degrees of literacy.[23]

The way such intellectual exclusion could work in practice is illustrated by the memory shared with me before I established the 'Reading Sheffield' project. Jessie Robinson, born in 1906, a generation before David Flather and Norman Adsetts, was actively dissuaded from exploring a world beyond. She was explicitly barred from material which might introduce her to a reading community regarded as inappropriate to her class. In 1920 she was scrubbing floors at a vicarage on the newly developed estate

23 Jonathan Rose, *The Intellectual Life of the British Working Classes*, New Haven, CT: Yale University Press, 2001, 394–401.

of Norfolk Park. The 14-year-old's great pleasure was to read the vicar's newspapers.

> I had a field day with them because we used to have an hour for lunch and the housekeeper she used to go to sleep and of course she seemed to resent me reading the newspapers. I don't know why... [The vicar] had some fantastic books ... all Dickens books and she had all these in the kitchen in her bookcase... She said to me one day, 'Now I think you will get more education, child,' (she never called me my name, always 'child') 'with Dickens's books.' [She] was so possessive with everything he had... She was a proper giant to me. She resented me; probably it was because I wanted to know things and I knew things ... but she lent me the Dickens because she resented me reading the papers, the London papers.[24]

Jessie was clear that the housekeeper was barring her access to a community that debated ideas and valued knowledge about the world beyond Sheffield. Jessie, like so many in domestic service between the wars, was made aware of and even gained access to a culture unavailable to the rest of her family; but she was also introduced, in a way few of our readers were, to the notion that she was not fit to read everything she wanted.

The culture of Sheffield's settlements: 'the Kingdom of God' in Upperthorpe

From 1864 when Toynbee Hall opened in the East End of London, Christian groups, university colleges and social reformers worldwide established inner-city 'settlements'. These institutions encouraged the highly educated, often students who had just graduated, to live alongside the poor in an attempt to share knowledge and skills. Toynbee Hall and the Rowntree Trust in York became hubs of social enquiry into the conditions of the poor. There were many such settlements in London, Manchester, Edinburgh, Glasgow and Birmingham from the end of the 1860s onwards, most founded by Oxford and Cambridge colleges, big civic universities or religious bodies. Critics, such as Seth Koven, criticise the patronising, possibly prurient attitudes of the educated, wealthy, middle-class women who involved themselves with such settlements, describing them as 'slumming' while remaining safely rooted in much more privileged communities.[25]

---

24 Jessie Robinson in conversation with Mary Grover, 20 June 1997.
25 Seth Koven, *Slumming: Sexual Politics and Social Policies in Victorian London*, Princeton, NJ: Princeton University Press, 2006.

It is difficult to level such accusations against the men and women who founded and ran Sheffield's three settlements between the wars. All three were founded by nonconformists with close links to the communities they served. The Croft House Settlement and Rutland Hall Settlements focused on social work in the slums to the immediate south and west of the industrialised valley of the River Don, though there were reading rooms in both and Croft House sponsored a dramatic society.[26] St Philip's Settlement, or the Sheffield Educational Settlement as it became known, was, in contrast with the other two, a powerful cultural force. It was only half a mile from both settlements, attached to St Philip's church, which served Upperthorpe, a hillside of Victorian terraced housing below the university and above the smoke-filled Don Valley. The area was significantly less poor than the Crofts and less dirty than the polluted area of Neepsend where Rutland Hall had been built. Its cultural programme had a profound effect on a notable Sheffield politician, Roy Hattersley, and on two of our readers: Winnie Lincoln from the streets around the settlement in the early 1930s, and Erica from a Derbyshire village in the 1940s.

The man whose cultural vision inspired both girls in the 1930s and 1940s was an Oxford graduate, Arnold Freeman, son of a nonconformist cigar merchant in London. Freeman arrived in Sheffield at the beginning of the twentieth century to work as an extramural tutor for Sheffield University. He was appointed warden of the Sheffield Educational Settlement by the Young Men's Christian Association (YMCA) in 1918. Both as warden of the settlement and as director of the adjacent Little Theatre, Freeman consistently worked to extend the imaginative and literary resources of the communities in which he worked.

In 1875, a mile up the same hill, John Ruskin had established St George's Museum, inspired by similar ideals. Ruskin aimed to expand the aesthetic sensibilities of skilled Sheffield craftsmen by establishing a treasure trove of beautiful artefacts and natural objects which would tempt them to climb upwards above the 'yellow fog' permanently settled on the city below, a city 'steady in darkness and blight all day long'.[27]

---

26 E.B. Spencer, 'Sister Edith', 'Reminiscences of Croft House Settlement, 1914–1953', undated, Sheffield City Archives, M.D. 3417; T. Alec Seed, 'Croft House Settlement Operatic Society', undated, crofttheatre.co.uk (accessed 14 January 2022).

27 John Ruskin's diary entry for Friday 28 April 1876. Quoted in Sylvia Pybus (ed.), 'Damned Bad Place, Sheffield': An Anthology of Writing about Sheffield Through the Ages, Sheffield: Sheffield Academic Press, 1994, 151.

In Sheffield's city centre, Ruskin's collection of natural wonders and of art inspired by the Italian Renaissance can still be enjoyed. It is witness to Ruskin's ambition to transform industrial workers from wage slaves, shackled by obedience to philistine masters, to craftsmen inspired by nature and high art. Both Ruskin and Freeman sought to create a net of enchantment which would draw participants from every side of the city.

Having appointed Freeman as warden in 1918, the YMCA withdrew support in 1921, alarmed by the costs and scale of his educational ambitions. Freeman continued the work of the settlement with a strong board of supporters, among whom were representatives from the University of Sheffield and the Anglican Church, the Quaker Arnold Rowntree from York and a radical intellectual with strong local connections, Edward Carpenter. Many of Upperthorpe's terraces would have housed the workshops of the skilled craftsmen known as 'little mesters'. These workers manufactured or finished goods in a small way themselves, but were often closely connected with the mightier enterprises in the Don Valley below. It was among these men and their families, a less impoverished area than that around the other two settlements, that Freeman aimed to establish 'the Kingdom of God'. When we read his definition of this Kingdom we can understand the YMCA's alarm.

> By the 'Kingdom of God' we mean streets along which it is a pleasure to walk; homes worthy of those who live in them; workplaces in which people enjoy working; public-houses that are centres of social and educational life; kinemas [sic] that show elevating films; schools that would win the approval of Plato; churches made up of men and women indifferent to their own salvation; an environment in which people 'may have life and have it abundantly'.[28]

Winnie, the daughter of a carter for the London, Midland and Scottish Railway, was born in Upperthorpe in 1923. She was from exactly the kind of background that the settlement movement of the late nineteenth and early twentieth centuries hoped to reach; the urban working classes without access to adequate education or the means to

---

28 The words appear on the letterhead of correspondence from the settlement. They are quoted in a short summary of the work of the settlement, 'Administrative/ biographical history: The Settlement, in Shipton Street, Upperthorpe', contained in a collection of papers held by the Sheffield University Library's Special Collections and Archives, MS 91, entitled 'The Educational Settlement Papers Scope: Papers from the Sheffield Educational Settlement during the period of Arnold Freeman's wardenship (1918–55). Dates: 1918–1955'.

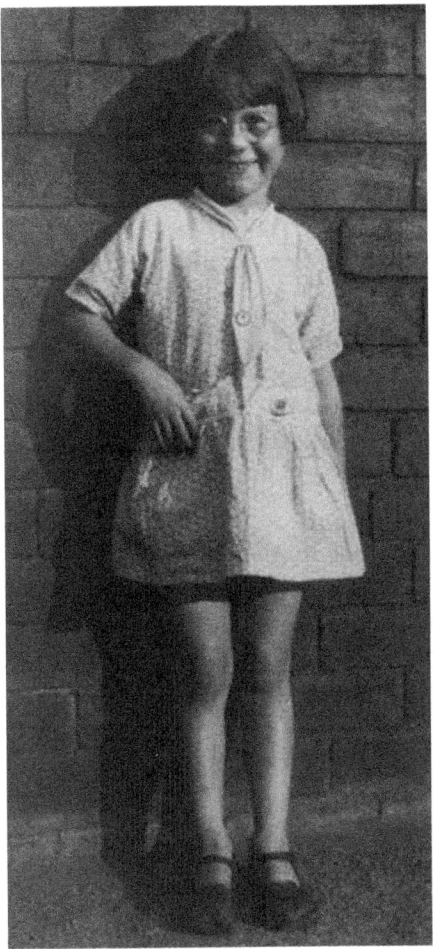

15 Winnie Lincoln in the 1930s

buy books. In the 1930s, when she was old enough to wander the streets alone, she discovered the 'abundant life' of the Little Theatre.

> A very famous man worked there, Arnold Freeman ... and he used to put on little plays – as you would expect, quite studious. He used to walk, sort of walk about in a study. But it was nice, we used to go, because I mean, probably, I can't remember even what we paid. We probably got in for free. 'Cos I was always hanging round t'door!

Freeman's 'little' plays were very ambitious, strenuously serious but not avant-garde. There was a clear intent to uplift culturally and spiritually:

no Gilbert and Sullivan or the ever-popular *Merrie England* for him.[29] Thomas Hardy's *The Dynasts* certainly qualifies as uplifting and serious. Hardy's own description of his verse drama gives a sense of its scale: 'an epic-drama of the war with Napoleon, in three parts, nineteen acts and one hundred and thirty scenes'. Though Hardy believed it was unstageable, Freeman thought otherwise. He gloried in his ability to overcome the problems of a six-foot stage. The future Labour politician Roy Hattersley never forgot this production, sought out when he was a grammar school boy in the 1940s.

> My disbelief hung willingly suspended well into the third hour. Then the six actors who had been Russian Infantry at the Battle of Borodino and the Grande Armée at Austerlitz turned into three Prussians under Blucher who joined with Wellington's three Grenadier Guards at Waterloo. I squeezed into the chip shop before the notice on the steam-streaked window was turned to 'closed'.[30]

Hattersley went on to study English Literature at Hull University, before entering politics. For Winnie, contact with Freeman inspired not a lifelong engagement with imaginative literature, but a deep respect for intellectuals who put their gifts at the service of the community from which she came.

We have met Erica before, the daughter of a manufacturer of mother-of-pearl goods whose anthroposophical beliefs caused him to delay his daughter's introduction to books lest they dull her sensory development. She, like Winnie and Roy, was mesmerised by Freeman's productions. She remembers *A Midsummer Night's Dream* 'very vividly'. The experience was 'fascinating, completely fascinating. And Faust, I do remember. Arnold Freeman was very keen on Faust.'[31]

It is clear that Freeman created a cultural scene experienced by children from a wide range of classes. His wardenship lasted from 1913 to 1955. In 1918 he published a unique account of working-class reading entitled *The Equipment of the Workers*. On the basis of what they read and what they knew, the 816 manual workers interviewed were judged to be intellectually 'well-equipped', 'inadequately-equipped' or

---

29 *Merrie England*, a patriotic comic opera set in Elizabethan England, was staged in 1920 by Croft House.

30 Roy Hattersley, *Guardian*, 23 January 1982, anthologised as 'How I Came to Casterbridge by Way of Rekjavik', in *In Search of England*, London: Little, Brown, 2009, 16.

31 Erica, born 1937, interviewed by Mary Grover, 9 February 2012.

'mal-equipped' (a categorisation echoing Charles Booth's maps of the degree of poverty in which the London poor lived).[32] Freeman's sense of cultural levels and their close connection with spiritual and economic survival underpins his choice of plays. As we have seen, the aim to engage with 'the best' rather than 'the available' was unfamiliar to the vast majority of Sheffield readers.

Drama made 'the best' to some degree accessible, the element of magic often deriving from the inventiveness with which cultural missionaries such as Freeman created a spectacle in spartan premises on streets where light itself struggled to penetrate the industrial smog. The historian of the Manchester University Settlement, based in the working-class district of Ancoats, describes the impact of the stage sets created for their nativity play sometime in the early 1930s: 'Those who saw the curtain rise on ... the sunset over Bethlehem will not easily forget the gasp with which an Ancoats audience met a sudden onslaught of beauty.'[33]

Perhaps it was the power to conjure another world that drew both the Sheffield and Manchester settlements to contemporary romantic Irish literature. The warden of the Manchester settlement in the 1930s wrote 'melancholy haunting plays of the Celtic twilight and produced them with great ingenuity'.[34] These plays inspired members of the audience to write plays themselves.[35] I can find no evidence that the Sheffield settlement at this period fostered this kind of creative literary engagement. Freeman seems to have driven the cultural agenda from the top, sometimes losing his audience. The production of a little-known play by the Irish poet W.B. Yeats staged at the Little Theatre in 1928 was badly attended. In June 1931 the 8-year-old Winnie, hanging round the theatre entrance, might well have been given free entrance to a production of the *Oresteia* dismissed by one member of the audience as 'too highbrow for me'. The *Sheffield Telegraph* drama critic had doubts about 'the desirability or need for staging such pieces at a workers' educational settlement'.[36] But Winnie recalls no distaste for anything she saw, her respect for Freeman undimmed over the eighty years since

---

32 Mary S. Morgan, Iain Sinclair and the London School of Economics, *Charles Booth's London Poverty Maps: A Landmark Reassessment of Booth's Social Survey*, London: Thames and Hudson, 2019.

33 M.D. Stocks, *Fifty Years in Every Street*, Manchester: Manchester University Press, 1945, 74.

34 Stocks, *Fifty Years in Every Street*, 91.

35 Stocks, *Fifty Years in Every Street*, 91–2.

36 *Sheffield Telegraph*, 1 June 1931, 7.

she first saw his productions. The audiences might often have felt baffled but they were never patronised.

Political and religious networks

There were, of course, political and religious networks which had a powerful influence on reading in Sheffield. The parents of our readers were rarely described as engaging in political activities or discussions. We have come across the painter and decorator who wrapped his political books in brown covers. Erica's anthroposophical father was much more intellectually and socially secure than Adele's father, but his political books were also concealed. He belonged to the Left Book Club in the 1930s.[37] During the Second World War he moved his factory out to the Hope Valley to the west of Sheffield to escape the bombing, and his family rented the house of a left-wing miner whom he had met at Cambridge a decade before. With him came the books he had bought with his Left Book Club subscription, 'all in these bright yellow covers'. In fact, hardbacks were bright red, and the paperbacks yellow, but it is interesting that Erica recalls how bright they were, a bold declaration of radical politics in the conservative valley outside Sheffield. Erica recalls that 'we were the only people to distribute political pamphlets from the Liberal Party'. When the family inherited a grandparent's books, safe Edwardian fiction, Erica's mother used them to conceal her husband's books.

In the homes of the two readers who mention their father's possession of political books (Erica and Adele), both fathers judged it wise to keep their political allegiances under wraps to an extent. This discretion would have made it unlikely that a child would be invited to discuss radical ideas even with a father sympathetic to them. The only reference to political discussion in the home is connected, rather dismissively, to intellectual snobbery. Edna's father was a steelmaker whose mother was illiterate. He married a woman who felt that her own family was superior to his because they discussed politics while her husband's didn't.

Religious engagement seems to have been less fraught than political involvement, perhaps because there was such a wide range of Christian denominations in Sheffield, Anglicanism and Methodism both attracting the rich and powerful. The Bible was noticeable in our interviews by its relative absence. It is possible, of course, that our interviewees just took

37 The Left Book Club (1936–48), founded by Stafford Cripps, Victor Gollancz and John Strachey, aimed to inform and initiate debate among its left-wing members

its presence in the home for granted and were more familiar with it than their interviews suggest. They would certainly have been made familiar with Christian teaching in schools.

Five of our readers described the effect of their church or chapel traditions on their reading, more frequently as adults than as children. Most of the religious texts that came into their homes as children tended to be remembered not as personal possessions but as family relics, Sunday School prizes earned by parents or more likely grandparents. As we saw in an earlier chapter, these copies were rarely read, the exception being Betty Newman's, whose grandmother's Sunday School prize, *A Peep Behind the Scenes*, was the first book she ever read and still rereads.[38] This novel was discovered in the 1920s by Janet Hitchman who, as the Reading Experience database records, 'acquired her literary education among the derelict bookshelves of an orphanage, which included a huge collection of "drunken conversion stories (*Christie's Old Organ*, *The Little Match Girl*, *A Peep behind the Scenes*)",[39] as well as everything by Dickens, old volumes of *Punch* and the *Spectator* and *The Life of Ruskin*'. She reflects, 'My undigested reading made me look at the world with mid-Victorian eyes.'

It is striking that these Victorian texts, usually acquired by parents or grandparents, were still preserved. These books first came into working-class families at the end of the nineteenth century and the beginning of the twentieth. This was the heyday of the Sunday School movement. Such schools had, following the 1870 Education Act, ceased to serve the secular function of increasing literacy. Nevertheless, attendance at Sunday Schools in Britain tripled between the 1860s and 1906.[40] The embossed and gilded books from the Religious Tract Society and other Christian groups were aiming not so much to promote literacy as to counter the sensationalism of the delectable 'penny dreadfuls', much as the Christian promoters of improving boys' magazines were doing at the same period.

Robert Roberts describes such books as *Uncle Tom's Cabin*, *The Old Curiosity Shop*, *Black Beauty*, *Heroes of the United Services* and *A Basket of Flowers* being awarded as prizes in 1920s Salford.

38 *A Peep Behind the Scenes* (1877) by O.F. Walton, https://www.open.ac.uk/Arts/reading/UK/browse_author_writings.php?s=Walton&f=O.F (accessed 27 January 2023).

39 *Christie's Old Organ* (1875) is also by O.F. Walton, https://www.open.ac.uk/Arts/reading/UK/browse_author_writings.php?s=Walton&f=O.F (accessed 27 January 2023); *The Little Match Girl* (1845) is by Hans Christian Andersen.

40 Jose Harris, *Private Lives, Public Spirit: Britain 1870–1914*, Harmondsworth: Penguin, 1994, 154.

Many of our sub-literates treasured these books, but, I discovered, seldom read them. They stood on the chiffonier as ornaments and were not looked upon as objects to be handled. Children were forbidden even to touch them.[41]

The survival of such volumes demonstrates the absence of other sources of treasurable texts. During the first half of the twentieth century no other agency attempted to introduce literature into the lives of the working-class child. These books survive because of the very poverty of such families who had little else to mark their achievements, but also because the books were so well produced. They persisted when the penny dreadfuls and tuppenny magazines had fallen to bits. This is one of the many contributing factors to what Jonathan Rose calls the 'conservative canon of working class reading', the ways in which the reading of working-class readers is bound to be outdated.[42]

For those who took such texts off the chiffonier or attended Sunday services beyond Sunday School, church or chapel culture did play a significant intellectual, emotional or spiritual part. Religious texts accustomed the reader to linguistic difficulty, introduced a wealth of poetic narrative and enacted the power of the written word. John Y came from a Wesleyan background and was born in 1929, two years before David Flather and Norman Adsetts. Members of his family had written respected devotional books and one had worked at the Wesleyan Reform book shop in Sheffield throughout the Second World War. His father was a crane driver and his mother came from a family of Methodist ministers, the religious life of the family fostering its bookishness. If John were to have just one book it would be a hymn book, in itself a book of literary and spiritual signposts because, as John puts it, 'it's the Bible in another form'.[43]

Why I like the hymn books, is because things like that you remember better, because my memory's very bad now, so I can't remember things. I remember this one verse in particular:

I am not skilled to understand
What God had willed and God has planned
I only know at God's right hand
Stands one who is my saviour.[44]

41 Robert Roberts, *The Classic Slum: Salford Life in the First Quarter of the Century*, Harmondsworth: Penguin, 1973 [1971], 174.
42 Rose, *The Intellectual Life of the British Working Classes*, 116–46.
43 John Y, born 1929, interviewed by Mary Grover, 6 June 2013.
44 Dorothy 'Dora' Greenwell, born 1821. This poem was included in a collection of her poems, *Songs of Salvation* (1874).

And things like that you remember, and it makes you remember them. This is what I try to do now, to sort of stoke up my memory.

So, the stories, the poetry and the values by which he lives are accessible still, in part because of the hymns repeatedly sung and therefore lodged in heart and head, an internal and portable library and a guide to the sacred book itself.

John's Methodist background also lent him access to new points of view, introduced by visitors from beyond Sheffield. Although he cannot remember individual titles from the chapel library, he does remember a constant flow of visitors from other chapels: 'aunts and uncles', he called them. The Methodist Circuit on which ministers travelled from chapel to chapel established a sense of the geographical context of Sheffield itself and the introduction of intellectual influences from beyond.

'The Brontë girls' and other Yorkshire writers

Sometimes a reader might be encouraged to read the classics because their authors were 'local'. Even though David Flather did not as a rule read classic novels, he did make an exception. 'Perhaps the only ones of the nineteenth century I've read particularly are the Brontë girls. I've read them all, largely because they're fairly local, but also because they're well read.' By 'well read' I presume he meant read by people he knows.

David's wonderfully compendious list of books read includes 'Brontë girls x 3', Winifred Holtby (best known for her novel *South Riding*) and J.B. Priestley. Of the half-dozen readers who mention Holtby, most came across her at grammar school or university. Both David and Alan noted her because she was 'local', but the nature of their interest in the geographical connection was rather different. David, whose ancestors had been part of Sheffield literary life for two centuries, was engaged by Holtby's historical connection with his family. He still has his copy of *South Riding* 'because in fact [Holtby is] buried in the village where my family came from'. Alan read her because she offered a rare reflection on the community of which he was a member. He read several of her novels because they were 'realistic and set locally'. He too had visited her grave.

The most famous Yorkshire writer in the 1930s and 1940s was probably J.B. Priestley: journalist, novelist, dramatist and broadcaster. A far greater proportion of men than women recalled reading him. Their responses suggest that it was the ideas rather than the narratives that were attractive. In the 1950s the adolescent Alan valued *The Bright Day*.

His engagement with the book was an engagement with a notional community:

> I found that really sort of useful in the sense that as an adolescent you had certain uncertainties and that is what he talked about. And knowing that other people had the same uncertainties, it's not just you.[45]

Peter Mason found this engagement with problems less heartening: 'sadness seemed to prevail'. Curiously, Peter B, who studied history at Oxford and became a judge, distanced himself mockingly from the Yorkshire identity that he felt Priestley paraded. Peter parodied a Yorkshire accent when he recalled Priestley's contention that 'he was a very simple man'. He said that he doesn't find the regional aspect of Priestley 'a bother' because he himself was from Yorkshire, but he 'can understand that those who weren't would find him a bit tiresome'. Peter's ambivalence about his relationship to any kind of Yorkshire scene is suggested by his statement that he himself 'was', not 'is', a Yorkshireman, the implication being that he has become an actor on a wider stage.[46]

Joan is a reader whose life was enmeshed with Priestley's. The fabric of her family's life was material for the Bradford author. Her grandfather, a joiner, was a friend of Priestley's. 'In fact, he wrote one book about me grandfather.' Joan is unusual among our readers in feeling herself in exile in Sheffield. She compares rather bitterly the livelier literary culture of her father's family in Bradford to the council estate on which she now lives.[47]

The Brontë 'girls', Priestley and Holtby were actively connected with concerns and debates that extended far beyond their local region. So, our Sheffield readers, by choosing these books according to instincts that could be described as parochial, found themselves in imaginative and ideological words which hugely extended the range of their literary experience.

Betty usually rejected fiction in favour of history but she made an exception in the case of one novel because she regarded it as 'local'. *The Crowthers of Bankdam* by Thomas Armstrong was published in 1940 and was enjoyed by three of our readers. This and subsequent novels form the saga of a mill-owning family in West Yorkshire, and are rooted in

---

45 Alan, born 1944, interviewed by Susan Roe, 2 May 2012.
46 Peter B, born 1930, interviewed by Susan Roe, 29 May 2012.
47 Joan T, born 1941, interviewed by Mary Grover, 8 May 2012.

Armstrong's own family background, far removed from Betty's own; her father was a member of the transport police. Betty remembers exactly when she bought the novel: in 1957 when she was 22 'to read on a long journey'. It is a journey that never ended. It is still her 'comfort read'. 'I've worn out so many copies, and I'm worrying now because the last two or three I've had have been from charity shops.' When her interviewer asked whether she could get it from the library she replied, 'Oh no, it's one of the ones they throw away.' Her present copy is in about five pieces now, 'which is easier to read in bed actually because I can pick a section up'. She reflected: 'I don't read very much fiction at all. That is my one.'[48]

Place played a significant part in how reading communities were formed. David's move from the countryside into Sheffield freed him from certain constrictions of his class and enabled him to access the riches of a municipal library. Sheffield's location in Yorkshire meant that readers not usually into Victorian fiction tackled the 'Brontë girls'. Winnie Lincoln and Roy Hattersley would not have entered the enchanted world of Arnold Freeman if they had not lived near 'The Kingdom of God in Upperthorpe'. We will hear about how Sheffield's hills put a municipal library out of reach of the encumbered young mother who found the local 'few shelves in a newsagent' less of a stretch.[49] Location, class affiliation, religion, politics and family networks all shaped the ways our readers perceived themselves as part of wider reading communities. The classroom, as might be expected, also created reading cultures but, as my next chapter shows, to a surprisingly limited extent.

48 Betty Newman, born 1935, interviewed by Ros Witten, 13 October 2011.
49 Mary Robertson, born 1923, interviewed by Susan Roe, 7 March 2013.

CHAPTER FIVE

'Getting them learned'

Books in the Classroom

Shirley Truswell was born in 1936, an only child. Her parents believed that books could provide their daughter with a living. Her father worked in the Town Hall and her mother was a Civil Service telephonist. Unlike most of our readers, Shirley can remember a bookshelf of library books in her junior school. Her cherished memory is of *The Pigeons of Leyden*, a historical novel by Agnes M. Miall about the siege of Leyden. Her grammar school education confirmed her desire to become a history teacher; the myths of the Romans and Greeks and the plays of Shakespeare became her great love. She treasures the edition of Shakespeare's plays illustrated by portraits of famous actors and actresses in character that her mother won at Crookesmoor Elementary School, a prize for 'Progress'. At university in London in the 1950s Shirley found she had enough spending money to buy volumes of poetry. By the time she married, and became Shirley Ellins, she and her husband had both accumulated extensive personal libraries. It was 'a marriage of two minds and the marriage of two libraries, too, when we got together'.[1]

1 Shirley Ellins, born 1936, interviewed by Loveday Herridge, 22 November 2011.

Reading ... I just couldn't fathom it.

Fred Jones, born c. 1922

We saw in previous chapters how many of our readers' homes lacked books and the habit of reading, and we might have hoped to find these deficiencies remedied by their schools. But for reasons partly of resource and partly of philosophy, the support that potential readers received from the education system was patchy at best.

The 8-year-old Fred Jones who, in the early 1930s, could not fathom reading had a lucky break; he was sent from the vast new Manor estate on the east of the city to the old Poor Law hospital on the west for an extended stay to treat his tuberculosis. A benefactor had donated piles of comics for the children exiled from home. 'That's where I learned to read through comics – just picking comics up and listening to others read. Once I got it, I've never put a book down.'[2]

The poet, novelist, historian and government advisor Sir Henry Newbolt, who produced an eloquent report on English teaching, would have been delighted by Fred's experience. In 1921 the Newbolt Report stressed the vital importance of improving the quality of elementary schools, which then provided the only education for 94 per cent of children. English was placed at the heart of the elementary school curriculum: 'It is not so much a subject as the body and vital principle of all school activity', a humanising rather than a fact-finding mission.[3] While Newbolt stressed the intellectual value of wrestling with the exact meaning and intent of short passages of well-written prose, he was especially passionate about the importance of reading for pleasure.

> The lesson will be a failure if it is not really a recreation, and the teacher who means the effect of his work to be lasting will start from what the children themselves enjoy, recognising that even though what they read may be rubbish, their being willing to read at all is a definite asset.[4]

Sir Henry would have applauded Fred's access to comics because he saw literacy as the route to higher things, but he also laid emphasis on the supposedly humanising effects of studying English literature. This

---

2 Malcolm Mercer, *A Portrait of the Manor in the 1930s: The Evolution of a Council Estate*, Sheffield: Pickard Publishing, 2002, 74.

3 *The Newbolt Report: The Teaching of English in England*, London: HM Stationery Office, 1921, 57, http://www.educationengland.org.uk/documents/newbolt/newbolt1921.html (accessed 20 May 2020).

4 *The Newbolt Report*, 84.

was, in practice, at odds with the encouragement of indiscriminate and voracious reading for pleasure. Creative and individual responses to works of English literature were often held to encourage empathy, moral discrimination and a resistance to the dehumanising effects of industrialisation. Throughout Newbolt's report the work of a Cambridge educationalist, Caldwell Cook, is approvingly cited because his methods helped pupils engage imaginatively with the great classics of English literature, freeing them from mechanical ways of studying the canon. His theories influenced the ways that many of our readers encountered books in the classroom, especially in the elementary schools established on the council estates built after the end of the First World War.

Cook's treatise on his teaching methods, *The Play Way* (1917), inspired a generation of teachers trained between the wars to encourage imaginative writing and drama rooted in works of high literary value or in the folk tradition. His chapter on the use of imaginative islands, or 'Ilonds' as he styled them, sketches created by children which gave them space to develop their own imaginative worlds, offered an antidote to the spelling tests and narrow focus on grammar that had dominated the elementary classroom, and that has arguably returned to deaden student responses.

For all the virtues of Cook's teaching methods, however, they came packaged with his violent dislike of popular literary culture. So, while elementary pupils were being encouraged to take fire from Shakespeare and even Chaucer, they were being turned against the very sources of print that would remain accessible once they left school: comics, magazines and pulp fiction from the tuppenny libraries and the popular authors stocked by municipal libraries. Cook's thundering dismissal of contemporary 'pulp' would have echoed in the ears of Sheffield's brave new English teachers between the wars.

> In the present disordered and ill-managed state of education a boy may satisfy his crude desire for novelty and sensation in the reading of books which have no spark of literary value, and in the shows at the cinema which are equally destitute of all dramatic or artistic taste. He may seek fun and the satisfaction of his sense of humour in the unspeakable halfpenny comics or in sheer brainless tomfoolery with his fellows. School gives but little guidance to his amusements.[5]

5 Caldwell Cook, *The Play Way: An Essay in Educational Method*, New York: Frederick A. Stokes, 1917, 270.

Cook wanted to change all this. He and many teachers since have seen themselves as cultural prophets unscrolling sacred reading lists, rather than as foremen in a workshop where apprentices can acquire the tools to make them omnivorous readers. Unlike Newbolt, Cook would have confiscated Fred's comics and would have been completely at odds with Sheffield's chief librarian, J.P. Lamb, who insisted that Sheffield's local libraries should stock many of the works that were the mainstay of the tuppenny libraries: Richmal Crompton's *Just William* stories, for example.

Sheffield schooling between the wars

In the 1930s there were many Sheffield children who, like Fred, failed to get the hang of reading in school, and unlike him never had the luxury of free and entertaining reading matter which overcame their fear and sense of inadequacy when faced with the printed word. The man who treasured Fred's story and preserved it in a history of the Manor was our interviewee, Malcolm Mercer. Malcolm, a head teacher and author of *A Portrait of the Manor in the 1930s* (2002) and of *Schooling the Poorer Child* (1996),[6] knew the cost to children who failed to become literate. He had worked all his life to improve the chances of primary school pupils and as a child had experienced the limitations of the school system at first hand.

In common with Fred, and with all children who were not privately educated, Malcolm, born in 1925, entered elementary school on the Manor, aged five. Here he was taught by generalist teachers, expected to take on all subjects. The small minority of pupils who passed a scholarship examination could leave elementary school at 11 for secondary education but everyone else, and this included Malcolm, continued their generalist education until the elementary school leaving age of 14. The provision of secondary education in Sheffield had been worse than in other industrial cities for the previous century. Whereas in Sheffield, with a population of 380,793 in 1901, there were 600 places in selective secondary schools offering opportunities to go on to university, in Birmingham, with a population of 522,204, there were 2,500 places in many more such schools.[7] In 1924 there were only 33 secondary places

6 Malcolm Mercer, *Schooling the Poorer Child: Elementary Education in Sheffield 1560–1902*, Sheffield: Sheffield Academic Press, 1996.
7 Great Britain Historical GIS Project, 'A Vision of Britain Through Time', https://web.archive.org/web/20110629044720/http://www.visionofbritain.org.uk/index.jsp (accessed 19 December 2020).

per 1,000 pupils in Sheffield. This ratio improved in the 1930s but by 1936 Sheffield's provision of secondary school places still compared badly to other cities.[8] In addition to this scarcity of places there were economic and social hurdles to be surmounted.

Those few who moved to selective secondary education might find themselves in an intermediate school or grammar school, both provided by the local education authority, or in a private school which offered council-funded places to students attaining the highest marks in the scholarship exam. Here they were taught by specialist subject teachers and prepared for further examinations. The School Certificate was usually taken at 16 and then the Higher School Certificate at 18. The HSC was the grammar school pupil's passport to a university education. Interestingly, pupils at the most prestigious private secondary schools in Britain had a tradition of only entering their pupils for the lower School Certificate, spending the remaining two years of their school education reading more widely than their grammar school contemporaries were able to do as they laboured over the extensive syllabus demanded by the Higher School Certificate.

After the First World War there was a brief period of economic expansion and optimism. In the late 1920s Sheffield established two of Britain's largest council estates, Manor to the east of Sheffield, where Malcolm Mercer grew up, and Parson Cross to the north, where he was a primary school head teacher from 1968 to 1983. Residents on these estates were usually young families from the skilled working classes, able to afford the relatively high rents for the new two- or three-bedroom houses, equipped with bathrooms and indoor toilets.[9] But with the onset of the Great Depression in 1929 aspirations were dashed and many families returned to poorer dwellings in Darnall or Attercliffe, back to the Victorian terraces from which they had moved and which were later severely bombed. Food, clothing and rent were the first priorities for these struggling families. In the early 1930s it was found that 'over 35 per cent of one-time tenants' on the newly built Wybourn estate had moved back to the areas from which they had come, unable to pay rents

---

8 David Hey, 'Sheffield Schools, 1918–60', in *The History of the City of Sheffield 1843–1993, Volume 2: Society*, ed. Clyde Binfield, Roger Harper, David Hey, Richard Childs, David Martin, Geoffrey Tweedale, Sheffield: Sheffield Academic Press, 1993, 320.

9 https://municipaldreams.wordpress.com/2014/11/11/sheffields-interwar-council-estates-the-pampered-pets-of-the-corporation/ (accessed 5 September 1919).

of 10/– a week that, for over 7 per cent of residents, constituted more than a third of their wages.[10]

It is no wonder therefore that Fred's family on the neighbouring Manor estate (like John D's in Darnall described in the last chapter) lacked the disposable two pence to borrow a book from George Austin's circulating library in the neighbourhood or the pennies to buy the comics beloved of Sheffield's chief librarian as a child. Clearly many families could not afford to buy reading matter, and the twentieth century had no equivalent to the religious tracts which flooded into poorer homes at the beginning of the nineteenth century, providing a kind of textual mulch – the yards of continuous print that are needed to convert poorer readers who struggle to decipher words into ones who read easily with a habit or passion for reading. If homes were often lacking in books, how did schools fare?

English teaching in elementary schools

Despite Newbolt and Cook's emphasis on reading and the enjoyment of reading, our readers' experience of books at elementary school was much more of listening, in part because old methods persisted, but also for lack of resources. The supply of library books was limited at least until 1944 when Sheffield Library Services aimed to provide 'one volume to every child over seven years of age in the primary schools'. This scheme was reported to have been 'carried out and was successful in every way',[11] but if our readers retain a memory of books for recreational reading in elementary schools from the 1930s or 1940s it is simply of a single shelf or a couple of boxes.

Many people remember teachers reading aloud, sometimes for a whole afternoon, to a class who had no accompanying text. Malcolm Mercer's elementary school teacher delighted the boy with his reading of whole books, most of them thrilling adventures: 'favourites included Mark Twain's *Adventures of Tom Sawyer*, Scott's *Ivanhoe*, Kingsley's *Westward Ho*, Ballantyne's *Coral Island* and the book that enthralled me most, John Buchan's *Greenmantle*'.[12] Betty, Malcolm's contemporary, was similarly fortunate. When she was unexpectedly moved up a grade at

---

10 municipaldreams.wordpress.com.

11 Sheffield Libraries, Art Galleries and Museums Committee, *The City Libraries of Sheffield, 1856–1956*, Sheffield, 1956, 53–4.

12 Mercer, *A Portrait of the Manor in the 1930s*, 82.

the age of nine or ten (her mother had already helped her establish the habit of reading), her first and pleasurable memories of books in school are of being read to by her new teacher. Like Malcolm, Betty was read whole books.

> At the end of the lessons, Miss Pashley would read a story for quarter of an hour. She'd stand up on that ledge ... with the lectern. We'd read, we'd have *Anne of Green Gables*, *Tom Sawyer*, *Huckleberry Finn*, *Robinson Crusoe*.[13]

Jean A, born in 1930, also remembers being read to at her elementary school in the late 1930s, 'every Friday, all afternoon... We used to enjoy that. Books like *Water Babies*, or *Wind in the Willows*.' *Treasure Island* was a particular favourite.[14]

Often individual teachers would take a private initiative to do what they could to help pupils access reading material. In the early 1930s Edna remembers her 'far-seeing teacher' in her elementary school in Wincobank gathering together 'a little library and we used to borrow those books from her bookshelf'.[15] The teacher requested that the children comment on the books borrowed. These private acts of generosity and engagement are not forgotten.

Not only were books in short supply, but traditional approaches to teaching often persisted. In 1934 an elementary school on the Wybourn estate, further down towards the city centre than the Manor where Malcolm grew up, drew praise from the school inspector. With fewer facilities than most, the English Department was to be commended: 'the children's speech, not only in formal Recitation, but also in reading as well, is unusually clear and pleasing'.[16] 'Clear' presumably meant relatively free of the Sheffield accent and idiom. Nowhere in this 1934 report is there mention of imaginative literature, only the 'fundamentals, 'systematically and usefully corrected' written work and children whose oral responses to questions were 'brisk and to the point'. Frank, whose story ends this chapter, concluded that the important thing in his 1940s elementary school in any lesson was simply to 'get it learned'. The teaching methods advocated by Cook in 1917 and Newbolt in 1921 are not reflected in our readers' memories of elementary schools in 1940s

---

13 Barbara 'Betty' R, born 1925, interviewed by Loveday Herridge, 26 September 2011.

14 Jean A, born 1930, interviewed by Loveday Herridge, 22 April 2013.

15 Edna, born 1928, interviewed by Ros Witten, 25 July 2012.

16 H.M. Thurston, 'Wybourn Council Senior Mixed School', 1934, 2 (it is unclear whether this is a formal or interim report).

Sheffield, deprived as they had become of resources and teachers in the war years and subsequent austerity.

In the 1930s, despite the interwar depression, Sheffield found some money to appoint young staff trained to make learning and books a source of pleasure. These newly qualified teachers who were appointed to the elementary schools serving Sheffield's modern estates did, in the professional opinion of Malcolm Mercer, a good job.[17] The delight that their progressive teaching methods introduced into the lives of elementary school children in the 1930s is reflected in the voices of two women who recall with warmth and affection their experience of poetry and drama in Wisewood Elementary School, on one of Sheffield's first subsidised housing projects.

The Sutton Trust estate, built in 1927 to the west of Sheffield, was funded privately by the money of a wealthy brewer and freight magnate, William Richard Sutton. The children who moved up from the smoky valleys below to the Wisewood estate not only came to live in well-built houses but went to a new elementary school staffed by newly qualified staff, heirs of Cook and Newbolt. His Majesty's Inspectors in 1935 clearly felt that the children from Wisewood Elementary School were served well. Within six months of the school's opening in 1933 it had put on a performance of *The Merchant of Venice*, followed by *The Tempest* in 1934.

> These productions, which have involved an immense amount of happy thought and effort on the part of the staff and the children outside school hours, reached a high degree of technical excellence, and apart from the healthy stimulus they have given to Literature studies throughout the department, their value as a help in fostering a good co-operative spirit between the children and the teachers, and also as a means of enlisting the interest of the parents in what their children are doing, has been very strongly felt.[18]

These children, like many on new estates, lacked a local library or the superior book provision of a grammar school, but they did, as Caldwell Cook would have hoped, have fun with literary classics. The missionary note in *The Play Way* is picked up by the inspector when he comments on the way the plays put on in school had moral, spiritual and social benefits for the community beyond the walls of the school.

17 Mercer, *A Portrait of the Manor in the 1930s.*
18 H.M. Thurston, 'Report of His Majesty's Inspector of Schools, January 1935: Wisewood Council Senior Mixed School', 1935, 2.

Two pupils at Wisewood recalled the excitement of their encounters with imaginative literature, memories of 'The Play Way' that they still treasure. Hazel and Dorothy H were both born in January 1929 and both came from families with little money. Hazel's family was on the verge of destitution, as her father had died when she was two. Hazel joined the school in the first years of its existence, the year when *The Tempest* was produced. She was not naturally confident ('I were always backward about coming forward') but she loved school and knew that she was part of something new:

> I went at Easter time and it was lovely... It wasn't a bit strict and things like that – it was lovely. Everybody wanted to go to school ... I loved it. There were no reason not to really because I think it was a new way of educating children.[19]

Dorothy H, like Hazel, joined Wisewood in 1934, where she played two starring roles: Shylock and Bottom, Bottom, of all Shakespeare's characters, being the least backward about putting himself forward. Dorothy's joy in acting and knowledge of Shakespeare did not, however, deliver a certificate that would demonstrate her imaginative gifts. Neither Hazel nor Dorothy could sit the School Certificate, which in the 1930s and early 1940s was available only to children at selective schools. Both girls left Wisewood at 14 with no qualifications and, despite their enjoyment of literature, without a reading habit.

Nevertheless, they entered adulthood with a vast store of poetry, memorised in lessons: ballads, 'Meg Merrilies' and 'Hiawatha'. Alma, who left Rotherham Central at the age of 14 in 1942, 'loved' her English teachers: 'they introduced us to lots of poetry; Walter de la Mare, John Masefield – that was very interesting'.[20] Jean H went to Hartley Brook Elementary, founded, like Wisewood, in the 1930s to serve a new estate. Like Alma, she excelled at reading and reciting poetry.

> Yes. I used to have to stand up in front of the class and read ... [laughs] and if we had visitors, I used to have to stand up ... and when the visitors came to school, I used to have to go round with them.[21]

Jean H, like Alma, left school at 14. She left with so great a love for drama and poetry that in her adult life she would take herself to the theatre, whether there was anyone to go with her or not.

19 Hazel, born 1929, interviewed by Mary Grover, 9 May 2012.
20 Alma, born 1928, interviewed by Liz Hawkins, 8 November 2011.
21 Jean H, born 1926, interviewed by Mary Grover, 8 May 2012.

Jean was interviewed with Winnie and Joan, in Winnie's front room, which she often filled with her friends. When Winnie encouraged a hesitant Jean to recite the poems she had memorised (Winnie: 'You've just got to be clicked on'), Jean responded with '"Hidden in the elder bushes, there they waited until the deer came" – I could go on and on', and Winnie recalled a gathering of widows that she organised to play cards or Scrabble on a Saturday.

> There were seven of us then, and we'd all be sat round and it would start up quoting a bit of poetry. And everybody would pick it up, what they could remember, or else they'd remember a song. And we'd all start singing until we couldn't remember whose turn it were to play a card [all laughing].[22]

So, in spite of the large classes, the economic depression and the lack of a chance to get a qualification, these girls from new, progressive elementary schools in the 1930s had entirely positive memories of their experience of English literature. What they did not get from school was any encouragement to read widely. Their homes were largely bookless and the new estates lacked local libraries. There never has been a municipal library serving the Wisewood estate. Jean H was the only one of the four pupils who attended a progressive elementary school who described using a municipal library regularly during her school days, four miles there and back from Shirecliffe down to Firth Park Library in the valley beneath. It was her parents who encouraged her reading and they had many books in the house. The school played no part in her explorations of novels.

The impact of war and austerity

The setback caused to children's education by the Second World War should not be underestimated. It was almost impossible to sustain imaginative ways of teaching involving drama, for instance. Education budgets were slashed, far fewer books were being published and paper shortages meant that existing books were being pulped. When a van was heralded to appear in the village for book donations on the coming Saturday, Betty R remembers her parents

> thinking which books should go. They said, 'That is for Betty, Paula and Cecily to decide. If they want them, they won't go. They should decide, but we'll tell them it's needed for the country.'[23]

22 Winnie Lincoln, born 1923, interviewed by Mary Grover, 8 May 2012.
23 Barbara 'Betty' R, born 1925, interviewed by Loveday Herridge, 26 September 2011.

Sometimes books were not even pulped. The urgent need to requisition buildings for the war effort meant that elementary schools were closed down and their book stocks simply thrown away. The school secretary of a junior school remembers that

> when the Army took over, we felt that the main object was to rid the school of all its books, files and papers. They were literally thrown outside. Many were beyond repair or completely destroyed.[24]

Set in the context of the impending blitz the very value of the written word, of educating children for a future, seemed imperilled. It is difficult to imagine how teachers managed to occupy, let alone teach, their elementary school pupils. Jean A, over the hill from Abbeydale in the suburb of Greystones, remembers, as a 10-year-old, being shipped off for a few hours a day into the neighbouring intermediate school and then into neighbouring homes.

> We used to congregate in other people's houses... So my mum offered our attic. It was a nice room up there, plenty of light. I think we had about four or five but ... we also had to go to the fishmonger's up the road; he had a room to spare and I think Peak's the Butcher's had.[25]

Even before the war, the hopes of a new way of introducing literature into the classroom had begun to wane. An elementary teacher in the late 1930s was less likely to consult the Newbolt Report of 1921 than the very practical chapter on teaching English Language and Literature in the Board of Education's 1937 *Handbook of Suggestions for Teachers*, 'For the Consideration of Teachers and Others Concerned in the Work of Public Elementary Schools'. The readers of the *Handbook* would have missed even an echo of the ideals of Newbolt to foster pleasure in reading, though they would have come across the kind of fear of popular culture we find in Cook's *The Play Way*. Thus, though the absence of books and library facilities in elementary schools is often noted (and deplored), the authors seem uneasy about the possible consequences of children's promiscuous access to print and of the entrance into their lives of the literary 'rubbish' which Newbolt had welcomed. It is as if the rise in literacy, which the *Handbook*'s chapter aimed to promote, was feared rather than applauded. We hear distinctly Leavisite tones in the section entitled 'The special responsibility of the teacher of English': 'The virtual

---

24 S.M. Badger, *Abbeydale Girls' Grammar School – Jubilee Year 1968*, Sheffield: Greenups, 1968, 7–8.

25 Jean A, born 1930, interviewed by Loveday Herridge, 22 April 2013.

disappearance of illiteracy has resulted in the production of a mass of reading material which appeals almost exclusively to cheap sentiment and facile emotion.'[26] The section concludes with this direction to the teacher:

> In a modern civilised community, it is his privilege and his responsibility to educate minds into toughness and sensitivity. To train children to think hard and clearly, and, at the same time, to recognise and enjoy, so far as children may, some of the finest and deepest experiences of humanity. Only if these aims are vigorously pursued can our society keep its sanity and wholeness.

It is clear from this that the authors who passionately desired that English teachers instil 'certain standards of taste which may last' felt that this task was not purely literary but linked to the urgent need to resist the power of fascism. The teacher teaches literary discrimination in order to create robust democrats. This conflation of mass popularity with mindless populism can be understood at that moment in history, but an integral part of this civilising mission was the rejection of the kind of literature that both Henry Newbolt and J.P. Lamb insisted was essential fodder if a habit of reading was to be formed.

When schools were reopened after the war, classes were big and teaching methods unlikely to be progressive. Meg, born in in 1936, recalls her post-war elementary school education at Chapeltown Lound in the large mining and manufacturing village of Chapeltown, just north of Sheffield. One day her teacher, Mr Brody, 'with just a blackboard, an easel and a piece of chalk', alerted his pupils that 'someone important was coming to see the class'.

> I remember vividly this gentleman coming in because we were doing reading poetry. For some reason I was often asked to read aloud in class and we were doing 'Old Meg she was a gypsy and lived upon the moors'. And this gentleman arrived and we all sat there quietly and he counted how many of us were in the room, and there were sixty-two of us. And, of course, I had to do my reading, so that was memorable.[27]

So memorable, apparently, that Mr Brody christened her 'Meg' rather than Margaret, so Meg she remained for the rest of her life. Making

---

26 The Board of Education, *Handbook of Suggestions for Teachers: 'For the Consideration of Teachers and Others Concerned in the Work of Public Elementary Schools'*, London: HM Stationery Office, 1937, 352–3.

27 Meg Young, born 1936, interviewed by Mary Grover, 6 June 2013.

students learn poetry by heart from battered old anthologies from the 1920s would have been a useful solution to the problems of teaching literature caused by the dearth of published books during and after the war and well into the 1950s.

Malcolm Mercer recalls that in his elementary school on the newly built Manor estate in the 1930s, the school curriculum for speaking in public was differentiated.

> Speech training for the boys was largely developed through debates, the reciting of poetry and occasionally through dramatic work. In the girls' classes there was a greater emphasis on elocution coupled with deportment.[28]

Judging by the poems Malcolm was introduced to at school there was probably a wider variety of poetry available to the boys: Matthew Arnold's 'Sohrab and Rustum' and Coleridge's 'Rime of the Ancient Mariner', for example, are both more demanding than 'Meg Merrilies', which figured in the memories of most of the women recalling their elementary schooling. It is likely that the emphasis on elocution was to help fit girls for work in service industries, such as shop work.

The emphasis on teaching the poorer classes, especially girls, to speak like their 'betters' persisted into the 1940s. Judith, born in 1939, experienced in her post-war elementary school a far from playful introduction to the word: 'I can remember the first lady teacher, Mrs Poole they called her. She was quite grand.' The first thing Mrs Poole tried to teach her class of illiterate 6-year-olds was to abandon their native tongue. Judith found the sight of forty classmates enunciating a, e, i, o, u into little round mirrors so absurd that she burst out laughing and was sent to stand behind the blackboard.[29]

The two pre-war elementary schools on the Manor which Malcolm rated highly contrast with others elsewhere in the city that were the source of unhappy memories well into the 1950s. Maureen L started elementary school in 1946. She thinks the appeal of Enid Blyton's Malory Towers school stories was their ability to remove her to 'another world', another and kinder school environment. She grew up on the Parson Cross estate, an enormous, principally post-war estate. Maureen felt trapped there 'because there weren't any buses locally at that time'. Maureen had loved her time at her home with her mother during the war and schooling was a shock. The school was

28 Mercer, *A Portrait of the Manor in the 1930s*, 82.
29 Judith G, born 1939, interviewed by Loveday Herridge, 14 February 2013.

in the middle of the estate, you know. I didn't enjoy school, I hated school, it was awful... The head teacher, until the year I left, I think was quite cruel. She would hit you, really, and she would leave finger marks there.[30]

Bob W, who grew up on the same estate as Maureen in the late 1940s, commented that 'Of course, you didn't have books in school, so I used to go to the library.'[31] For most children on any of the new estates there was no 'local' library until the 1950s or 1960s, when there was more money to provide community services. Bob's library was a two-mile tram ride away. We have almost no mention of commercial 'tuppenny libraries' on these new estates.

The municipal library service did, however, try to reach school children. Throughout the 1930s the number of books lent to schools by box delivery grew. In wartime, when junior libraries were closed, these deliveries must have been significant and an extraordinary achievement in the circumstances.[32] In 1946–7 420,354 books were issued to fulfil the council's aim, stated in 1944, of issuing one book to every primary school pupil over five years old. Yet Margaret H has no memory of a school library in her primary school in the 1950s.[33] Although Sheffield Libraries circulated library books in post-war primary schools they made little impact on 'Delia'. She remembers 'a few', but her most memorable source of narrative delight was Miss Garth, reading aloud from Aesop's Fables – folk stories and fables very much part of a progressive curriculum.[34]

Mavis was therefore lucky, in the early 1940s, to go to an elementary school within walking distance of a library. Her school, like others near a municipal library, made it its business to teach pupils how to use the public library.

They took us all to the library: they got us all to get library tickets, they sent us all home with a form for our parents to sign and they carried on taking us for maybe the best part of half a term. We seemed to do the walk quite often. And those were the days when they could say, 'Right, you can go home when you've finished.' And some kids would pick a book, rush to the desk, get it stamped, and they'd got an extra quarter of an hour... Sometimes I'd stay there for an hour. You just went home from the library. But to keep it

30 Maureen L, born 1941, interviewed by Mary Grover, 30 April 2012.
31 Bob W, born 1940, interviewed by Trisha Cooper, 19 February 2012.
32 J.P. Lamb, *The City Libraries of Sheffield 1856–1956*, Sheffield: Sheffield Libraries, Art Galleries and Museums Committee, 1956, 28.
33 Margaret H, born 1945, interviewed by Susan Roe and Mary Grover, 10 May 2018.
34 'Delia', born 1942, interviewed by Trisha Cooper, 10 November 2011.

up long enough for it to become familiar to us. And our parents thought nothing of it. I wasn't the only one; occasionally I'd bump into other people who just used to use it as spare time. You could walk there from school – it was two sides of a triangle to go home – it was for many of the children.[35]

Intermediate grammar schools

Until 1947 only selective schools offered a child an education beyond the elementary stage. Sheffield's provision of selective school places was notoriously inadequate, especially for girls. Throughout the 1920s it provided fewer selective places than any of the eight major boroughs in Britain: as we have seen, only 33 selective places for every 1,000 elementary school pupils.[36] In an attempt to address this problem, the Sheffield educational authorities created a form of cut-price grammar school, which came to be known as an intermediate school. Although the teachers in such schools were as fully qualified as those in the city's higher-tier grammar schools, the opportunities for intermediate pupils were more limited in many ways. In order to cut costs there were usually no playing fields, no libraries and no lessons that were not strictly focused on getting the pupils through a five-year syllabus in four years. The funding of the Roman Catholic Intermediate was described as 'niggardly'.[37] No wonder five out of our seven intermediate school pupils have no memories of school extending their reading pleasure. Whether before or after the war, it is only the libraries of higher-tier grammar schools that figure in our readers' memories.

Parents of children in both categories of grammar school signed a contract to keep their children at school until they sat the School Certificate, and were heavily fined if this contract was broken. Roger Longden observes that, nevertheless, throughout the 1930s staff of intermediate schools 'fought a determined but seemingly hopeless battle to persuade both the pupils and their parents of the value and importance of completing the full four-year course'.[38] If the options were a decent apprenticeship at 14 at a time of great economic insecurity or two years

35 Mavis, born 1937, interviewed by Mary Grover, 12 March 2012.
36 Roger Longden, 'The History of Secondary Education in Sheffield 1902–1939', thesis submitted for the degree of Doctor of Philosophy for the Division of Education, University of Sheffield, 1979, 35.
37 Longden, 'The History of Secondary Education', 'Summary', n.p.
38 Longden, 'The History of Secondary Education', 263–4.

studying a favourite text of the examiners, such as George Borrow's *Lavengro* (1851), it is not hard to see why schools struggled to retain their pupils. Those leaving probably included some of the most able, who were therefore the most likely to get an apprenticeship.

Irene Hailstone went to Southey Intermediate in 1932, one of only two pupils from her elementary school to pass the scholarship examination. Her history illustrates the difficulties for children from working-class backgrounds in investing time to acquire a post-elementary education.

> I was going to stay on to take the certificate but I became ill, I think in the March, so it was October before they let me go back again, but the Head Master said I must do the whole year again, and I thought I could have managed it.[39]

Her mother thought otherwise and judged that an extra year would make her too old to be staying at school, so she left at 15 and went to the labour exchange. In 1936, the year she left, only 17 of the 79 pupils initially recruited to her intermediate grammar school stayed on to take the School Certificate examination.[40]

The two girls who attended post-war intermediate schools that merged into mainstream grammar schools had a different experience when they became members of a regular grammar school. They remembered inspirational teachers, individually generous. Though Anne's school had a very small library, in the second or third year her teacher encouraged her to read for pleasure: 'she had one of those big, wooden school cupboards. It was full of books which we were allowed to go and choose from which I used to love to do.'[41] Carolyn W had a similar experience in the mid-1950s. Her English literature teacher in the first two years of her secondary schooling 'was great she was':

> and I think maybe then that's when I started reading, as I say, more school sort of books. I did end up going through all the ones girls were used to read in those days. Like Jane Austen and *Jane Eyre*, all that sort of stuff. And then I don't remember much apart from the book you were doing that year at school.[42]

The closing down of exploratory reading as the public examinations loomed was marked even for those at the prestigious grammar schools,

39 Irene Hailstone, born 1921, interviewed by Susan Roe, 28 February 2012.
40 Longden, 'The History of Secondary Education', 261.
41 Anne, born 1944, interviewed by Susan Roe, 5 April 2012.
42 Carolyn W, born 1944, interviewed by Trisha Cooper, 19 February 2012.

but Carolyn was left with an awareness of a literary tradition because of her grammar school attendance. Unlike the older Mary Wilkinson who, though a voracious reader, had not been to grammar school, Carolyn knew that there was a 'sort of stuff', nineteenth-century classics, that she was expected to read and that she might expect to enjoy. This awareness has been called 'cultural capital', and from the 1950s to the 1970s might have eased entry to a middle-class occupation such as teaching. Interestingly, such equations between familiarity with the classics and fitness for a profession are made much less readily today.[43]

'I could have gone there': high-tier grammar schools

Judith, who was assigned an intermediate school place, wished passionately to go to the better-resourced High Storrs grammar school, its art deco building still pristine when she sat her 11-plus in 1949. She now lives down the road from the elegant building looking over the moors. In 1949 it would have been three miles away from the city centre where Judith lived. Both High Storrs and the striking Sheffield Central Library building were job creation projects in 1935. As Judith watches today's pupils make their way to what is now a comprehensive, she can't help reflecting, 'I could have gone there.'[44]

The barriers to gaining and taking up a place at one of the top grammar schools in the 1930s and 1940s were many: the lack of places available even to those who did well in the examination, poverty, a family's lack of conviction that such an education would better the economic future of their children and a child's fear of social ostracism by their peers. Thirty-five of our 65 readers went to grammar or intermediate schools. Another five passed the scholarship examination but didn't take up their places. Of the five, four were girls. They accepted that, usually for financial reasons, the family judged it impossible. The only boy who did not take up his place did so by his own choice; James could not face 'the solo run' in his grammar school uniform across town to a school in a middle-class suburb to the west.[45] Even if the place was taken, economic

---

43 Pierre Bourdieu's *Distinction* (1986) is a seminal discussion of the relationship between culture and class. In *Social Class in the 21st Century*, Harmondsworth: Penguin, 2015, Mike Savage describes the way this relationship has changed in the twenty-first century.

44 Judith G, born 1939, interviewed by Loveday Herridge, 14 February 2013.

45 James Green, born 1936, in conversation with Sue Roe and Mary Grover, 27 July 2017.

pressures made it common for pupils to be pulled out of school before being able to take the School Certificate and thus capitalise on the value of their education.

The lucky few in the 1930s who not only passed the scholarship examination but were also able to take up their grammar school place rarely laughed or smiled as they recalled their English lessons. In contrast to the group of women recalling their progressive elementary schools in the 1930s, grammar school pupils remember English lessons as serious affairs, narrowly exam-orientated. The lack of joy in their reminiscences has much to do with the extraordinarily unchanging curriculum imposed on grammar schools throughout the first fifty years of the twentieth century. David Shayer's question in 1972 about the narrowness of the School and Higher School Certificates is still difficult to answer: 'Why do Hardy, Wells, Conrad, Shaw, Mark Twain, Kipling, Wilde, Yeats – or for that matter George Eliot or Jane Austen – not appear more often in syllabuses after 1915?'[46]

From 1932 to 1942 the Joint Matriculation Board's School Certificate paper usually, but not always, offered an opportunity to write on a work of prose, not always fiction. The teachers of candidates between 1932 and 1934 could choose one prose text from the two set: R.D. Blackmore's *Lorna Doone* or Borrow's semi-fictional *Lavengro* in 1932; *Northanger Abbey* or *A Tale of Two Cities* in 1933 and Thackeray's *Henry Esmond* or W.H. Hudson's *A Shepherd's Life* in 1934. For three years fiction was not offered at all; then in 1938 there was a choice of Bunyan's *Pilgrim's Progress* or Dickens's *David Copperfield*, after which in 1939 there was only Charles Reade's *The Cloister and the Hearth*, in 1940 only *Gulliver's Travels* (3 parts), in 1941 the examiner's favourite, *Henry Esmond*, and in 1942 Conrad's *Four Tales*. Of these eleven choices set between 1932 and 1942, two were semi-autobiographical, descriptive and lyrical (*Lavengro* and *A Shepherd's Life*) and two (*Pilgrim's Progress* and *Gulliver's Travels*) profoundly unlike the kinds of novel likely to be read for pleasure in the 1930s or 1940s. Judith found *The Cloister and the Hearth*, back on the syllabus as her O level set text in the mid-1950s, 'the most dreary book I've ever read'.[47] Not so dreary for some: an unusual primary school in 1946 unlocked this text for a class of 8-year-olds. As we have heard,

46 David Shayer, *The Teaching of English in Schools*, London: Routledge and Kegan Paul, 1972, 115.

47 O levels were the examinations for 16-year-olds which succeeded the School Certificate in 1951.

Erica attended a private school in the tradition of the Parents' National Educational Union, with its child-centred and liberal philosophy.[48] Charlotte Mason, the founder of the PNEU method, promoted the reading of 'living books' in schools: 'Children must have books, living books; the best are not too good for them; anything less than the best is not good enough.'[49] The material could indeed be transformative with well-trained teachers and small classes, such as were offered by private schools.

Unlike the much older Judith in Greystones Intermediate, 8-year-old Erica loved *The Cloister and the Hearth*, which along with *Pilgrim's Progress* was read out aloud to her small class: 'And they were so exciting and I do think that was formative.'[50] These 'classics' became 'living books' for the listeners in that private junior school, because of what followed the reading. Each child was expected to 'narrate back' to the rest of the class and do creative work inspired by the stories. So for Erica, listening was far from the passive process described by Judith, the 'dreary' experience of mugging up medieval history in order to write about the novel for O level.

Though Charles Reade might no longer be regarded as a 'classic' author, Thackeray certainly is. It was *Henry Esmond*, not the far more approachable but equally morally equivocal *Vanity Fair*, that was regularly set for School Certificate from the 1930s through to the 1950s. *Vanity Fair*, never out of print and regularly televised, did make a showing on the Higher School Certificate syllabus, where it was encountered with joy by the privately educated David Flather after the war. Madeleine was the only other reader to record that she enjoyed Thackeray – in the early 1950s.

> And then when I got to grammar school when I was, what 14, the Head of English was our form teacher and she had a book, a cupboard full of books and we were allowed to borrow anything we wanted and then I really got into reading, I used to stay up reading half the night you know. I'd not turn my light out but I read them too fast and I can't remember ... there was *The Virginians*, there was *Henry Esmond* ...[51]

48 The Parents' National Educational Union was co-founded in 1892 by Charlotte Mason (1842–1923) and Emmeline Petrie Steinthal (1855–1921). The Union fostered a broad and liberal education. See note in Chapter 1.

49 Charlotte Mason, *Parents and Children*, London: Kegan Paul, 1897, 279, https://amblesideonline.org/CMM/M2complete.html.

50 Erica, born 1937, interviewed by Mary Grover, 9 February 2012.

51 Madeleine Doherty, born 1940, interviewed by Trisha Cooper, 29 October 2011.

'The cupboard full of books' sounds like a privately assembled collection, all the more enticing for being in the gift of an admired teacher. *Henry Esmond* contains no character as seductive as Becky Sharp from *Vanity Fair* and does seem a curious choice for adolescents to pore over in school. Like *The Cloister and the Hearth*, *The Tale of Two Cities* and *Lorna Doone*, it has the intellectual respectability of being a historical novel but the romantic interest has a suggestion of incest unusual in a set text. The hero loves his foster-sister but opts to marry his foster-mother. Although most of our grammar school pupils would have come across Thackeray, only Madeleine, indebted to her English teacher's cupboard of treasures, was inspired to read the sequel to *Henry Esmond*, *The Virginians*.

No doubt the unchanging nature of the books set for School Certificate owed a huge amount to the blows dealt to the book trade and to education funding in the economic depression of the 1930s, followed by poor resourcing of schools during the war and post-war austerity. Few schools could have afforded to replace their sets of *Lavengro* with anything appealing. Poet and academic Jan Montefiore, who attended the Perse School in Cambridge in the 1950s, remembers at 14 being bored by 'battered old volumes of essays by Addison, Hazlitt and Lamb... Textbooks got newer as one went up the school. I guess they were gradually replacing their stock.'[52]

Sadly, few of our Sheffield readers seemed to have come away from grammar schools with a love of the English classics.

Post-war: secondary modern schools

In 1947 the school leaving age was raised to 15. Those who passed the 11-plus examination went to grammar schools, the vast majority of which in Sheffield were in the west and middle-class areas of the city. Most 11-year-olds went on to secondary modern or technical schools. Post-war austerity meant that the hopes for the quality of these schools were not fulfilled in the 1940s or 1950s. None of our interviewees who attended a secondary modern school in the 1950s remembers a school library.

Barbara Green was deeply disappointed at not being able to take the place she had gained at grammar school in 1955. She went on to do an English degree in 1992. Her mother's determined and enthusiastic enjoyment of romantic novels had established the reading habit far more powerfully than any English lessons at Burngreave Secondary Modern.

52 Janet Montefiore, in conversation with Mary Grover, 8 January 1920.

Reading, it was much more regimented, more prescribed, and you weren't discussing books *per se*; you were more or less reading by rote. Or at least that's my experience. They were more interested in whether you could read and write and whether you wrote properly, between the lines. And that you were equipped for your role in life.[53]

Unlike Barbara, Alan B failed his 11-plus but, like her, he developed a taste for reading. He started at a secondary modern in Rotherham in 1955 where he observed that

> there were very few books actually in school in those days ... and the ones that were, I think they were trying to make us realise how good books were but they were so sort of reverential about books that, you know, I wouldn't have dared go to the library and borrow one.[54]

Alan and his friends at his secondary modern were entertained with adventure stories: Jack London's adventure stories of life in the Canadian forests, *Call of the Wild* and *White Fang*; and the great story about wartime escape, Eric Williams's *The Wooden Horse*. Alan overcame his fear of libraries and went on to read widely and independently, seeking out more adventure stories of many different sorts: John Buchan, John Masters, C.S. Forester, John Wyndham, Nevil Shute and Graham Greene. But not just adventure stories – he was omnivorous.

> Well, I started reading classic books like Charles Dickens and I remember trying to read *Paradise Lost* and finding it absolutely totally beyond me... I can remember going to Rotherham City Library and saying I'd like to join the library and them trying to direct me to the children's library. I wouldn't have that, no I wanted these other books... I liked to read sort of light-hearted things. The easy things like G.A. Henty but I also knew that there were all these *important* books [chuckles] which I felt I ought to try and read as well. Sometimes I was unsuccessful but I remember I had no concept of what people would refer to as good books or lightweight books. So they were all the same to me.

Christopher Isherwood's *Goodbye to Berlin* he enjoyed 'in a sort of [pause] disturbed way'. Though Rotherham Central Library was Alan's main source of books, he was unusual in buying books and having family members who bought him books from Harper's Bookshop, 'a rabbit warren of shelves'. A particular family friend was the chair of the

---

53 Barbara Green, born 1944, interviewed by Mary Grover and Susan Roe, 27 July 2017.
54 Alan, born 1944, interviewed by Susan Roe, 2 May 2012.

local education committee in Rotherham. 'If I ever mentioned a book in his presence, he would get it for me.' Alan was lucky. Most of the boys he was educated with would not have had these social resources. It is difficult to imagine that the cultivation of wide reading was any better in the post-war secondary modern schools than it was in the pre-war elementary schools.

With no guidance but with some sense that some books were more 'important' than others, Alan embarked on a solitary journey to discriminate between the books that did and did not matter, while maintaining a taste for both. Determined and enquiring, Alan was one of the huge proportion of children emerging from school without much of a literary map. This absence possibly liberated him from inhibitions and snobbery. Born in 1944, he was, unlike the 94 per cent who left elementary school at 14 in 1921, able to go to a secondary school and stay on till he was 15, but it was the richly stocked municipal library, not school, that satisfied his literary curiosity.

Opinionated teachers and clever friends: reading outside the syllabus

Although the choice of fiction in exam-orientated secondary schools was limited and the syllabus not designed to inspire wider reading, a specialist subject teacher with pronounced personal tastes was in a position to promote them. Pupils might sometimes catch fire from these extra-curricular enthusiasms. This certainly happened to a number of our readers, and it was not always their English teachers who inspired them.

If a boy was in the top percentile of scholarship boys in the 1930s, he could get a place at the otherwise fee-paying King Edward VII School. There Norman Adsetts had the good fortune to be taught by the classical scholar Edward Fairchild Watling. Watling, who translated Sophocles' three Theban plays, nine plays of Plautus and a selection of Seneca's tragedies for Penguin Classics, was also actively engaged in local theatre as an actor and producer. Through him Norman encountered texts he would never be examined on, and engaged with the local theatres he would later, as a highly successful businessman, do a huge amount to support financially.

The most unlikely classroom epiphany was experienced by Ken when he went to the Catholic De la Salle Grammar School in 1936:

> I expect it's when I went to grammar school that I first got on to other things. An English master who was a brilliant man put me on to all sorts of good books. And he was a very opinionated bloke. He used to think that

all the best writers were people like Lytton Strachey and all that lot. You know – the Bloomsbury outfit and all those people.[55]

To Ken, Lytton Strachey may have been part of an 'outfit' whose politics were unconnected to his own left-wing convictions, but he respected the evaluation of the 'opinionated bloke' who shared Strachey and other stylists with his pupils, despite their absence from any examination syllabus.

Quiller Couch – he was great. According to my English master, Quiller Couch – Sir Arthur Quiller Couch – was the greatest writer of English there had ever been. He was an essayist, you know, and a teacher. Wrote *The Art of Writing* and all that sort of business. Really good… Oh, Lytton Strachey's *Eminent Victorians*. Fantastic book, that. Elegant writing, you know. Really stunning.

Selective schools introduced many pupils to literary texts outside the experience of most Sheffielders, and they also introduced bookish children to each other. Not only the book but the pen was an object to be valued. There were, in Edna's memory

lots of children – they'd been to private schools to get to grammar school – they were from professional backgrounds, and the difference showed. You know, I mean they'd have an expensive fountain pen and you hadn't.[56]

Those at the higher-tier grammar schools do remember using school libraries. Shirley, who went on to one of these schools, has a 'half recollection' of a bookshelf in her elementary school classroom where one of her few delights was *The Pigeons of Leyden* (Agnes Mackenzie Miall, 1945).[57] 'Whereas there was a whole room at High Storrs! Full of books!' The grammar school curriculum invariably included stories from Greek myth, not only a source of glorious and terrible narratives but a key to unlocking the meaning of so many key works of English literature. It is not the set texts from English lessons at her grammar school in the 1940s that Shirley remembers with excitement, but the Greeks. Anne too, ten years later, remembers the tales of Greek heroes. 'It's the sense of adventure isn't it? Being transported away from real life.'[58] Anne's contemporary, Barbara Green, who went to a secondary modern, remembers not Greek myth but Bible stories. She comments on the power of her familiarity with the Bible to unlock texts when she

55 Ken, born 1925, interviewed by Clare Keen, 16 November 2011.
56 Edna, born 1928, interviewed by Ros Witten, 25 July 2012.
57 Shirley Ellins, born 1936, interviewed by Loveday Herridge, 22 November 2011.
58 Anne, born 1944, interviewed by Susan Roe, 5 April 2012.

came to be a literature student in the 1990s: 'We read from the Bible quite regularly which really helped me when I went to university because so much of our literature finds its roots there, so I was able to give input that the younger ones weren't.'[59] Barbara felt unable to share her pleasure in literature with anyone at her secondary modern, but used every tool she was given to explore books on her own or with her mother.

Betty Newman found a novel in her grammar school library which might have changed her life had there been a film industry in Sheffield. The novel was called *Continuity Girl*: 'and I got it out of the school library and it was about a continuity girl in the film industry.[60] And that was my short-term ambition, I was going to be that.'[61]

Grammar school students, unlike Barbara, often had friends to be their guides. In Anne's case it was not the superior library, teaching or curriculum that changed her reading when she moved from an intermediate school to Central Grammar.

> I read what you'd call children's books right up to going into the sixth form. When I was 15 I moved across to City Grammar, for the sixth form, and that is when I became friendly with a girl who was doing literature and so was very much more into *proper* books [chuckles], adult books. She started taking me to the Central Library and I actually started to read grown-up novels. I got into Jean Plaidy, oh was that then? Yes, I think I did start with Jean Plaidy. Yes, I was doing history and I remember we were recommended it for the period, we were doing the Tudors… I was also doing RE and so I started to read things like *The Robe* [Lloyd C. Douglas, 1942, about the crucifixion of Jesus].

'Delia' too had a school friend who transformed her reading. She went in the 1950s from the rural suburb of Stannington to the prestigious Ecclesfield Grammar in the countryside seven miles to the north of Sheffield. Her first job after leaving school was in the city centre and it was then that she discovered the thrill of a library. She started using the Central Library thanks to 'a friend who's a lot cleverer than me'.

> She was in the top stream all the way through school and she was the one who introduced me to Sheffield Library because I started work and used to meet her there. And we used to exchange our books, you know.[62]

59 Barbara Green, born 1944, interviewed by Mary Grover and Susan Roe, 27 July 2017.
60 Perhaps Martha Robinson, *Continuity Girl*, London: Oxford University Press, 1946, a story about film production.
61 Betty Newman, born 1935, interviewed by Ros Witten, 13 October 2011.
62 'Delia', born 1942, interviewed by Trisha Cooper, 10 November 2011.

The physical mobility of the child travelling first from Stannington to Ecclesfield and then qualifying for a job in the city centre translated into an increased access to varied reading matter thanks to the friend who had the cultural confidence to introduce her to the Central Library. 'Delia' became a journalist, without getting a degree. Nearly all our grammar-educated female readers who were able to go on to do a degree direct from school became teachers. In the 1940s and 1950s this would still have been the most familiar, perhaps the only, role model for a female graduate that they had encountered. All these retired teachers had an inclusive acceptance of the legitimacy of any reading taste.

In fact, it is surprising how little selective school pupils absorbed a sense that one sort of reading was more impressive than another or might place you in a position superior to someone else. If anyone was going to encounter literary or perhaps even social prejudice at school it would have been Mavis. She won top marks in the scholarship exam in 1948 which entitled her to go to the fee-paying Sheffield School for Girls, at the council's expense. There she found herself making up stories with the future novelist Margaret Drabble, over lunch. Margaret and her sister Antonia were the daughters of writers with a comfortable income; their father was a barrister.[63] Mavis seems simply to have enjoyed Margaret's inventiveness without being intimidated by the cultural confidence that went with it. As we will see later, Mavis was hard to intimidate.

University education

Three of our female interviewees went straight to university from school: Mavis, Shirley and Erica. All were humanities students and none of them went to Sheffield University. In the 1930s Sheffield University struggled to recruit students to humanities degrees. The number of women undergraduates plummeted. Although this was a national trend (because the Board of Education ceased to support those wanting to go into teaching), Helen Mathers points out that 'the decline in Sheffield was far greater than the national average'.[64] Sheffield University was dominated by courses serving the city's industries. Industrialists such as Mark Firth were its chief funders. Hence the global reputation Sheffield University developed and still has for courses in metallurgy

---

63 Antonia Drabble publishes her novels under the name A.S. Byatt.

64 Helen Mathers, *Steel City Scholars: The Centenary History of the University of Sheffield*, London: James and James, 2005, 101.

and engineering. Science teaching in girls' schools remained poor until the 1970s, so few women could aspire to go to the local university. Our female interviewees who went straight from school to college did secretarial courses in Sheffield, library training on the job or two-year teacher training courses in Yorkshire or Nottinghamshire. Two went into nursing.

Mavis studied English Literature at Leeds University, Erica French at King's College London and Shirley History at Bedford College London, all in the 1940s. All three gained that opportunity by passing their 11-plus with such high marks that they earned places at the top girls' schools in Sheffield, one at a grammar school and the other two as scholarship pupils in a private school. Selective boys' schools taught Latin, a requisite for a humanities degree in the 1940s, but girls at similar schools did not always get that opportunity. Jean A, a pupil at a reputable grammar school, wanted to study English at university, but she couldn't. 'I didn't have Latin so I couldn't go to any of those posh universities so I had to do one of those social sciences certificate courses', not a three-year degree course.[65] Grammar school boys who had the opportunity of going on to higher education would have been more likely to have Latin than their female counterparts. Nevertheless none of our male readers opted for a degree in non-vocational humanities. Engineering was the most common choice; two took law degrees. Interestingly the economically most successful of our interviewees did a degree that was unique among our readers. Norman Adsetts chose to switch from Natural Sciences to Philosophy, Politics and Economics at Oxford. This was a degree that enhanced his competence with the written word and gave him a platform for his career.[66] His range of skills eventually helped him to manage the biggest distributor of insulating materials in Europe.

Our female readers came out of school in the 1940s and 1950s ill-equipped for any job in industry and with a fairly narrow set of employment options; but, as we will see, their confidence with the written word made them better able than many of their male contem-poraries to adapt to the changing economic landscape of the 1970s and 1980s. Their literary competence and habit of seizing rare opportunities to extend their skills were to serve Sheffield well.

65 Jean A, born 1930, interviewed by Loveday Herridge, 22 April 2013.
66 Norman Adsetts, born in 1931, interviewed by Mary Grover, 17 February 2014.

17 Frank Burgin in the early 1950s

Boys only: English for apprentices

The only two of our readers to gain postgraduate research qualifications were Malcolm, with an MPhil in History from Sheffield University, and Frank Burgin with a PhD in Physics from Sheffield Hallam University. Yet both men had failed the scholarship exam that would have gained them places at a selective school and left school at 14, Malcolm to go into shop work in 1939 and Frank to become an engineering apprentice in 1948. Their failure in the scholarship examination, which for most children marked the end of hope for further education, did not blight the lives of these two bright children, in part because they had acquired a habit of reading which gave them a sense that they could be independent learners, but also in part because they were boys.

In the 1930s and 1940s a girl unable to win or to take up a place at a selective school could not expect a second chance. If boys left school at 14 and went into a skilled trade, they were often encouraged to take classes at night school or offered further training by their firm. This rarely happened to girls who became, at 14, part of a workforce whose skills were not usually considered valuable enough to develop. Many were automatically laid off once they were married. Linda Sibley got a 'dowry' from the Civil Service when she was laid off as a telephonist with the General Post Office on her marriage in 1965.[67]

67 Linda Sibley, born 1942, in conversation with Mary Grover, 18 January 2021.

Malcolm Mercer was born in 1925 and throughout his life seized any chance that came his way, always supported by his wife Jean, who came, like him from the Manor and Park, estates on the hill to the east of Sheffield railway station. Jean had, unlike Malcolm, passed the scholarship, but her family judged it impossible to justify the financial pressure that grammar school attendance would create. Together Malcolm and Jean described the family reasoning:

> Malcolm: Yes, Jean passed to go to grammar school but her parents couldn't afford it. And this happened to a number of children.
>
> Jean: But Peter [her brother] was important because he was a boy you see.
>
> Malcolm: If there was only a limited amount the boy had it and they wore uniforms.

As Malcolm appreciated, it was Jean who minded the children while he worked towards his increasingly ambitious educational goals. Women could rarely be spared from domestic duties to attend evening classes. The women we interviewed who got second chances to attend further or higher education classes did so in the 1960s and 1970s when domestic appliances were more affordable and further education was funded.

We gathered few accounts of the content of classes available to young apprentices in the 1940s and 1950s, but we have one remarkable memory that may have been unique to the apprentices at the Birfield Group of which the Sheffield engineering firm Laycock's was a part. Most industrial organisations included some communications courses in their apprenticeship training in the second half of the twentieth century, but even in the 1980s, the 'English' or 'Communications' classes on offer to apprentices in a wide range of industries were limited to basic literacy rather than the encouragement of any kind of reading habit.[68] Yet in the early 1950s Frank Burgin, a young apprentice at Laycock's, found himself in Goldicote Hall, a mansion in the Warwickshire countryside. Each year, apprentices from subsidiaries around the country were sent there by the Birfield Group for the weekend. 'A holiday was it?', asked Loveday, his interviewer.

> Oh God, no. It was a course. You had to go and learn how to talk to Brummies and people like that without fighting! It was all very posh catering, sort of thing, you went to breakfast with your jacket on.

68 See D.E. Wheatley, *Apprenticeships in the United Kingdom*, Social Policies Services no. 30, Brussels: European Economic Union Collection Studies, 1978.

The boys were taken to a Shakespeare play in neighbouring Stratford-upon-Avon, but the session that Frank will never forget, and which possibly changed his life, was the evening in which each boy had to present a book to his fellow apprentices. This was in striking contrast to his school experience: 'We didn't do projects in school and things like that. We weren't encouraged to go and look for things. We had to sit there and get it learned.'[69]

A few weeks before the weekend away Frank was given an Ernest Hemingway novel, the title of which now escapes him, but the memory of that evening does not.

> I talked about it. I presented it. I can remember doing it. I'm sure very very hesitantly, and I wasn't as articulate then as I am now but at least I didn't sort of stand there tongue-tied and say, 'Aye, well it were crap', like some did.

Frank cannot remember how, but somehow his tepid reaction to Hemingway prompted him to explore other pre-war writers, and he came across the novels of Graham Greene, 'who I did relate to'. When Loveday asked Frank why he thought the training officer had encouraged the boys to read, he replied,

> It was to get us away from the back page of the 'Star' and things like that. I mean they hadn't invented page 3 then. No, it was all done to make us think. Some of us did think. It certainly woke up things in me that I didn't know was there. I think it also made me think that perhaps there might be life beyond knocking very precise spots off big lumps of metal which I'd gone into engineering to do and was quite happy doing.

Few young employees in the 1950s would have had the opportunity to develop their communication skills in precisely this way, and it was moreover an opportunity that could only have been offered to a boy. Even in 1974 only 7 per cent of girls under 19 were offered apprenticeships, compared to 43 per cent of boys, and the great majority of those apprenticeships were in hairdressing. When a girl left school in the 1940s and 1950s the chances of her then being offered an educational experience which would improve her reading confidence were minimal.[70] The significance of not gaining an 11-plus place was far greater for a girl than a boy.

The failure of schools of every sort to encourage reading for pleasure before, during and after the Second World War contrasts with Sheffield

69 Frank, born 1938, interviewed by Loveday Herridge, 21 August 2012.
70 Wheatly, *Apprenticeships in the United Kingdom*, 8.

Library Services' success, described in previous chapters, in establishing a sense of the abundance and variety of books that could be enjoyed. The striking encounters with books in the school context were nearly all inspired by personal relationship: the shy elementary school girl encouraged to play Bottom in *A Midsummer Night's Dream* by a disciple of Caldwell Cook; the Catholic grammar school pupil who learned to value the independent judgement and wide reading of his 'opinionated' teacher; and the scholarship girl (daughter of a colliery weigh station manager) at the private girls' school, who whiled away the lunch hour by playing verbal games with two future novelists (daughters of a barrister). The world after school, especially for girls pulled early out of selective schooling, could close down the possibility of such productive encounters, but for some, the world outside the classroom increased the possibilities of developing new tastes and new ways of connecting with other readers.

CHAPTER SIX

The 1937 'Confession Book' of Mary Wilkinson

Reading and the Second World War

Mary's early adult tastes were shaped by a lodger whom the family took in just before the war and whom Mary would later marry. Mary's weekly wage was only 10/– so Maurice Soar's rent was a huge help. He arrived not only with a car but with as great a love of reading as his landlords.

The reading life of Mary Wilkinson between 1937 and 1942 is more fully documented than any other that we have collected. Mary, later Mary Soar, and her daughter, Frances, have shared with us over many years their unique archive, a testament to Mary's awareness that her reading was formative. Mary's entry into adulthood coincided with a sudden loss of educational opportunities, the threat and onset of the Second World War and family tragedies rapidly followed by marriage and parenthood. Her reading choices reflect and are influenced by these personal and public events.

Mary, whose father was a printer, came from a home that had an explicitly bookish culture. The only other reader from a relatively unmoneyed home to describe a family habit of sharing and discussing books was Pat Cymbal, whose father was an immigrant to Britain and had been a furrier. As we have seen, children from both wealthy and impoverished homes could end up spending little time with their parents, while children of parents with limited space but some disposable income, some leisure time and a habit of reading might get more of the father and mother's attention. For both Pat and Mary, the bond between father and daughter was key to engagement with books, not just as a form of entertainment but as a topic of conversation, a shared family activity.

Mary's parents were both from Sheffield. Before she was married, Mary's mother had worked on a market stall selling 'books and things', and she was encouraged to read bits of the books so that she could discuss them with customers. Mary's mother left Duchess Road Elementary School at the age of 12 at the turn of the century, with her head full of 'chunks of verse' and passages of Shakespeare that she would recite 'at the drop of a hat'.[1] Words were also the trade of Mary's father. The family printing business was long-established, with lucrative contracts with railway companies. In the 1930s the business had also become highly reliant on its contract with the city council, publishing 'recipe books and things for schools'. When, in 1935, the council set up its own printing division, the family firm went out of business. Its collapse might not have been inevitable in a city less reliant on the metal and mining industries. These did not generate a demand for marketing and communication materials to the same extent as the more diverse trades found in cities such as Leeds, Birmingham and Manchester.

On the collapse of the business, the 14-year-old girl was removed from the little private school she attended and went to secretarial

1 Frances Soar, in conversation with Mary Grover, 17 February 2022.

college. Reading was not only a substitute and solace for the higher education she missed but soon became a social asset. At 16 she was earning enough as a secretary to purchase ballroom dancing classes at 'Miss Lockwood's', the first few having been paid for by her two devoted, much older brothers. There she met and danced with a group of scholarship boys from the most prestigious boys' grammar school in the city: King Edward VII. Not only did the young people enjoy dancing 'in a room with a lovely bouncy floor above the garage on Psalter Lane',[2] they fostered their friendships by joining in the contemporary craze for 'Confession Books'. Mary still had the Confession Book that she drew up in 1936 and 1937 when she was in her mid-teens and had just left school. All the headings are written out by herself. Informants were invited to list favourite composers, tunes, dance bands, radio stars, film stars and authors. Unsurprisingly, in an exercise designed to foster flirting, the questions on the questionnaire all focused on the person: not 'your favourite film', but 'your favourite film star', not 'your favourite book' but 'your favourite author'.

The final three headings in particular were cues which revealed the real point of this diverting exercise: your favourite girl, your favourite boy and a sentence to complete – 'I shall marry for...' While the sons of wealthy steel manufacturers, such as David Flather for example, were able to meet similarly educated boys and their sisters at private functions in their large suburban or rural mansions, scholarship boys and girls in jobs had to work harder to create a social set. Judging from the number of responses she collected, Mary was well fitted to play a role in encouraging her friends to transform themselves from a group of acquaintances into a social set who both identified themselves with or, playfully, defined themselves against other members of the group.

The dancing classes were held in the leafy suburb of Nether Edge to the south-west of the city, offering a wide range of housing affordable to wage-earners who were highly skilled working class, senior clerks and a large number of teachers, artists and writers. There were a significant number of schools in the area, King Edward VII Grammar School an easy walk away. Mary's daughter Frances believes most of Mary's male friends were pupils at King Edward's.

Fifty-four friends and acquaintances exchanged information about their tastes with Mary. Their responses to the musical and film questions were

2 Mary Soar, née Wilkinson, born 1921, interviewed by Loveday Herridge, 3 December 2012.

always up-to-the minute and what you would expect from a group who had met each other dancing: Gershwin and Irving Berlin were favourites.[3] The pages were an arena for musical appreciation and for lively mockery of musical tastes not shared. The pages would have been prompts, if such were needed, to debate the rival musical merits of Nat Gonella and his Georgians or Henry Hall (of the BBC Dance Band), who won on points.

It is difficult to imagine that the reading tastes of Mary's dancing partners would have inspired such cultural 'banter'. Authors are not condemned in these pages, whereas the entries under 'Pet aversion' included many musicians or types of music: 'Swing Music', 'Opera', 'Harry Hall' or 'Leonard Henry' (a regular performer of songs and comic sketches on the radio in the 1930s). Just as frequently, under this heading, the boys and girls expressed distaste for 'snobs', 'self-satisfied people' or 'conceited persons'. None of the favourite authors reflected tastes that would have been regarded as stuck-up or pretentiously literary and seemed to provoke no dissension. Most of those chosen were authors who were first popular in the 1920s or earlier: authors such as Rafael Sabatini (the boys' favourite), Ian Hay, 'Sapper', Edgar Wallace, and T.C. Bridges, one of the many authors of the Sexton Blake stories. These authors of thrillers and adventure stories might well have been found on the shelves of parents, but it is just as likely that recent film adaptations made them attractive to a younger generation.

These young people were clearly filmgoers and the range of film stars they admired suggests that they were attending the cinema fairly regularly. Dancers such as Fred Astaire and Ginger Rogers, and the singer Bing Crosby, are frequently mentioned. Most of the stars of the mid-1930s made an appearance: Robert Taylor four times; Robert Donat three times; Gary Cooper, Errol Flynn, Charles Laughton, Myrna Loy, William Powell, Franchot Tone and Spencer Tracey twice. But the contemporary films in which these actors starred were based on novels that were distinctly 'old hat'.

Sabatini's *Captain Blood* (1922), a tale of heroic survival in the pirate-infested Caribbean of the seventeenth century, was a superb vehicle for Errol Flynn in the 1935 film adaptation. John Buchan's *Thirty-Nine Steps* (1915) was filmed by Alfred Hitchcock in 1935 with Robert Donat in the lead. The first Bulldog Drummond novel came out in 1920. Was it a father's copy of the novel, the long run of affordable 'yellow back' sequels

---

3 The greatest divergence of preference was for favourite dance band: Harry Roy's seems to have been the 'Marmite' band; loved by some, hated by others.

with their menacing covers in the 1930s, or the 1935 film, *Bulldog Jack*, starring Jack Hulbert, that accounts for the popularity of its author, H.C. 'Sapper' McNeile, among both girls and boys? No doubt all of these.

The popularity of film in the 1930s stimulated an appetite for certain kinds of book and the persistent popularity of earlier thriller writers was used to promote film adaptations of their novels. Robert James describes how throughout the 1930s the magazine *Kineweekly* used the established popularity of Edgar Wallace's novels to promote film adaptations. Libraries for their part used popular films to reveal the literary treasures that could be borrowed. For example, Coventry Library in 1937 used the launch of *Bulldog Drummond at Bay* to arrange a special exhibition of the novels of 'Sapper' McNeile.[4] Those in the publishing and movie industries acknowledged the mutual dependence of these two kinds of leisure activity.[5]

In addition to novels which had been made into film adaptations, Mary's friends enjoyed more recent authors such as the mystery writers Bruce Graeme[6] and Agatha Christie and the thriller writer Sydney Horler. The popular novels read by the 23 girls were the most contemporary of the titles mentioned: modern but in the traditional romance genre. Staple authors of Mills and Boon such as Denise Robins, Anne Duffield and Margaret Pedler were popular, as were the violent versions of the 'punishing kiss' by Ethel M. Dell.[7] The 16-year-old Kathleen Greaves selected Michael Arlen as her favourite author. This risqué writer of the lives of bright young things in the 1920s seems a sophisticated choice, but it, like so many other choices, might well have been linked to a film adaptation rather than to a taste for twenties comedy. Arlen's bestselling 1928 novel, *The Green Hat*, had been filmed, sanitised and retitled as *The Outcast Lady* in 1934.

It tended to be the grammar school boys who read Wodehouse. Unlike the much wealthier and privately educated David Flather, who was their exact contemporary, they did not seem to reject Wodehouse as belonging

4 Robert James, *Popular Culture and Working-Class Taste in Britain 1930–1939*, Manchester: Manchester University Press, 2010, 26.
5 James, *Popular Culture and Working-Class Taste*, 25.
6 Bruce Graeme (1919–82) wrote over a hundred detective novels, and was perhaps at his most popular in the 1930s.
7 Dell's romances often feature violent and abusive sex. Notoriously, the heroine of E.M. Hull's 1919 bestseller *The Sheik* is repeatedly raped by the eponymous Sheik, with whom she falls in love. Not a Sheik at all, he is in fact half-English and half-Spanish.

to a previous generation. Neither did they dismiss him as snobbish. Both girls and boys mentioned Charles Dickens and 'Sapper'. Only the boys listed non-fiction authors as favourites. Some had clearly been a help to them in their studies. I presume 'Prof. Law' and 'David Hulme' [*sic*] fell into this category.

Among the Sheffield boys' grandiose and vague desires to be wealthy, a film star and to get to the top, are more realisable goals: 'to play cricket well', 'to scat-sing for a "hot band"', 'to have breakfast in bed', 'to repair our wireless' or the decadent dream – 'to do nothing'. The chief ambition of both boys and girls was to travel, Egypt being by far the most popular destination. One of the girls had literary ambitions: 'to write a story and to be a surgeon'.

Two boys answered the questions with a set of strikingly coherent and purposeful responses. These were two German exchange students whom, in her nineties, Mary remembered well. One lists as his favourite author an Austrian writer, Mirko Jelusich, a fascist sympathiser who wrote historical novels in the 1930s dramatising the qualities of 'great leaders' of the past. The other listed his 'pet aversion' as 'girls who are not really girls and boys who are not really boys'; his idea of happiness was to become 'an officer'. There are three English entries that also suggest sympathy with fascist values. Mussolini and Mosley were favourite authors of two English boys, and one of the girls listed her favourite boy as Hitler. The proto-fascism of Sapper's novels might well have made the attitudes of Mussolini and Mosley less startling and more acceptable to these teenage readers.

A wartime reading diary

Mary Wilkinson kept two detailed records of her own extensive reading: one for the years 1936–9 and the other from 1939 until the first few months of 1942. We can see from the first notebook that while compiling her Confession Book in 1936 Mary read virtually nothing but novels, about six a month: the comedic novels of Ian Hay, the accounts of the evil doings of master criminal Fu Manchu by Sax Rohmer, the thrillers of Edgar Wallace and the comic novels of P.G. Wodehouse.[8] From 1936

---

8 Ian Hay, whose real name was John Hay Beith, was hugely successful with his thinly fictionalised account of army life during the first year of the First World War, *The First Hundred Thousand* (1915). In the 1930s Mary was reading his entertaining novels and his plays, co-written with P.G. Wodehouse among others.

to 1937 she read ten of the witty and varied works of Beverley Nichols, nearly everything he had written in the 1920s and 1930s, the most popular of which were entertaining accounts of his homes and gardens. In 1938 non-fiction made an occasional appearance in the shape of biographies of Mussolini, Rasputin, T.E. Lawrence and Lenin.[9] Then in the second half of 1938 she began to read less fiction. The novels she did read still tended to the comedic: John Glyder,[10] Michael Arlen and J.B. Morton's satire on the Oxford Movement *Skylighters* (1934). Delisle Burn's *Democracy: Its Challenges and Advantages* (1929) is the first of the many discursive works that dominated her reading throughout the next two years.

By the beginning of 1939, like many other library users, she was clearly reading with an urgent purpose, to inform herself about the world beyond Sheffield and to try to understand the appalling course of events. During the seven months leading up to the outbreak of war she read 33 books, many of them travel books: *Mystics and Magicians in Tibet* by the spiritualist opera singer and explorer Alexandra David-Néel (1929), Muriel Innes Currey's *A Woman at the Abyssinian War* (1936) and then two published in 1939: the Danish writer Mielche Hakon's *Let's See if the World is Round* and Gordon West's *By Bus to the Sahara*. Both of these were read in Travel Book Club editions, Mary's father's subscription to the club enabling the family to access recently published titles.

Mary read two accounts of contemporary Germany, Gerald Bullet's *Germany* (1930) and *I Was Hitler's Prisoner* (1935) by the journalist and photographer Stefan Lorant. In March she read Somerset de Chair's satirical portrait of the British Labour Party, *Red Tie in the Morning* (1936), and in May, Phyllis Bottome's bestselling anti-fascist novel, *The Mortal Storm* (1937).[11] Perhaps her exploration of Julian Huxley's *Essays in Popular Science* (1927) helped compensate for the science education she missed by leaving school unexpectedly early. Most surprisingly she read the Penguin edition of *Britain by Mass-Observation*, by the founders of the Mass-Observation project, Tom Harrisson and Charles Madge. She is the only one of our readers to mention this pioneering work

9 Charles Petrie's *Mussolini* (1931); Charles Edmonds's *T.E. Lawrence* (1935); *My Father* by Maria Rasputin (1934); the biography of Lenin is probably that by the communist Ralph Fox, published by Victor Gollancz in 1933.

10 John Glyder's comic novels tended towards farce and were compared by critics to P.G. Wodehouse.

11 A dramatisation of the novel was staged by Arnold Freeman's Little Theatre in 1939, and the film adaptation came out in 1940.

of social observation, which came out in January 1939 as a Penguin Special, just four months before she read it. Mary's recorded reading is remarkably up-to-date (apart from the comedy or adventures she read for entertainment). Given the family's financial circumstances, most of these books must have been borrowed from the municipal libraries.

Mary shared her turn towards non-fiction with other users of the Sheffield libraries at this period. Margaret Simpson, a diarist in the *Sheffield Telegraph*, noted on 12 September 1939 that

> Mr. J.P. Lamb tells me that since September, 1938, there has been a great demand for books on world affairs. First-hand accounts of the rise of Nazism, such as *Inside Europe* (1936) by John Gunther, *Insanity Fair* (1938) by Douglas Reed and *Reaching for the Stars* (1939) by Nora Waln were much requested, as was *Mein Kampf*.[12]

The article goes on to report that 'the war has caused such a rush on non-fiction books at the Central Library that some stocks have had to be heavily duplicated'.

Mary's reading, like that of most other library users, fell off dramatically in the first months of the war. A Mass-Observation survey of wartime reading put this down partly to shorter library opening times because of the absence of blackout screens, but it is likely that families were preoccupied in coping with imminent call-up, creating domestic blackout screens and, if possible, constructing bomb shelters.[13] No titles were recorded in Mary's notebooks for November 1939. Joseph Lamb, Sheffield's chief librarian, noted a decrease in borrowing in the first week of war – 'less than two-thirds the normal daily average' – but this was a temporary reduction.[14] As people settled to their new wartime existence and leisure activities were resumed, borrowing also went up. There is evidence that adults joined the library who had never thought of doing so before the war. As Julia Banks notes: 'My mother borrowed books from the library in the war, and, you know, afterwards as well', the implication being that this was not the case before war broke out.[15] In November 1939 the number of books issued was 59,332, only 417 fewer than in November 1938, and totals continued to rise. Readers continued to probe the causes of the war. As books wore out, replacing them was

12 Margaret Simpson, 'A Sheffield Woman's Diary', *Sheffield Telegraph*, 20 December 1939, 8.

13 Mass-Observation File Report 47, March 1940, 'Wartime Reading'.

14 Simpson, 'A Sheffield Woman's Diary'.

15 Julia Banks, born 1939, interviewed by Liz Hawkins, 15 February 2012.

hard and costly, given shortages of paper and other materials necessary for book production. To make matters worse, the massive air-raids on London destroyed many publishers' stocks. Katie Halsey notes that twenty million unissued volumes were destroyed in the Blitz and four hundred libraries bombed.[16] Sheffield was fortunate that the far-sighted Joseph Lamb had early on bought a vast amount of fiction – enough for all the new library centres and 40,000 books in reserve – at nominal prices from publishers keen to empty their warehouses.

Val Hewson's research into Sheffield's library culture reveals how successful Lamb was in maintaining stock during the time of war and in monitoring provision.[17] Simpson's newspaper article, quoted earlier, reveals that classics were popular:

> the libraries' 10 copies of [*Lorna*] *Doone* were all on issue, also the full stock (six copies) of *Adam Bede* and the eight copies of *The Cloister and the Hearth*. *Wuthering Heights* and *Jane Eyre* are in great demand. Of the stock of 89 Dickens books 18 were out. Five out of 205 Galsworthy books were out.

Municipal libraries in Britain were generally wary of 'light fiction', leaving it to the commercial tuppenny libraries. But while promoting cultural standards in general, Joseph Lamb had championed popular fiction for years, on the grounds that it drew people in. He had the vast, cheaply acquired stock mentioned above, and we know from one of his staff (not in fact sympathetic to this policy) that just after the Blitz Lamb was 'flooding the libraries with fiction, in Central Lending for example we were buying, for example, forty copies of the latest Edgar Wallace'.[18] According to the Sheffield Libraries report for 1939–47, the most popular fiction books over the war were *Gone with the Wind* (Margaret Mitchell, 1936) – the one most often mentioned by our interviewees; *How Green Was My Valley* (Richard Llewellyn, 1939); *The Rains Came* (Louis Bromfield, 1937); *All This and Heaven Too* (Rachel Field, 1938); and *War*

16 Katie Halsey, '"Something light to take my mind off the war": Reading on the Home Front during the Second World War', in *The History of Reading Volume 2: Evidence from the British Isles, c.1750–1950*, ed. Katie Halsey and W.R. Owen, Basingstoke: Palgrave Macmillan, 2011, 86.

17 Val Hewson and Mary Grover, 'Running up Eyre Street: Sheffield Reading and the Second World War', paper presented at a conference at Leeds Library to celebrate its 250th anniversary, 21 September 2018, https://www.readingsheffield. co.uk/wp-content/uploads/2018/09/Running-Down-Eyre-Street10.8.18withPics-2. pdf (accessed 27 January 2023).

18 Charles Taylor, quoted in James R. Kelly, 'Oral History of Sheffield Public Libraries, 1926–1974', MA thesis, University of Sheffield, April 1983.

and Peace (Tolstoy, 1869). All, apart from *War and Peace*, were also popular films of the period. From 1945 to 1946, all library records were broken – 3.75 million books issued in twelve months.

Lamb thought that Sheffield's 'reading throughout the war did not differ to any marked extent from that of previous years'.[19] Fred Hutchings, his deputy in the early war years, disagreed. He felt that 'war became a release spring, taking the compression from dull lives and making people think beyond their narrow corners into the world around them'.[20] A Mass-Observation survey bears out Lamb's rather than Hutchings' view. It is true that the first few months of the war saw a flurry of requests for books on Germany, Europe and war in general. As well as *Mein Kampf*, readers borrowed journalist John Gunther's bestselling *Inside Europe* (1936) and *Inside Asia* (1939) and the ever-popular *Seven Pillars of Wisdom* (1926) by T.E. Lawrence. Mary read two biographies of Lawrence before war broke out but never read *Seven Pillars*. She did read *Revolt in the Desert* (1927) in July 1939. But within a few months, borrowing returned to its pre-war patterns: 75 per cent of lending being fiction and 25 per cent non-fiction. The Mass-Observation report also points out that only a small percentage of non-fiction borrowed was about current affairs and that 'war interest' was only 'a very small fraction of reading on the whole'. They noted that public libraries

> issue on an average only about 25% non-fiction, and a large proportion of this has nothing whatever to do with current events. Technical books on engineering and other subjects, biography, language, music, fine arts, hobbies, poetry and religion are all included in 'non-fiction' and account for by far the greater part of it.[21]

Mary was clearly unusual in the way her interest in travel, history and contemporary affairs, begun in 1938, was intensified during the war.[22]

---

19 1939–47 Sheffield Libraries report. Lamb goes on: 'The English people are not easily shaken out of their habits, nor are they given to making any great show of unusual states of mind in Sheffield', 7.

20 From a speech at the 1952 library annual conference, a draft of which is in the Sheffield city archives.

21 Mass-Observation File Report 47, March 1940, 'Wartime Reading'.

22 It is interesting to compare the reading experiences of the Mass-Observation respondent Hilary Spalding in County Durham. Spalding used her boarding school library and attended a course in English Literature at Newcastle University in the 1940s. Her choices are, on the whole, more literary than Mary's, with a greater proportion of fiction. Her responses are discussed in Halsey, '"Something light to take my mind off the war"', 88–98.

Non-fiction had, from the early 1930s, formed a much smaller proportion of books issued than fiction,[23] but this proportion grew even smaller during the war, especially in London and Birmingham. Curiously non-fiction borrowing held up more strongly in the provinces than in the big metropolitan centres.

The war certainly stimulated children's newspaper reading. Like Meg Young, who was encouraged to read her father's newspaper in order to follow the advance of the Eighth Army in Egypt, James Green, aged eight in 1944, read his father's copy of the *Express* to follow the course of the war: 'And I can remember reading – and I was interested, I weren't just reading for the sake of it – because I wanted to know.'[24] The slightly older Peter Mason read the papers with an even greater urgency as his brother, a pilot, had disappeared in the Far East, his body not found until sixty years later.[25] It was not simply what was read that changed (choice was, nationwide, diminishing), but the way in which books and newspapers were read.

The war impinged on the reading experiences of our interviewees in ways that often seem contradictory. On the one hand, the paper shortage, the lack of funds to buy new books, petrol rationing and the scarcity of new titles limited access to books. In Sheffield, children briefly faced an extra barrier when, as a safety measure, the council temporarily closed its more central libraries, moving some of the junior stock to suburban centres. Most of these closed libraries, except for those without air-raid shelters, reopened in November 1940. Although none of our readers mentioned reading in shelters, Helen Taylor's respondents to her questionnaire on how *Gone with the Wind* was read often mention the solace it offered during an air-raid. Immersion in the book rendered the Manchester reader Hylda Fletcher 'oblivious to the noise of falling bombs and anti-aircraft guns'. She also recalled that an air-raid led to a temporary suspension of the ban on reading all night.[26] The disruption of routines possibly led to greater ingenuity in finding opportunities to read and the war certainly sharpened intellectual curiosity. Mary read *Gone with the Wind* in 1942, immediately after Julian Huxley's *Democracy Marches* (1941). The juxtaposition of the two titles is a reminder that the

23 Q.D. Leavis, *Fiction and the Reading Public*, London: Bellew, 1990 [1932], 7.
24 James Green, born 1936, interviewed by Jean Gilmour, 12 October 2011.
25 Peter Mason, born 1929, interviewed by Susan Roe, 28 September 2011.
26 Helen Taylor, *Scarlett's Women: Gone with the Wind and its Female Fans*, London: Virago, 2014 [1989], 213.

novel's appeal was not simply the romance and the epic film but its topicality – set as it is at a time when, to its protagonists, civilisation itself seemed to be under threat. It is difficult to say whether the film or the book was the more important to our readers. For Florence, the book came first. She went to the film presumably in 1942 or 1943 because 'it was the "in" book at the time, wasn't it?'[27] Mary was reading the book when the film came out. She planned the trip carefully: 'it was very very long and we took sandwiches with us.'[28]

Couples who had courted at the cinema were sometimes reluctant to abandon the pleasure of watching films once children began to arrive. Perhaps because she felt (mistakenly) that we regarded film-going as inferior to book-reading, Mary Robertson apologised for sharing her passion for films as a young mother in the early 1950s.

> I mustn't keep you, but when Andrew was a baby I would get him washed, or whatever, and then run all the way to the Abbeydale [Picture House] and watch the first house and run all the way back and then David would have got Andrew to bed and then he would go to the second house.[29]

So, watching the film was both a private pleasure and a social one: husband and wife collaborating in setting up the film–child relay.

Literary guidance during the war

Mary's notebooks suggest, as Lamb did, that at the beginning of the war the demands of adjusting to wartime conditions left little time for reading. In 1940 she records nine titles, only one of them a novel: Evelyn Waugh's *Decline and Fall* (1928). She was still concentrating on non-fiction as she had in the first half of 1939. She listed Julian Huxley's *What I Dare Think* (1931) and R.W.B. Clarke's *The Economic Effort of the War* (1940), but there was a return to Dornford Yates, whose novels were linked by Alan Bennett to those of John Buchan and 'Sapper' as 'practitioners' in the school of 'snobbery with violence'.[30] During this period (1938–42) Mary was not exploring the classics of English literature. Oscar Wilde's *The Picture of Dorian Gray* and a few works by Kipling would

27 Florence, born 1923, interviewed by Susan Roe, 24 November 2011.
28 Mary Soar, born 1921, interviewed by Loveday Herridge, 3 December 2012.
29 Mary Robertson, born 1923, interviewed by Susan Roe, 7 March 2013.
30 Alan Bennett, *Forty Years On* (1972). Colin Watson entitles his study of English crime novels *Snobbery with Violence: English Crime Stories and their Audience* (London: Eyre and Spottiswoode, 1971).

perhaps be described as 'classic', but there is no mention of Jane Austen, the Brontës, Walter Scott, Charles Dickens or George Eliot, for example. Mary Wilkinson's contemporary, Mary Robertson, wondered, at the age of 92, why she had neglected Jane Austen and the Brontës. She concluded that they were too 'prissy'. 'I liked a little bit more get up and go in my books. I know they are wonderful classics and I do like them now they have been made into television.'[31]

It was only grammar school educated readers who mentioned reading Austen in their school years, chiefly after the Second World War. Shirley Ellins, born in 1936, succumbed to chicken pox in the mid-1950s having exhausted herself by long evenings revising for her O levels. She 'read the whole of Jane Austen, one after the other to take my mind off the itching'.[32] Yvonne Bland, born a year later than Shirley in 1937, felt that Jane Austen was 'a bit girly' but she 'stuck at it because she writes in a way that leaves one to believe that the women were downtrodden. And I got on all right with that. Things like *Northanger Abbey* and *Mansfield Park* and stuff like that.'[33] Peter Mason, educated at the boys' grammar school next door to Shirley's, made Austen his own but in a curiously equivocal way.

> I enjoyed … Jane Austen, I found, from a grammatical point of view. I thought she was great, but to me there was always a darkness about Jane Austen, in a way. I was being drawn into her world, which was fair enough and what she should do as an author, but I wasn't happy about it if you know what I mean. There was a bit of misery attached to her work but, don't get me wrong, she was a great author.

Mary Wilkinson and her father did not seem concerned to read 'great' authors. Together they were more engaged by what was contemporary. Mary's daughter Frances, who transcribed both the Confession Book and the book lists, describes how Mary

> read newspapers and magazines regularly and listened to the BBC a lot, so probably took notice of reviews and serialisations on the radio. She and her father used to spend a lot of time together listening to plays and readings on the radio.[34]

This experience of listening to any spoken word other than the news is

---

31 Mary Robertson, born 1923, interviewed by Susan Roe, 7 March 2013.
32 Shirley Ellins, born 1936, interviewed by Loveday Herridge, 22 November 2011.
33 Yvonne Bland, born 1937, interviewed by Susan Roe, 24 June 2019.
34 Frances Soar in conversation with Mary Grover, 2018.

the only recorded example among our readers, who usually associated the wireless with music. Whereas Mary's exploration of fiction was not dissimilar to that of her female friends (though her tastes were for adventure stories not romance), her exploration of ideas and the contemporary world is exceptional and was clearly social. She shared her tastes and discussed them with the family: both her parents and possibly her two much older brothers. Frances records that Mary regarded herself as 'not academic', but her appetite for the new and challenging demonstrates her intelligence and keen intellectual curiosity.

A major source for the family's awareness of the latest publications would have been the local paper. Every Thursday, the *Sheffield Telegraph and Daily Independent* printed 'Books of Today' on page 5, alongside religious reporting and the radio schedules. Precisely because the national newspapers had low penetration in the provinces, regional papers (most commonly the *Sheffield Telegraph*) were where newspaper readers looked for both political and cultural news. Since these local papers were read by members of all classes, this meant that reading tastes would have been more transmissible across class and ideological divides than they are today. There were regular reviews of history and travel books. Though reviews of local books were given prominence, they did not dominate. Only about half the reviews were of novels, which were easily accessible and from a wide variety of genres. They were never disparaged as high- or lowbrow and there was a general tendency to be appreciative rather than dismissive. On page 4 of the 'Books of Today' column on 23 November 1939 Mary could have found reviews of an adventure story by the Poet Laureate John Masefield, which 'sounds pretty wild but is breathless reading'; of a family chronicle by Naomi Royde-Smith, 'a mild tale very pleasant in its mildness'; and of two collections of poetry.

Most reviews were anonymous; only one reviewer signed his name. Dr Frederick T. Wood was, alongside the anthroposophist Arnold Freeman, one of the few public figures who sought to shape the tastes of Sheffield readers. He was a significant presence in Sheffield cultural life from the 1930s to his death in 1967: a scholar of linguistics, a teacher at Firth Park Grammar School, a lecturer for the library services and a literary reviewer. The quotations from the reviews above are rather backward-looking, but in fact his range was wide and his tastes discriminating. On 12 January 1939 he gave a respectful if restrained review of H.N. Wethered's account of Thackeray's artistic development ('written with adulation'). On 4 May 1939 he described as 'well-written ... moving and terrifying' Louis Golding's novel *Mr. Emmanuel*, which deals with the persecution of Jews in contemporary Germany. And on 10 August there was a warm appreciation of Robert Lynd's anthology *Modern Poetry*, which encouraged the reader to explore the unfamiliar. Although hugely well-read, Wood never indulged himself with a knowing or intimidating reference, possibly because he came from and worked in communities not likely to be impressed by a parade of literary sophistication.

Wood was from Kent, like Lamb, from a working-class background. Unlike Lamb he had managed to study beyond school, gaining a doctorate from London University. Though he could have been an academic, he opted to teach in schools. Firth Park was one of the grammar schools in Sheffield. It was on the north side of the city, which was middle-class at the time but less affluent than the west of the city where the majority of the grammar schools were based. One of his pupils, not one of our interviewees, shared a portrait of him which is a testament to his gifts as a teacher.

> He never preached, but we always seemed to behave as though we were in a cathedral in his classroom. I remember him as being intensely, yet quietly and calmly, interested in any topic discussed, and would wander around the room, up and down the aisles, with the text book in his hand, and his eyes on the passage read. It must have penetrated my mind that he was so committed for me, and all, to understand, and enjoy this bit of the English Language that he so obviously did, that I regarded him in a strangely noble light, and respected him as such.[35]

Of the thirty books Wood published, the majority were on English grammar and current English usage. These appeared in a dozen languages, including Serbo-Croat, Japanese and Arabic, and are still readily available. It is as a descriptive linguist that he must have been offered a professorship 'abroad', which he turned down to stay in his adopted city. Impossible to say why he did so but his active involvement in the strong Unitarian community in Sheffield may have been a part of this. Sheffield's eighteenth- and nineteenth-century readers owed a great deal to this religious community, which fostered book societies and civic library provision. In an obituary, Wood's reputation for high principles and rationality was linked to his religious faith: 'He was never afraid of being in a minority of one. He conceived it to be the right,

---

35 The obituary was posted on the website of Firth Park Grammar School and used in a blog post by Mary Grover on the 'Reading Sheffield' website, 16 November 2016: https://www.readingsheffield.co.uk/tag/frederick-t-wood/ (accessed 27 January 2023). The Firth Park Grammar School website has since been taken down.

and the duty of each individual to proclaim and indicate the truth as he sees it.' It is interesting that this obituary, posted on a website associated with the school at which he taught, attributed Wood's stature in the community of Sheffield to his moral probity, high intellect and professional competence, not to his literary gifts, which possibly reflects the relatively low value put on the literary and the bookish in the city at that time.

A family reading community

The shared family interest in literature does not seem to have linked Mary Soar and the Wilkinson family with other wider social networks. During this time of personal and national crisis, the family created instead a commonwealth of ideas focused on the home and the municipal library. In the early years of the war, the reading circle widened further. The family took in Maurice Soar as a lodger, probably in 1940. Having trained as an engineer at Loughborough University, he had just joined Firth Brown Tools. He himself owed his grammar school education to his mother's insistence that he should not go into the Derbyshire pottery factory managed by his father but should have the chance to complete his grammar school education, like his brother. He was soon integrated into the gregarious and bookish family in Sheffield.

Maurice used to read to them all in the evening. The group's relative literary sophistication, their engagement with contemporary ideas and their openness to different idioms are reflected in his choice of *The Egg and I*, Betty MacDonald's satirical account of trying to be a chicken farmer in 1930s America. This exceptionally enquiring household fostered an oral as well as a written literary culture: reading aloud, poring over the same newspaper, listening to radio broadcasts together and, of course, discussing the experiences they shared.

On Mary's twenty-first birthday in 1942 Maurice gave her the complete set of Rudyard Kipling, one of his own favourite authors. Before his arrival, she had already read G.C. Beresford's 1936 *Schooldays with Kipling*, and Kipling's *Debits and Credits* (a collection of stories with accompanying poems) and *Stalky & Co*. In spite of her truncated schooling, the absence of her better-educated friends from dance school (many now in the forces) and the diminishing social and cultural resources of wartime Sheffield, her home became an arena for intellectual growth, and for the courtship of Mary and Maurice.

The richness of this shared culture and connection with the

contemporary can be appreciated by comparing Mary's exposure to a wide range of books with the experience of her near contemporary, Jocelyn, equally enquiring and also from a reading household. Jocelyn was born into the steel aristocracy and lived in a large house full of books. Petrol rationing made the libraries used in peacetime less 'handy', as she put it. So on her return from her boarding school, itself evacuated to Cornwall without the school library, the teenage girl explored the books on her mother's shelves: Mary Webb and the classics. Rather reluctantly she acted on her father's recommendation that she read the adventures of Henty and Surtees ('heavy-going' felt Jocelyn). 'But there was so little choice. And I think that's one of the things we forget now 'cos there are so many books of every kind, good and bad. And then there were very, very few.'[36]

Of course, Jocelyn is right. As Katie Halsey says, in her essay on wartime reading, 'Demand for books … consistently outstripped supply',[37] but to a lesser extent in Sheffield than in many other places. The municipal libraries were, as Mary's experience demonstrates, full of delectable books. It was in part the affluence of Jocelyn's family that drove the school girl back to her parents' bookshelves during the war. Her family lived in the spacious outer suburbs of the city. Unable, because of fuel-rationing, to call on the family car, they did not walk the mile and a half to the nearest municipal library or take the bus to the centre, so Jocelyn was deprived of the municipal resources that sustained Mary and her family. It meant that Mary's reading was more closely linked with the contemporary than that of Jocelyn who, after the war, did go on to use a municipal library with her children and was a wide and curious reader.

Reading, the war and National Service

In 1939 fewer of our readers were conscripted than might have been the case had they been in cities less relied upon to supply armaments. Nevertheless, for most of our male interviewees, the war meant a geographical dislocation which sometimes led to a discovery of genres never before encountered. Only one of our interviewees describes taking a book with him to war.[38] Malcolm Mercer's meticulous reading diary,

36 Jocelyn, born 1926, interviewed by Mary Grover, 17 October 2011.
37 Halsey, '"Something light to take my mind off the war"', 86.
38 Malcolm Mercer, born 1925, interviewed by Mary Grover, 10 August 2010.

explored in an earlier chapter, stopped in 1942. At 17, the determined autodidact joined the crew of a minesweeper. He has no memories of any reading on board but he took with him one book.

> I had it throughout the war until [pause] we were anchored ... and we drifted and the bottle of ink that I had went all over the pages of Palgrave's *Golden Treasury [of English Verse]*, the copy that I had – so that was the end. I've got another copy but it's not the same. But that was the only book. I didn't have a Bible, although I was a churchman.[39]

Without books of their own, servicemen were reliant on the resources of their friends or on the libraries provided by the Navy, Army and Airforce Institutes (NAAFI), a not-for-profit organisation which ran catering and recreational establishments for the armed forces. Although few of our interviewees described their reading while on service, Peter Mason did. He is fairly dismissive of the NAAFI libraries but shared with us, rather apologetically:

> [U]nfortunately a lot of the books I read I wouldn't admit to reading today because they were all sorts of, what shall we say, blue books and very blue books... In the NAAFI areas and quarters you could get paperbacks which were the modern, y'know, genre.[40]

Peter was still embarrassed when talking about such 'blue' fiction, sexually more explicit and violent than anything he had come across before.

From 1949 to 1963 able-bodied young men were required to do initially 18 months and then from 1950 two years of military service. This period of National Service extended literary as well as geographical horizons. The pulp fiction on offer in the NAAFI continued to make an impression. Hank Janson's pseudo-American hard-boiled novels were quite often mentioned. Janson was the pseudonym of the British author Stephen Daniel Frances, born in South London in 1917. The titles of his novels (over 200 of them) reveal their genre, style and content: *Honey Take My Gun* (1949), *Don't Dare Me Sugar* (1950), *Frails Can Be So Tough* (1951), *The Filly Wore a Rod* (1952). They have all been recently

---

39 Francis Turner Palgrave's *Golden Treasury of English Verse* was an instant bestseller on its publication in 1861, and remained a staple of secondary school English teaching until the 1970s. See Martin Spevack, 'The Golden Treasury: 150 Years On', eBLJ 2012, Article 2, https://bl.iro.bl.uk/concern/articles/97e9035b-7614-4463-b5e8-11de2fb57360?locale=en (accessed 26 January 2023).

40 'Blue' and 'genre' are Peter's code for salacious and hard-boiled.

reprinted by Telos and other publishers – each a pastiche of Hammett and Chandler, but with more sex and lurid covers, each featuring a half-naked girl in jeopardy. This kind of literary entertainment would have been taboo in Sheffield public libraries and even in the tuppenny libraries, such as the local Red Circle, which supplied men with Westerns and horse-racing thrillers. Accounts of Red Circle use suggest that men's fiction was collected by wives or daughters while men were at work. Whereas Zane Grey's *Riders of the Purple Sage* would have caused no blushes, it was difficult to imagine a female relative feeling comfortable walking up busy Snig Hill with a copy of *Broads Don't Scare Easy* (1951).

One of the ways in which military service could improve the lives of servicemen was by teaching basic literacy, and these novels were a highly effective aid in overcoming a young man's fear of print. It was with one of Janson's novels that my neighbour, a professional teacher in civilian life, lured an unconfident serviceman to tackle print.[41] It is not unlikely that Peter Mason, who discovered 'blue' books in the army, used them when he responded to the educational needs of 'the chap in the next bed'. He was

> a boy that had been offered the army or six months inside and he'd chosen the army which as he said afterwards was his biggest mistake – he should have gone to prison, but his problem was that he was illiterate. He could neither read nor write and I know I used to write home, I used to write his letters for him and I used to read his letters back for him and I did encourage him and I've got to say he did go to the army education people and he did learn to read and write, so at least something came out of his military service.

None of our female readers suggest that service in the armed forces extended their reading. Betty B, a driver in the Air Force in 1941, was from a family that had fostered her reading, her bond with her father leading to a delight in Edgar Wallace. Though she received parcels of books from her family, she found that dancing topped reading on her nights off. The NAAFI library never became as attractive to the young woman as the Carnegie Library in Walkley had been, and was to become again.[42]

41 John Gilbert in conversation with Mary Grover, 2002.
42 Walkley and Tinsley libraries, both opened in 1905, were endowed by Andrew Carnegie, the Scots-born American philanthropist who made his millions from steel. Walkley was on the terraced slopes to the west of Sheffield's industrial centre. Tinsley was then an independent township to the east of the Sheffield city boundary. It was surrounded by working-class housing, collieries and industry.

Reading and the radio

In 1944 Mary Soar's short-lived community of readers was diminished by the death of her father and the subsequent illness of her mother. As Mary adapted to the loss of her father, to the demands of married life, to motherhood and the need to care for her mother, it is unsurprising that she left no further records of her reading in the 1940s or 1950s; but had she had the time, there were many opportunities that might have put her in touch with a wider community of readers. In 1946 the parallel national and regional radio services were replaced by the Home Service, Light Programme and the Third Programme. There was huge controversy at the time about how the new tripartite service was undermining the principle of the first managing director of the BBC, John Reith, that every variety of culture should be available to every kind of listener, on the same channel. But for the young mother, the post-war ghettoising of the popular and elite cultures on different stations should have made contemporary literary debates and analysis of current affairs much more readily accessible. Compared to the meagre intellectual stimulus provided by pre-war radio programming, there was, in the late 1940s, a far wider range of debates and intellectual voices available, at many different times of the day. In 1946 the Third Programme's Living Writers series, which ran on Saturday evenings at 8.30 p.m., offered the following:

1   Denis Johnston on Sean O'Casey

2   Arthur Calder Marshall on Graham Greene

3   W.J. Turner on Christopher Isherwood

4   L.A.G. Strong on Elizabeth Bowen

5   Geoffrey Grigson on Wyndham Lewis

6   Edward Sackville-West on Ivy Compton-Burnett

7   Rose Macaulay on E.M. Forster

8   V.S. Pritchett on George Orwell

9   Dylan Thomas on Walter de la Mare

10 Peter Quennell on Aldous Huxley

11 John Betjeman on Evelyn Waugh

12 Desmond MacCarthy on Sir Max Beerbohm.

Sadly, the demands of motherhood, marriage and caring for her mother meant that Mary has left us no record of how these suggestive pairings might have shaped her reading. She would have needed time to tune in and the permission of the other members of the family who shared the living room or the kitchen's wireless set. She may not have been able to access the wider literary world opening up after the war, but it is difficult to imagine she ever lost sight of the significance of her reading choices.

Today's readers are drawn to literary memoirs, for example Sheila Kaye Smith's *All the Books of My Life* (1956), Lucy Mangan's *Bookworm* (2018) and novelist Francis Spufford's *The Child that Books Built* (2002), because their authors are authors; what they read made them write the way they do and what they write is publicly noteworthy. Our Sheffield readers never anticipated any interest in the literary building blocks of their lives, but Mary's personal records reveal her sense that her adult identity was being shaped by what she read. It is impossible to trace the ways their reading might have contributed to the kind of mothers, fathers, teachers or seamstresses our interviewees became, but it is clear from their conversations with us that they, like Mary, took great delight in becoming the authors of their own literary narratives.

CHAPTER SEVEN

'You can read and dance'

Reading in Early Adulthood

Doreen Gill was born in 1934. Her father was a great reader and there were books in the house. Her childhood reading sustained her through her years in the orphanage in Leeds where she was sent when her mother died in 1943. There she passed the 11-plus and gained a grammar school place. On her father's return from the war, Doreen was returned to Sheffield and attended Sheffield Central Girls' Grammar. She was unable to sit her School Certificate because her father and stepmother insisted she leave school at 15.

First, she worked at Firth Brown steelworks, then in a shop where she became an expert operator of the new Borough Sensormatic Machine, processing wage slips. In the evening she went to dances. Lunch hour was always reading hour: 'Very unsociable but I used to do it': Nevil Shute, Edgar Allan Poe and Terence Rattigan's plays. When asked if she tended to avoid books that would prove so gripping that she would be distracted from her job, she laughed: 'Oh no, no! I just let me job wait.'[1] When I suggested to Doreen that dancing might have put paid to reading she was quite tart with me: 'You can read *and* dance, Mary!' Perhaps because Doreen's reading never advanced her education or career in any obvious way, it became, for her, primarily a source of delight.

---

1 Doreen Gill, born 1934, interviewed by Mary Grover, 18 May 2012.

Hazel, born three years earlier than Doreen in 1929, also lost a parent when she was very young. Her father's death left her mother with four children to support, the family constantly on the edge of destitution. When Hazel was 14 she needed to start earning, so she found herself in 1942 in the office of a careers adviser, her mother in attendance. The two women agreed over the head of the quiet school leaver that she should go into the shirt factory because she liked sewing: 'Well I came home *furious*. I didn't want to make shirts! Oh I came home and I were *angry*, you know, "I'm not going there".'[2]

She saw an advertisement for a needlewoman in an upmarket dressmaker's in the western suburbs of Sheffield, applied independently of her mother and got the job. Hazel, whose widowed mother had brought up her and her three brothers and sisters on Public Assistance and by taking in washing, found herself a wage-earner. She loved her work and she loved to dance. Though she had taken herself off on her own and joined the library at the age of seven, bringing Enid Blyton into a home that was almost empty of books, then graduating on to 'Gone with the Wind and them sort of things', once she left school she stopped reading, the poetry she had learned at elementary school remaining her private, portable compendium. She no longer went to the public library and never regained the habit. After dancing came marriage and three children whom she struggled to keep silent while her husband slept in preparation for his night shift. Once married she gave her children her full attention, 'because you do everything you can for them – you live for them and do everything'.

Living for others became part of the adult life of most of our readers. Whether caring for children or providing the money that supported them, these men and women were under pressures that often pushed out reading. But the adult worlds of work, courtship, marriage and parenthood could extend as well as restrict reading opportunities. It is at this stage of our readers' lives that there is the greatest divergence between those who were born before 1939 and those who were born afterwards. In 1947 the school leaving age was raised to 15. All children were able to access some sort of secondary education whether or not they passed the 11-plus. During the post-war years libraries were gradually restocked, books became more affordable and Sheffield's numerous literary networks flourished. But access to these riches was

2 Hazel, born 1929, interviewed by Mary Grover, 9 May 2012.

not guaranteed. Poverty, ill health, work and the demands of bringing up a family meant that, for many young adults, reading was a luxury that had to be fought for.

The word and work

The only three readers who described receiving reading suggestions in their place of work were all secretaries: Mary Soar (born Mary Wilkinson) and Kath in the late 1930s, and Margaret H in the 1960s. Mary was a secretary until she became a mother. As we have seen, her interest in Kipling was formative in her courtship and it had been in the office that she discovered *Stalky & Co.* 'It was the first one I read. I think somebody at work persuaded me to read that.'

Kath was lucky enough to find a colleague who fostered her responsiveness to language. In the late 1930s she had already found a companion who could share her love of 'well-written' books: her husband Ken. Their shared reading led them both to 'sort of pick up extra words'. This was encouraged by a woman she met at the first office she worked in.[3]

> At work when I was a young lass there was a woman who was a wonderful person. She read everything. And every day I could see her coming and she'd say a word and I'd have to memorise this word, a long word that'd fit a certain subject. I can't just think off the top of my head, you know. But it really taught me a lesson, to look, and then I'd get the dictionary out and start looking through for words that I'd baffle her with, you know, but ... [laughs] I never did, like, but that was the idea behind it.[4]

Margaret H went to work in an architect's office when she left school at 15 in the early 1960s. Her curiosity about the world, her openness and her quickness to respond to new avenues of thought clearly attracted many people who offered her reading matter as an adult. One of the first of these mentors was the secretary of the firm's partner, a glamorous and generous woman. All the people in the office 'were good people and nice people and were very kind to me', but the senior secretary 'was just wonderful to me'.

3 Possibly inspired by the *Reader's Digest* magazine's popular section, 'How to Increase your Word Power'. The first 'Word Power' column was published in the January 1945 issue.
4 Kath, born 1928, interviewed by Clare Keen, 16 November 2011.

I learned an awful lot from her. She gave me a lot of encouragement and helped me with things when I was taking dictation from whomever and I wasn't sure about things and I hadn't had the knowledge really.[5]

She encouraged Margaret to read books and was the first person to introduce her to magazines because the girl had never had a magazine or a newspaper in her home. The warmth, sophistication and generosity of this woman inspired Margaret's gratitude but also a slight unease about the world to which she was being introduced. 'Posh' magazines such as *Vogue* – 'I remember thinking that they were quite irrelevant to what was going on in my life.' For Margaret to suddenly discover the joy of reading in young adulthood was an enormous gift, but also a shock. The reader of the unfamiliar book or magazine would learn not only that there were worlds elsewhere but also that one's own world, until then so normal and inevitable, was unfamiliar to others. That new perspective might mean that in time the reader's world would come to seem limited or even questionable. Such encounters could trigger a sense of aspiration, but they could also engender a kind of shame at not being good enough or lead to outright rejection of the culturally unfamiliar. For Julia Banks such engagement with the unfamiliar was less complex: 'I think if you read of other people's situations you can see your situations alongside. And it's just learning isn't it?'[6] But Julia had read books throughout her childhood. The habit of encountering the unfamiliar was a long-standing one.

Although the jobs our female readers got in the 1940s were not well paid, if they became secretaries their skills would have been explicitly linked to a relatively high degree of literacy and would have introduced them to people who might take an interest in their development. A much higher proportion of our male readers went into employment where they shared the educational background of their co-workers, but there is little evidence of sharing reading in the workplace during the 1930s and 1940s (except, of course, for surreptitious exchanges of *Lady Chatterley*). David Flather, a voracious reader of mostly popular fiction throughout his life, found that his reading fell off when he was studying aeronautical engineering at Cambridge in the late 1940s. Then when he started to work back in Sheffield it was clear that he would not have talked about his reading at work.

---

5 Margaret H, born 1945, interviewed by Susan Roe and Mary Grover, 10 May 2018.
6 Julia Banks, born 1939, interviewed by Liz Hawkins, 15 February 2012.

You tended to some extent to compartmentalise your life … and this was particularly so when I went into our own family business. You tended to have to keep yourself a little bit aloof from the staff, although some became very, very good friends of mine over the years. The family position relaxed considerably over the years, but there was very little influence there. Very little influence there. There wasn't a great crossover at all between work and social life, including reading. We tended to keep it separate.[7]

By contrast, a number of David's forebears found that books were an asset in their working lives. David was descended from a number of prominent Sheffield families: the Leaders (politics and journalism), the Waterhouses (literary life, commerce and philanthropy) and the Flathers (manufacturing and Masonry). Members of two of these dynasties belonged, in the nineteenth century, to the Sheffield Book Society: a Waterhouse and a Leader.[8] Founded in 1806, this Society survived until the Second World War when a shortage of books caused it to close. This small network was originally dominated by Unitarians but over the nineteenth century and into the twentieth came to include academics, journalists, lawyers, manufacturers, politicians (the Leaders were Liberals) and religious ministers. Members met to choose the books the Society should buy and the newspapers to which it would subscribe. For most of the nineteenth century the books chosen (both fiction and non-fiction) were circulated among members and helped establish intellectual connections between these various kinds of Sheffield 'worthy', as they were termed in the 1906 report on the Society's centenary dinner by the *Sheffield Daily Telegraph*.[9] Such reading networks based on book societies and private libraries were common across Europe and North America until the interwar period in the twentieth century. They helped establish select, but non-domestic, forums for debates about books, the social pleasure bringing the benefit of professional advantage.[10]

---

7 David Flather, born 1931, interviewed by Mary Grover, 31 May 2012.

8 Thomas Waterhouse, a member between 1816 and 1825, Robert Leader Junior (1816–85) and Robert Eadon Leader, who in his article 'The Sheffield Book Society and its first Members', *Sheffield Daily Telegraph*, 5 January 1907, 8, comments that 'acting as a book carrier was often my lot', presumably before the Society employed a boy for that purpose.

9 'Sheffield Book Society: Centenary Dinner', *Sheffield Daily Telegraph*, 28 December 1906, 6.

10 The richness of this early period of book culture is examined by two members of the 'Reading Sheffield' team, Loveday Herridge and Sue Roe, in their essay 'Reading Sheffield: Sheffield Library and Book Clubs, 1771–1850', in *Before the*

Such groups had established cultural exchange between the different professions in the city, but David's reading did not serve that function. Instead, it was an avid but private pleasure shared with his wife, Sally, explicitly outside his working life as a member of a family engineering firm.

A couple of novelists seem to have connected with his new working life, Nevil Shute and Francis Brett Young, who both, like David, had a scientific background and training. Young's series of 'Mercian novels', about trade in the thinly fictionalised West Midlands town of Halesowen, were first published in the 1920s yet seemed to be about the modern world as David knew it. He recalled of Halesowen: 'we bought a steelworks there'. Nevil Shute was of interest professionally. 'Being an aeronautical engineer, I was interested in his autobiography to some extent.' Whereas in his late teens David described a reading set among the sons and daughters of wealthy manufacturers, he felt that when he started work reading 'diminished' because of 'family, houses to run, social activities, community activities, whatever'. He and Sally resisted the temptation to distract themselves from work and family duties. They 'restricted' their reading 'to about twenty minutes in bed at night … just as a complete change and to relax and get away from it all, that sort of thing'. Despite their very different economic status, both Doreen and David, in early adulthood, had to fight for privacy and for the reading time that had been one of the few luxuries of a lonely childhood.

Theatre

If an adult were single or childless, with some disposable income and time that he or she could call their own, the theatre could offer a chance to engage with imaginative literature. Local drama groups flourished in Britain both before and after the Second World War. Ken, whose wide literary tastes were fostered by his keen political engagement and love of elegant writing, would have liked to go to the commercial theatre in the late 1930s, but he could not afford it so supported his friends' amateur efforts.

> I don't know whether it was, er, nourishment or punishment! [laughs] But …
> lots of people, when I was a kid, lots of people like my parents and my sister
> and all my friends were all in amateur dramatics, whether belonging to the

Public Library: Reading, Community, and Identity in the Atlantic World, ed. Kyle B. Roberts and Mark Towsey, Leiden: Brill, 2017, 174–99.

church or the chapel or whatever it was they were mixed up with. So, you always used to be going to see these things but they were pretty rubbish, you know.[11]

Shakespeare was often staged, but, for some, his plays were simply baffling or intimidating. Ken was very amused by the memory that when he was on curtain duty at a production of *Hamlet* at St Cuthbert's Church,

> they said the first three words and this bloke got up and walked out. [laughs] I've never forgotten it. This bloke right at the front. He was sort of incredulous. He got up and walked straight out.

This experience is a reminder that theatre might seem to combine the sociable and the imaginative, but an audience member is plunged into a potentially challenging cultural environment. Attending a play is to some extent a public act, whereas a novel reader is alone with a text that appears unmediated.

Only Jean, born in 1926 and elementary school educated, described visiting the commercial theatre and the opera, probably in the post-war period when she was a shop-worker. She went on her own, not with a convivial group, so, unusually, it was a private pleasure. Her confidence to do this may well have been fostered by the curriculum of her progressive elementary school, which was inspired by the ideals of Caldwell Cook and his 'Play Way' discussed in Chapter 5. Though she was not a great reader she had acted in Shakespeare plays at school in the 1930s.

The attraction of amateur theatre to young Elsie Brownlee in the late 1940s was not literary. She volunteered to be a ticket seller because she 'got a crush on one of the men'. 'I was roped in on the understanding that no way was I going to do any acting. I'd do anything else but no acting … those were the happiest times of my life.'[12] From the theatre aisles, Elsie was introduced to post-war favourites of amateur societies, plays by Rattigan and J.B. Priestley that were both serious and popular, in language accessible to audiences from all social classes.

Doreen Gill too saw a play by Terence Rattigan. It was probably an amateur production of *The Browning Version* in the Teachers' Training College next door to her grammar school in 1950, the year she started

---

11 Ken, born 1925, interviewed by Clare Keen, 16 November 2011. Industrial works, such as Hadfields, also supported theatre groups.
12 Elsie Brownlee, born 1925, interviewed by Mary Grover, 21 February 2013.

work.[13] 'I think that Terence Rattigan play opened my eyes a bit... It certainly opens your eyes from children's books.' It may have been the infidelity of the wife of the ageing Classics master that 'opened the eyes' of the teenage Doreen, but the contempt in which the master's scholarship is held by his pupils and fellow teachers may have been a poignant reminder to Doreen of the low value put on her own academic promise. Doreen's skills on the Sensormatic earned her keep rather than any validation of the 'book-learning' she might have won if she had been allowed to stay on at school and get her School Certificate.

Reading in early marriage

All but six of our readers married, and marriage was usually followed fairly rapidly by parenthood. Norman Adsetts, like David, remembered that work and marriage checked his reading habit.

> I did, for a time, stop when I was in the Air Force [post-war National Service] and when I got married. I was working hard to keep the family going and establish the marriage and so on. But when it was necessary to succeed in my job, I reverted to being a general learning machine and devoured the physics and mathematics books which reading enabled me to become a thermal insulation and acoustics specialist![14]

When Norman became 'more settled' he started reading non-vocational books again.

Newly married women usually had different kinds of calls on their time. In the 1930s and 1940s women's domestic duties were usually unrelieved either by help from a husband, paid help or by expensive appliances. Even women who married in the late 1950s or 1960s struggled to read once they had young families. Wynne discovered magazines at that period in her life. She recalls reading *Woman's Own*, the *People's Friend*, 'all those' in the 1940s when she was a young mother. This sounds like an expensive habit, but it is clear that these magazines were 'going around', the women pooling their magazines and creating another reading community. Wynne enjoyed the kind of stories in the *People's Friend* because they were short, 'not a full story or book'. She was particularly fond of stories connected with Scotland. Wynne cannot

---

13 'One Act Plays', a review of two one-act plays performed by the Brincliffe Players at Sheffield Teacher Training College, *Sheffield Daily Telegraph*, 29 April 1950, 3.
14 Norman Adsetts, born 1931, interviewed by Mary Grover, 17 February 2014.

20 Norman Adsetts and his daughter in the 1950s, exploring together the paperwork brought home from Fibreglass

remember owning a book or going to the library on her own account, but after the war she took her children to the library at the end of her road and now her children, her niece, her sister and her grandchildren swap books and reading suggestions regularly.[15] Madeleine Doherty, a keen reader before her marriage in the early 1960s, was never able to recover the habit. Her husband was not a reader, she had children and then cared for her incapacitated husband.

By contrast, Winnie Lincoln, from a family with virtually no books, married a man with whom she read companionably throughout her married life. Her recollection suggests that he steered her towards non-fiction: 'books on nature, so we always read things like that. Shooting, nature, whatever. But since then, I like, more or less, factual books.'[16]

Winnie and her husband, Carolyn and Bob W, Ken and Kath, and Jean and Malcolm Mercer read in tandem. The couples who chose to be interviewed together knew exactly what their partners were reading and when, their interviews a duet of mutual prompting and commentary. Jean and Malcolm got married in the late 1940s. Both of them had the

15 Wynne, born 1919, interviewed by Jan Chatterton, 18 October 2011.
16 Winnie Lincoln, born 1923, interviewed by Mary Grover, 8 May 2012.

reading habit, but parenting and Malcolm's successful attempts to acquire the qualifications denied him by his non-selective schooling meant that he turned his evenings over to studying history and education through extra-mural classes, while Jean looked after the family and the house. For both, recreational reading was suspended. Carolyn and Bob W still share books with the children they had in the 1960s. They stopped reading themselves when the children were small but when they were a bit older picked the habit up again: 'We used to read in bed, didn't we?'[17] Even if a couple didn't share a taste for reading they could respect each other's interests. Dorothy recalls her married life in the 1950s.

> Derek was always very, very practical. He had his own business as a plumber and heating engineer... He liked fiddling, doing things... He wasn't bothered about television and I, so often at night, I'd read and he'd be in the garage doing something.[18]

In the early days of their courtship and marriage, Kath and Ken explored their shared political commitment. In the late 1930s they read with a keen sense of purpose: a desire to equip themselves to carry the political message to their fellow citizens. Unusually among our readers, they read contemporary and foreign fiction. It was Kath who took the lead.[19]

> Ken: Kath introduced me – and I met her very early on – to all Sholokhov's books. *Quiet Flows the Don* and all those Russian novels.

> Kath: And Chinese books. Famous Chinese novels.

> Ken: And we were very serious then, weren't we, about politics?

> Kath: Revolutionaries, really. I think a bit that way anyway.

> Ken: And there were loads and loads of pamphlets, political pamphlets. They were all the rage then.[20]

Their politics meant that they were part of circle which established what was 'all the rage'. It is only from Kath and Ken that we hear echoes

17 Carolyn W, born 1944, and Bob W, born 1940, were interviewed by Trisha Cooper, 19 February 2012.

18 Dorothy Latham, born 1931, interviewed by Clare Keen, 17 October 2011.

19 Kath, born 1928, and Ken, born 1925, both interviewed by Clare Keen, 16 November 2011.

20 *And Quiet Flows the Don* by Mikail Sholokhov is about the life of the Don Cossacks during the Russian Revolution, civil war and the period of collectivisation. It came out in four volumes, between 1925 and 1940.

of their contemporary, the far wealthier David Flather, who, before marriage, was conscious of a reading 'net' among the sons and daughters of his father's fellow industrialists.

Even when reading was a shared interest, a book could create marital discord. Books were an important prop for Maurice and Mary Soar in their courtship, but in the first years of her marriage Mary found her new husband a little threatened by her absorption in a book. He didn't really like it if she took up a book to read on her own – she thinks that it made him feel 'jealous'. As Maurice sought to establish his career and Mary to bring up two children, both must have recalled the evenings before marriage when books were a communal pastime: listening to episodes on the radio or the reading aloud of *The Egg and I*. Instead of making her accessible, the book now temporarily removed Mary from her husband's world.

Only one of our readers, Jocelyn, read more in the early stages of her marriage than she expected to.

> I do remember when we went away on our honeymoon to Switzerland and I hadn't taken enough to read. [laughs] Because my husband had come back from the war and he was totally exhausted and so he slept a lot in the warm weather and I was very bored. Luckily, in this nice little hotel on Lake Maggiore there were a few English books and one of them was Hardy, *The Woodlanders* and one of them I can't remember. I was so pleased to find them; I would have read anything! [laughs] Nobody tells you to take books on your honeymoon! [laughs] [21]

'They're not doing that to me again': motherhood and reading

In the early 1960s Maureen L encountered an unforeseen obstacle to picking up a book again. During the period of courtship and early marriage she had let her library membership lapse. With her first baby well on the way she decided to rejoin the library. She was 20 years old.

> I went up to Southey Green library, which was quite a hill from where I lived – I was heavily pregnant at the time, and they wouldn't let me join because I had to go back and get my husband's signature because I wasn't 21.[22]

Once the baby had been born it would have required considerable determination for a young mother to use the library at all. Nearly every

21 Jocelyn, born 1926, interviewed by Mary Grover, 17 October 2011.
22 Maureen L, born 1941, interviewed by Mary Grover, 30 April 2012.

21 Josie Hall, 1960s

Sheffield library is up a hill, and before the age of light collapsible buggies, small children severely restricted a mother's mobility.

Mary Robertson, comparatively well off in the mid-1950s, was a good two miles from her local municipal library when her first child arrived.

> I lived in a flat on Carter Knowle Road and my husband was away a lot so I was on my own an awful lot of the time and I would push [the baby] in his pram down to the bottom of Carter Knowle Road and there was a very good library there in one of the newsagent's shops. And I would always get books out and as soon as he had gone to bed I would read and read. As soon as I had got him down.[23]

These 'few shelves' from the newsagent's library supplied her with all she needed to entertain herself on her solitary evenings. The reason why these small private libraries survived as long as they did might have something to do with the difficulties of young mothers reaching the much better stocked city libraries.

23 Mary Robertson, born 1923, interviewed by Susan Roe, 7 March 2013.

Josie was one of the youngest of our interviewees, born in 1942. She married in the early 1960s and had four children in quick succession. The meticulous diary she has kept of her reading from 1962 to 2005 is a testament to her determination to get back to her books as soon as possible and to their importance to her. Josie commented with disapproval that during her first pregnancy, in 1964, she had read not a single book. In 1966 she got going again, reading two books a month, chiefly thrillers and historical romances. Then in 1967 she had twins: 'I didn't stop reading. I thought, "they're not doing that to me again"', and from then on she continued her gallop through romantic and historical novels, in particular the novels of Georgette Heyer and Jean Plaidy.[24] Josie was of a generation when paperbacks were increasingly affordable. When interviewed she was surrounded by hundreds of cheap editions of her favourite novels. In the 1960s she consumed the Pan editions of the James Bond spy novels and the Arrow editions of Dennis Wheatley's strange thrillers (but 'not the black magic ones').

Grown-up novels

Most of our readers who mentioned Wheatley were born between 1936 and 1942 and encountered him in the late 1950s or 1960s when they were just starting work. Yvonne Bland at Firth Brown Tools in the late 1950s gave him a go on the recommendation of a friend: 'Dennis Wheatley stories ... I thought that were good. Always lots of things going off there.'[25] The affordability and disposability of cheap paperback editions in the 1950s and 1960s made it easier to share reading tastes. Like Yvonne, the Methodist Meg Young picked up a Dennis Wheatley in the late 1950s but found that what was going off was too unnerving and laid him aside unexplored. It was an older reader, Peter Mason, born in 1929 who took to him most wholeheartedly, grouping him with Edgar Wallace as a master of improbable adventures. Peter had a totally matter-of-fact attitude to their very improbability: 'you knew for a fact they were out of this world y'know and that was it'.[26] In 2018 members of the Trefoil Guild shared with 'Reading Sheffield' their memories of the first novel felt to be an adult rather than a children's book. Four out of the 17 retired Girl Guiders chose Dennis Wheatley. One, coming to

24 Josie Hall, born 1942, interviewed by Mary Grover, 4 May 2012.
25 Yvonne Bland, born in 1937, interviewed by Susan Roe, 24 June 2019.
26 Peter Mason, born in 1929, interviewed by Susan Roe, 28 September 2011.

adulthood in the late 1950s, explained that it was 'the alcohol and the characters who were all grown up' that impressed her.

A very different kind of adult novelist mesmerised the young Madeleine Doherty. Born in 1940, she was 17 when she was introduced to the novels of Charles William by a charismatic church curate. 'We used to go to his flat on a Sunday evening after church for coffee. It was like a youth club type thing really but I was the only one that ever took the books home to read.'[27] Madeleine and her interviewer, Trish, struggled to pin down the exact nature of the fiction which 'absolutely hooked' Madeleine. The novels of Charles Williams are far stranger and more uncategorisable than any of the novels of his fellow Inklings, the Christian group of authors that included C.S. Lewis and J.R.R. Tolkien. Though the themes of the novels are the traditional Christian ones of redemption, sin and the self-destructive power of egoism, the props to the narrative are fantastical rather than spiritually metaphorical. The representatives of demonic forces are far more unsettling than Tolkein's 'Gollum' or Lewis's 'White Witch' because they are embedded in a semi-suburban world. Succubuses, doppelgangers and African fetishistic objects burst through the cracks of the everyday into the Home Counties villages where the stories are set.

They proved impossible to place in any genre category. 'Thrillers? Were they thrillers?' asked Trish. 'Science Fiction? Fantasy?' 'Not quite.' Madeleine tried hard to evoke their allure.

> They were not religious ones. They were … not spiritualist either, what's the word I'm looking for? … Well they were fantasy in a way but that is not the word I would use to describe them. It's not magic either, it's like magic but I don't mean magic, I just can't think of the word to describe, a bit Dracula-type things… What would you put Dracula under?

Madeleine paused, the compelling quality of these novels apparently derived from what they were not rather than what they were. Consumption of the books was unconnected to her Christian faith, the fascinating curate himself or a desire to read books that were a reference point for a group fellowship. Williams's novels became compulsive reading, read addictively and alone.

> I read too many, too fast. That was it. I would bring one and I would stay up, I can remember one night I woke. I was reading in bed and there was this spider and I'm terrified of spiders. I had been so absorbed reading this

27 Madeleine Doherty, born 1940, interviewed by Trisha Cooper, 29 October 2011.

book, it was probably two in the morning or whatever and I thought, "I'll 'ave to stop, shut me book, there's a spider hanging straight in front of me". It absolutely terrified me. I just couldn't put them down. So there was something about them but...

Impossible to nail down, these books seem to have been an initiation into adulthood in some way, but not into a reading community.

Second chances

It is no wonder that when the demands of marriage or parenthood grew less overwhelming our female readers sought to resume their connection with books and to re-enter formal education. In the 1960s Edna moved back into the city of Sheffield from the depths of Derbyshire and seized the opportunity to attend a further education college. As a consequence, the eldest of her three children, aged 15, was required to collect the youngest from nursery and push the pram home, accompanied by the mockery of his classmates. When Edna announced that she was going to Richmond College, 'my mother went mad. "You've had three children and there you are going to college!" I thought "Mother, I'm nearly going out of my head here."' Her college course rescued her from 'a black hole'.

> I'd be putting the washing in the washing machine and I thought he said for this essay we've got to have a good start, a wholesome middle and a good end. And I'd be planning it in me head, and me mind worked on more healthy things. It was a lifesaver going up there.

As her interviewer drew the discussion to a close, Edna added, 'well it didn't do me marriage any good I'll tell you but it kept me sane'.

The secure foundations of further education from the 1960s until the beginning of this century changed the lives of many women. Edna, Pat, Gillian, Josie, Maureen, Betty and Jean, all born between 1928 and 1942, got the chance to resume the education that had been cut off when they were 14 or 15. Their barriers to further and higher education had been many and varied: failure to pass a scholarship exam; the reluctance of hard-pressed families to permit a child, especially a daughter, to take up a scholarship place or to stay on at secondary school beyond 15; early marriage and parenthood; or middle-class expectations that an educated daughter should support the social and professional life of a husband.

The seven women listed above may have had doubts about whether they had the right skills to cope with an A level or access course, but they had comparatively little fear of books. It is possible that the absence from their lives of people who monitored their reading enabled them to pick up a text free of daunting preconceptions. If they had fears about re-entering education in their maturity (and most mature students express such fears), the pleasure they had come to expect from reading helped overcome the barriers to learning in a public place. And the provision was there. Our readers, who attended further education colleges and universities when their domestic responsibilities eased, were fortunate that 1960s and 1970s Britain was, uniquely, a period of second chances. No longer is such further education affordable and abundant.

We recruited many of our readers from community groups: exercise clubs, library events and weekly lunches in community centres. Such groups are still well attended and a rich social resource. Although literary and discussion groups were organised by the library service in the 1930s or 1940s none of our readers mentioned them. In 1937 and 1938 the new Central Library hosted fortnightly talks by nationally known figures, such as Vera Brittain, Bertrand Russell, Desmond MacCarthy, Osbert Sitwell (a local resident), the broadcaster Val Gielgud and the popular Yorkshire novelist Phyllis Bentley, but these authors seem to have been on the radar of few of our readers.

Earlier, in 1929, before any of our readers had reached adulthood, the BBC launched the Wireless Discussion Groups in cooperation with Sheffield and Coventry Municipal Library Services. Groups could choose from a series of programmes which would be listened to communally and which would be followed by discussions chaired by a local group leader. Libraries in Walkley and Hillsborough were chosen to pioneer this collaborative project: residential areas which attracted members of the clerkly and skilled working classes. The rooms in which the radio programmes were listened to were made attractive and at the end of the first series of meetings at Walkley, the attendance was 120. Despite this, the talks in Sheffield never had the success hoped for and ceased after two years. A history of Sheffield City Libraries gives us a few clues as to why that might have been so:

> The speakers who broadcast were men and women of note and worth; the subjects were interesting; but the talks were not altogether suitable. They seemed intended for a public prepared to receive instruction and to study the subject in a methodical way, whereas the people who came to the meetings merely wanted something interesting to talk about. The Wireless Discussion Groups did not survive the Depression; they have their place in the gropings

of that period for some means of satisfying the intellectual hunger of people unversed in methods of study but greatly desiring knowledge.[28]

So, the Wireless Discussion Groups did attract people unafraid of talking about their tastes but these people were alienated by the formal attempt to improve them intellectually, much as present students in adult education classes protest that they don't want a GCSE – they just want to speak Spanish.

The Workers' Education Association was actively concerned to reach the working class and explicitly explored the problems its offerings might present. Of all the subjects offered by the WEA in the 1930s, literature was the most frequent, a preponderance often deplored by the organisers of the WEA who hoped that economics and politics might have been a greater lure to students whose organising and campaigning skills they aimed to develop. In fact, a report that it commissioned in 1938 suggested that students with little educational background faced more hurdles in a literature class than they did in a subject such as economics, which, despite its fearsome reputation, had few cultural expectations of them.[29] Edmund Poole, the author of the report, perceived that the aims of the WEA and the University Extension Movement to help working men achieve university standards meant that inexperienced learners were offered 'slices of university hard-bake' and 'tutors have been so anxious to supply the deficiencies in the workers' past education that the starving man has been stuffed almost to choking'.[30] Poole pointed out that a literature teacher, unlike a teacher of science or mathematical subjects, relies on a socially determined set of cultural reference points and a shared tone of debate. A teacher's jokes, designed to put students at ease, could unintentionally exclude them. The kind of class barrier that dogged adult education is captured by the thinly concealed contempt for his rural students of a fictionalised WEA lecturer in Henry Treece's 1955 condition of England novel, *Ask for King Billy*.

> I'm in that line of business. W.E.A. lecturer and organiser – you know, talks at village institutes every Wednesday, on Chekov and Ibsen and what have you, eager farmers' wives out for a bit of culture. They are dears, really, but

28 Sheffield City Council, Libraries, Art Galleries and Museums Committee, *The City Libraries of Sheffield, 1856–1956*, 1956, 39.

29 Ben Knights, *Pedagogic Criticism: Reconfiguring University English Studies*, Basingstoke: Palgrave Macmillan, 2017, 27–8; and H. Edmund Poole, *The Teaching of Literature in the WEA*, London: British Institute of Adult Education, 1938.

30 Poole, *The Teaching of Literature in the WEA*, 43, 47.

very wearing. So intensely anxious to read the right things, you feel quite a fraud, if you have any literary conscience, at advising them.[31]

These fictionalised readers in Lincolnshire in the late 1940s bear no relation to their Sheffield sisters. None of our readers was 'intensely anxious' about their reading or desirous of reading 'the right things'.

The reading pleasures remembered from our readers' early adult years are usually private pleasures, but often in a social context: reading on the bus surrounded by strangers, in the living room with the radio playing programmes that someone else has chosen, or alone while the non-reader is 'fiddling around' with a plumbing problem. As the material world around the reader temporarily recedes, the reader's sense of personal freedom to explore new mental worlds is intensified. Attempts to draw readers out of this personal world into a shared world of 'improvement' carry risks. The precious growth in all sorts of kinds of confidence (cultural, intellectual, imaginative and linguistic) may well be dented by exposure to a new language of debate, a new physical space or an unfamiliar and uncohesive social group.

In my next chapter, I do not move on to a further stage of our readers' lives, but set the formation of their adult reading tastes in a wider context. I trace their connections to some of the books that we now regard as canonical or as exemplifying the tastes of 'the thirties' or 'the forties'. Were they aware of such categorisations and how did any such awareness affect the way they made their reading choices?

31 Henry Treece, *Ask for King Billy*, London: Faber and Faber, 1955, 95.

CHAPTER EIGHT

'Anna Karenina, you know, and all the normal things'

Sheffield Readers, Classics and the Contemporary

When asked what she studied at Bingley teaching training college Julia replied,

> Well in literature we did *Anna Karenina*, you know, Henry James, and you know all the normal things... Funnily enough I think the books that I enjoyed more were like Bertrand Russell, you know the really hard stuff. You think, 'well yeah, I never thought about that before but yeah'. You know? It was that you were learning something new, new situations.[1]

1 Julia Banks, born 1939, interviewed by Liz Hawkins, 15 February 2012.

When Julia gained her grammar school place two years after the 1944 Butler Act raised the school leaving age to 15 and provided for the establishment of secondary schools for all 11–15-year-olds, she increased her chances of, one day, opening *Anna Karenina*. Without the opportunity to train as a teacher, Julia would have been less likely to acquire a sense that Henry James and Tolstoy were 'normal' reading, let alone the confidence to say 'yeah' to Bertrand Russell. Her contemporary, Mavis, a Leeds University graduate in English, was the only other of our readers to mention Henry James. When Julia was tackling Russell, Mavis was being approached to go to Italy on a research grant to 'do some ferreting' into James for one of the staff in the university's English department. 'But I was getting married, so I, regretfully, had to turn it down.'[2]

Both Mavis and Julia entered a world where Tolstoy and Henry James were 'normal', having been nurtured in worlds where they were not. Julia was one of only a few of our readers to make a connection between reading and social mobility. Although her training as a teacher gave her the intellectual tools to analyse the relation between class and culture, it was the social relations in her early life that had heightened her awareness of the links between the two. Though supported by her sisters, Julia's mother had to bring up her daughter on her own, training as a corsetiere when she separated from her husband in Julia's infancy. Her resourcefulness is reflected in the variety of social classes with which her skills brought her into contact. Not only did Julia's self-employed mother travel by train out to wealthy clients in the neighbouring towns of Retford and Worksop, but she also made corsets for villagers in Woodhouse who would pay her by instalment.

The class composition of this village on the outskirts of Sheffield is not unlike that of Wadsley, discussed in my Introduction. Both communities were socially mixed in a way that was unusual in Sheffield. Elsewhere in the city, miners and steelworkers lived in densely populated areas around their place of work, surrounded by families in occupations similar to their own. Growing up surrounded by neighbours employed in similar ways and often by the same employer as one's own father made it difficult to understand how class structures shaped the nature of the city as a whole, or how they might shape one's own personal future.

By contrast, in the semi-rural and semi-industrial communities of Wadsley and Woodhouse, agricultural workers, miners and people

2 Mavis, born 1937, interviewed by Mary Grover, 12 March 2012.

servicing middle-class households lived alongside each other, and middle-class employers such as vicars, teachers and landowners often played a cultural role in the community. Unlike Wadsley, Woodhouse had its own grammar school which attracted children from more densely populated inner-city areas of Sheffield. Unlike the working-class grammar school children in the east of Sheffield who had to cross the city to attend schools in the more affluent west of the city, Julia's grammar school was on her doorstep. Although she grew up on a predominantly working-class council estate on the edge of Woodhouse, unlike most of our working-class readers she was not removed from her place of origin by gaining a grammar school education.

Julia still lives in Woodhouse, the village in which she was brought up, but in a sense, she has been socially mobile from her earliest years. Every Sunday, as a child, she was gathered up by a 'big girl' from the local Methodist church to attend Sunday School in the older part of the village. Every evening her mother or her aunts would read to her from the books which, unlike the children in the same street, Julia had in her home. Despite the family's economic situation, Julia, as a child, was exposed to a far wider range of cultures and social classes than most of our readers.[3] Recalling the way the bookcases and art deco décor of the children's section of Woodhouse Library seemed to 'lift' her, she goes on to say, hesitantly and apologetically, 'And ... that ... I probably shouldn't say, I found that quite middle class.' Judith was aware both of class signifiers, and of the class sensitivities of those around her, including her interviewer's. She was also more keenly aware than most of the subjectivity that governs our perceptions of class and of the kinds of culture that are associated with particular classes.

'Are you looking at me?' Ways of examining working-class tastes

Even before the Second World War and National Service threw together people from widely differing backgrounds, the mutual incomprehension of the differing classes and differing regions in Britain was, for the first time, becoming a matter for concern and investigation. Q.D. Leavis, in 1932, did comment on class differences of taste but from a position of perceived superiority to those whose tastes she was commenting on.[4]

3 Julia Banks, in conversation with Mary Grover, 4 March 2022.
4 Q.D. Leavis, *Fiction and the Reading Public*, London: Bellew, 1990 [1932].

The anthropologist Tom Harrisson's intentions were very different but, like Leavis's, his observations are coloured by his membership of a certain class, removed from those whose behaviour he sought to describe. Harrisson called into question the ways in which the press and cultural pundits of the 1930s characterised the British working classes. His first enquiries were conducted between 1936 and 1937 in the mill town of Bolton, just over fifty miles from Sheffield on the Lancashire side of the Pennine uplands. His study of working-class behaviour and attitudes in Bolton, or 'Worktown' as he named it, marked the beginning of the Mass-Observation project whose findings underpin most current studies of life in Britain in the 1930s and beyond. However, if we turn to later Mass-Observation material to help us understand the reading experiences of our Sheffield interviewees, we struggle.

In David Hall's recent history of Harrisson's 'Worktown' project there is no mention of libraries, reading or fiction because Harrisson and his pioneering observers were not, at first, interested in print culture among the working classes, except newspaper reading.[5] In countering the assumptions of middle-class commentators about what working-class life was like, the pioneer observers sought to get down into workplaces, pubs and homes to assemble raw data, observed first hand. They sought to bypass the arrogance towards, lies about and contempt for the working classes to be heard in the voices that dominated print culture. It is highly likely, however, that Harrisson and his colleagues would have shared some of the intellectual distaste for popular fiction rife in the 1930s and 1940s. Cultural commentators from Marxists to Cambridge academics argued that the emotional life depicted in popular fiction was in some way unreal, that genre fiction dulled readers' powers to argue critically or act politically, and that the print industries were controlled by capitalist conglomerates that instilled in readers a willingness to pay for repeated and formulaic narrative pleasure that reduced consumers to a passive, addicted mass.

When the Mass-Observation triumvirate of Charles Madge, Humphrey Jennings and Harrisson, from 1937 to 1947, started asking volunteer observers throughout Britain to record what they themselves read the findings were enormously interesting, but reflect the tastes of people with a much keener sense of what was available than most general readers, tastes shaped, for example by the Left Book Club and the *New Statesman*. Many Mass Observers were recruited, as was Harrisson, from

---

5 David Hall, *Work Town: The Astonishing Story of the 1930s Project that Launched Mass-Observation*, London: Weidenfeld and Nicolson, 2015.

Madge's 1937 advertisement in the *New Statesman* which Harrisson read in Bolton municipal library. Herbert Jennings reflected that observers tended to be of a certain class, privileged but left-leaning.

The relatively confident and sophisticated readers who were recruited as observers often named Orwell and Auden as favourite writers, but Auden never appears in our readers' memories of reading from the 1930s and the 1940s. Ken, whose left-wing tastes in the 1930s might have attracted him to Orwell, in fact turned to Chinese novels. Orwell and Auden are both absent from Sheffield newspaper reviews. Nor do our readers mention reading the *New Statesman*.

We did have one reader, Mary Soar, who engaged with the Mass-Observation project itself. She mentions reading *Britain* by Charles Madge and Tom Harrisson very soon after it came out in 1939. As we have seen, she and her father took an unusually active role in exploring contemporary issues, their reading prompted by reviews in the national as well as local papers and by the books sent to them by the Travel Book Club. This made them readers of contemporary publications in a way that few of our readers, whatever their economic circumstances, were. To what extent were our older readers, born between 1919 and 1929, able to access the kinds of literary culture associated with the 1930s and 1940s by such cultural commentators as Harrison, Madge and their cohort of observers?

Not my thirties: Sheffield readers and twentieth-century authors

Jonathan Rose has made us aware of what he calls the 'conservative canon' of the British working classes during the 'industrial era', when 'the reading of the British working classes consistently lagged a generation behind those of the educated middle classes'.[6] Rose suggests that working-class readers in London were more likely to be aware of the contemporary than those in the provinces.[7] It is likely that, in many respects, Sheffield was even further removed from the contemporary than other northern industrial cities. On Wednesday 18 October 1950, J. Warwick Buckler wrote to the *Sheffield Daily Telegraph* to complain that films arrived in Sheffield a year after they arrived in other cities. He judged Sheffield to be 'a backwater in the entertainment world':

6 Jonathan Rose, *The Intellectual Life of the British Working Classes*, New Haven, CT: Yale University Press, 2001, 116.

7 Rose, *The Intellectual Life of the British Working Classes*, 139.

Leeds, Manchester and Birmingham receive annual visits from Covent Garden and Sadler's Wells Opera and Ballet Companies, whereas all we receive is Carl Rosa and Dolin without the Markova that other cities had.[8]

In his view, Sheffield was not considered as profitable a market for new productions as other industrial cities. This indicates the absence of a sizeable social group interested in or able to afford what was new, even in the 1950s when the range of drama being performed by amateur groups, for example, had increased.

Born between 1903 and 1909, Evelyn Waugh, George Orwell and Graham Greene tend to be associated with the 'thirties'. Works by all three were available in paperback soon after publication. Graham Greene's *Stamboul Train* was filmed in 1934. Waugh and Greene had a presence on the National Radio in the 1930s and Orwell was to be heard on all three BBC services in the 1940s, after the war. Nevertheless, the works of these authors seem to have meant little to those of our readers who had come to adulthood in these decades. Why was this? They were available in municipal libraries and in bookshops, and they were reviewed in national journals and newspapers. Of the 29 readers interviewed who were born between 1919 and 1929, seven mention these authors, not often with enthusiasm. The fathers of five of the seven were skilled workers in Sheffield industries who encouraged their children's reading. Most read them well after the Second World War.

I began the chapter on our readers' memories of reading in the home with Mary Robertson, pictured on the beach at 'Brid' in 1928. Though her father was a highly educated man, and could afford to send his daughter to a private school, Mary was actively discouraged from going into higher education or training of any sort. She became a wide and adventurous reader and, unlike our other readers of Greene and Waugh, encountered them in the 1940s rather than the 1960s. She was unimpressed. Her Catholic convent school education did not appear to have helped her forge a connection to Greene: 'a bit holier than thou... He didn't grab me at all', and Waugh's scabrous novels left no impression at all. 'I have read some of Evelyn Waugh but I can't tell you what it was.'[9]

Eva, born in 1925, two years after Mary, also encountered Greene in the 1940s (she thinks), and not in an educational environment. Her father was an engineer and turner. She became an optical glazier. Though she won a place at a grammar school, her parents directed her to the local

8 Warwick Buckler, 'This Film Lag', *Sheffield Daily Telegraph*, 18 October 1950, 2.
9 Mary Robertson, born 1923, interviewed by Susan Roe, 7 March 2013.

non-selective secondary school, one of the early examples of what was to be called a secondary modern school. 'They didn't bother with the girls then, you know. Boys could have anything, but...' It is probable that she borrowed Greene from her local library, Burngreave, which she used regularly. Although Eva now owns a few copies of his books and is not very enthusiastic, she did pick them up: 'Yes. Graham Greene, I've got two or three of his. He's a bit peculiar though, isn't he?'[10]

Edna's father was a steelworker and the family's sole source of books was the municipal library. Born in 1928, she went to a grammar school and was encouraged to stay on to do her Higher School Certificate and become a teacher. As the family could not afford to support her, she had to leave school at 16. Of the six readers who mention authors associated with 1930s literary culture, Frank Burgin and Edna are the only readers who appear to have an appetite for Graham Greene. As we have seen, Greene's novels made a personal impression on the 15-year-old Frank when he came across them during the courses connected with his apprenticeship at Laycock's engineering firm in the early 1950s. 'I did relate [to him].'[11] Edna also came across Greene because of her education as an adult. She read 'lots' of Greene in the 1960s when her children had grown up. 'I'd be much older when I read Graham Greene ... because I did a course at Richmond College.'[12] Anne B also read Greene in the 1960s when she did her teacher training in Leeds. There she read Greene and Waugh because she was required to write essays on them, part of a curriculum rather than personally chosen.[13]

Peter Mason, born in 1929, a grammar school boy and a graduate, responded to the novels of Evelyn Waugh in a spirit of historical curiosity well after the Second World War.

> I've read a couple of his books – now he again, to me he brings back the twenties and thirties – and more or less, not the upper class, but the upper-middle class, their parties... It's interesting to see how they formed ... without having to work very hard.[14]

Peter meant that by reading such novels he did not have to work hard to acquire some knowledge of this remote social group.

Ken, like Peter, was a grammar school boy in the 1930s. He read 'all Evelyn Waugh's books, you know, *Vile Bodies* and all that business ...

---

10 Eva, born 1925, interviewed by Susan Roe, 16 May 2012.
11 Frank, born 1938, interviewed by Loveday Herridge, 21 August 2012.
12 Edna, born 1928, interviewed by Ros Witten, 25 July 2012.
13 Anne B, born 1944, interviewed by Susan Roe, 5 April 2012.
14 Peter Mason, born 1929, interviewed by Susan Roe, 28 September 2011.

all those', probably in the 1940s.[15] 'All that business' was geographically and socially remote to an extent that made it another business, almost another time. Yet Ken was driven to read them all, despite or perhaps because of his left-wing political convictions. Both Peter and Ken read Waugh's novels retrospectively, as a source of historically interesting information to be obtained 'without', as Peter put it, 'having to work very hard'. Peter commented that Orwell's were not the kind of books he particularly wanted to read, but he could 'appreciate what's behind it'. These readers had, for different reasons, access to national forums for debate: Ken by virtue of his political activism and Peter because of his access to higher education and work as a civic administrator.

It was James, born in 1936, who read Orwell with some degree of personal engagement. It is difficult to tell how James discovered Orwell. His parents encouraged his reading and were readers themselves: 'it were just a natural thing'. His mother read romances and his father the swashbuckling and larky Jeffery Farnol and Raphael Sabatini. James discovered Orwell's *Road to Wigan Pier* when he was 16, a year after he had left school in 1952. The book was published by the Left Book Club in 1937, the year after James was born. He said it 'really opened my eyes, you know',

> because living as we did, we were living as he were describing, the conditions we was born into. And the first dawnings in my mind were 'This ain't right. We shouldn't be living like this, and we've no need to live like this.'[16]

It is possible that James was encouraged to read Orwell by a teacher. Though he felt unable to take up his grammar school place, his secondary modern had specialist English teachers, not the generalist elementary teachers that he would have had if he had been born six years earlier. He is one of the few readers who mentioned that his teachers encouraged general reading, 'steering' him to whatever they thought 'you should be reading at that time'. 'And best things they ever said to me at school was, "Right – we've got a spare half hour where if you've got something to read, read." Perfect.'

James continued to read and reread both Orwell and Dickens, because they were the first authors he read who overturned his 13-year-old assumptions: 'I did think we were the greatest nation on this earth anyway. God is an Englishman.' This secondary modern pupil is the

---

15 Ken, born 1925, interviewed by Clare Keen, 16 November 2011.
16 James Green, born 1936, interviewed by Jean Gilmour, 12 October 2011.

23 James Green, 2017, in front of Attercliffe Free Library

only reader who read Orwell as a young man, who regarded him as contemporary.

If the now well-known novels of the 1930s were not known to the majority of our readers, the groundbreaking novels about working-class communities written in that decade, such as Walter Brierley's *The Means Test Man* (1935), were never mentioned at all. The most famous of such novels was Walter Greenwood's bestselling *Love on the Dole* (1933). This realist depiction of the lives of the urban working class in Salford's Hanky Park during the Depression was serialised in the *Sheffield Independent* in 1935, dramatised and then made into a popular film in 1941. Yet none of our readers, not even Ken and his equally left-wing wife Kath, referred to it.

As Chris Hopkins observes in his examination of the implied reader of Greenwood's novel, the author contrasts 'the limited viewpoint of those in the novel' with 'the relative freedom of perspective of those implied to be reading the novel'.[17] The suggestion is perhaps that Greenwood did not expect working-class readers to read and appreciate *Love on the Dole*, but since Greenwood was himself from Hanky Park, and from a very disadvantaged background, he must surely have expected some of his own class to be able to share his perspective, and there is no reason to suppose that our readers in the 1930s could not have done so. That they don't seem to have accessed realist books about the working classes before the war suggests the absence of a reading 'net' between avid working-class readers, which meant their reading tended to be solitary, idiosyncratic or confined to familiar genres and authors already known.

D.H. Lawrence: 'hoo-ha' and 'lah-de-dah'

Boys and girls in post-war secondary schools were certainly exposed to one of the few literary authors from early twentieth-century Britain who wrote about the life of the working classes. Although much of what they read by Lawrence was written at the beginning of twentieth century, he seemed contemporary to many of our readers in the mid-twentieth century. The Nottinghamshire mining community in which D.H. Lawrence was raised would not have been dissimilar to the mining communities within and just outside Sheffield's city boundaries until the 1980s.

English department stock cupboards in schools and colleges throughout the 1960s and 1970s were full of Lawrence: his short stories, his poetry and his novels, *Sons and Lovers* (1913) and *The Rainbow* (1915). The presence of these two novels on university syllabuses across the globe in the second half of the twentieth century owes a great deal to Q.D. and F.R. Leavis, their initial distaste for Lawrence matched by a later enthusiasm. In 1948 F.R. Leavis placed Lawrence in the pantheon of novelists in 'the great tradition' and in 1964 wrote one of the first full-length studies of Lawrence's novels. Leavis's tastes influenced the post-war generation of English teachers.

Teaching mixed-ability classes in an inner-city boys' secondary school in the 1970s, I found the stories by Lawrence in David Holbook's anthology *People and Diamonds* a rich resource, as did teachers in Further Education colleges across the country. Its four volumes came out

---

17 Chris Hopkins, *Love on the Dole: Novel, Play, Film*, Liverpool: Liverpool University Press, 2018, 30.

between 1962 and 1966, just at the time when many of our readers found the opportunity to resume their education. Holbrook's anthologies were among the first to include literature that reflected the lives of working-class students. As Peter B, a careful reader of Lawrence, observed,

of course, he advanced literature in the sense that it was the first time that sort of thoughts had been attributed to the working class. You had to be either a business man or a lawyer or something to be written about.[18]

Apart from Mavis, who did an English Literature degree at Leeds, our other readers' responses to Lawrence are scant and usually focus on a novel of his that was never on any school or university syllabus: *Lady Chatterley's Lover*. Although it is difficult to pin down the exact date at which each reader read *Lady Chatterley*, it was clearly not read for reasons that would have cheered Leavis or Holbrook. When on 2 November 1960, after a well-publicised trial, Penguin's unexpurgated edition was judged not to be obscene, it was avidly bought and read by people who hoped that it would be. Nothing is said about its content. What is remembered, by those of our readers who read it, was the thrill of getting hold of a copy. Most of these encounters seem to have been in the 1960s, though two readers record exploring the expurgated edition before the court case.

Anne B, born in 1944, read *Lady Chatterley* at the time of the trial when she was about 14 or 15. 'I didn't know what the fuss was about for most of it.' These are exactly the words used by Peter Mason, who read Lawrence because he 'wasn't meant to'.[19] Eva, born in 1935, only acknowledged reading *Lady Chatterley* when asked a direct question.

Eva: I didn't think it was shocking! I did think what all the fuss was about! … I don't know why I read it. But that sort of thing, I'm not interested in.

Susan: The sex thing.

Eva: No, I'm not.[20]

In 1934 Richard Hoggart, in West Yorkshire, brought home the novels of Lawrence to share with his grandmother; 'she had only been, and that occasionally, to a dame school', but she read many of the books brought home by her grandson. 'I remember especially her reaction to D.H. Lawrence; much of it she admired, and she was not shocked. But

18 Peter B, born 1930, interviewed by Susan Roe, 29 May 2012.
19 Peter Mason, born 1929, interviewed by Susan Roe, 28 September 2011.
20 Eva, born 1925, interviewed by Susan Roe, 16 May 2012.

of his descriptions of physical sex she said, "'E makes a lot of fuss and lah-de-dah about it.'"[21] Hoggart went on to write the 1961 introduction to Penguin's unexpurgated edition of *Lady Chatterley*. He began by dealing with the sexual encounters, comparing them with extracts from earlier bodice rippers and demonstrating persuasively the tenderness and mutual respect between Mellors and Constance. This eloquent and moving introduction might well not have been read by those who turned only to the notorious thirty pages, reading them out of context. It is perhaps a measure of how little Lawrence's ambitions have been realised that his attempt to speak of sex 'naturally' was interpreted as 'fuss' and 'lah-de-dah'.

Dorothy Latham was perhaps the only reader to be touched by the book, because it was shared with her by her husband. Born in 1931, she read the abridged version in the 1940s and the unexpurgated version in the 1960s after the court case. She got hold of the unexpurgated text because her husband brought it home from work, 'for me'. The husband of Dorothy H also decided that his wife should read the book: 'It was my husband that I got it through and it had been in their office. So, he brought it home for me.' In Anne's case too, a man had been the means of getting hold of the unexpurgated version of the book. At the time of the trial her father was reading it 'surreptitiously' and had hidden it under a pile of newspapers. 'There was always a half hour part of the day, when I got in from school before they came back from work, that I'd got to myself and I used to read it. I worked my way through it.' So, not just those thirty pages.

In fact, the expurgated version was circulating in Sheffield before the court case. Jean Wolfendale mentions that in the later 1940s or early 1950s, when she was still at school, 'everyone wanted to get their hands on *Lady Chatterley's Lover*'.[22] There was at least one unexpurgated copy in Sheffield lying dormant. Betty Newman was privileged to be working in the cavernous stacks in the basement of Sheffield University Library at the time of the trial, so she and her colleagues hunted it down.

> I don't think we knew it was there, really until all the court case, the hoo-ha came up about it. But we all read that. And then when it was released, on general release I went to buy it and they asked me if I was old enough. [laughs] I was a married lady by then, but they asked if I was old enough.

So among female librarians, in the privacy of a library basement, among men 'at the office' and in families where the husband and wife trusted

---

21 Richard Hoggart, *The Uses of Literacy*, Harmondsworth: Penguin, 1958, 13–14.
22 Jean Wolfendale, born 1935, interviewed by Sahra Ajiba, 14 August 2011.

one another enough to share those 30 pages, *Lady Chatterley*, though not contemporary, had contemporary currency, initiating talk about books and possibly discussions about sex.

But our readers returning to education in the 1960s and 1970s were encouraged to engage less with Lawrence's representations of sex than with his representations of class. Holbrook was involved with the Workers' Educational Association. He and other educators hoped that Lawrence would connect with post-Butler students because he represented the working class in ways that were promoted as 'authentic'.

Josie Hall, the daughter of a miner then steelworker, did not appear to find any connection with her family in the works of a man whose economic and social background was much like hers. Looking through a list of authors that we shared with our readers, she came upon D.H. Lawrence. 'I can read him but definitely not one of my favourites.' He made so little impression that she hadn't included any of his novels in the comprehensive reading diary she had compiled since 1962. Josie moved schools constantly so never got the education she craved until, with the support of her husband, she worked her way through the exams to enable her to do a Film and History degree at Sheffield Polytechnic in the 1970s. One of our most omnivorous and eclectic readers, Josie was of a generation blighted by the rigidity of selection at the age of 11, but was also able to take advantage of the boom in adult education in the 1960s and 1970s. It was then that she came across Lawrence, and read him as historically rather than personally significant.[23]

Peter B, born in 1930, his father an engineer, had family from 'D.H. Lawrence country'. Peter went from grammar school to study Law at Oxford, returning to Sheffield where he later became a judge. When asked if he had read *Lady Chatterley* during the period of the 'hoo-hah' in the 1960s, he replied, 'Yes, but it was written in the Thirties – read it, of course, even before copies were generally available. Yes. Lots of that.' When asked if he thought it was 'a good book' he responded in terms that would have dismayed both Lawrence and Leavis: 'It's a bit like *Forsyte Saga* if you know what I mean – it's a bit dated…' Like the older male readers Peter Mason and Ken, this Peter read Lawrence in a spirit of historical enquiry rather than because he responded to the mining communities with which, because of his father's background, he was familiar.

A similar lack of personal identification is reflected in a 1990s response to the nude wrestling scene in *Women in Love*. A mature

23 Josie Hall, born in 1942, interviewed by Mary Grover, 4 May 2012.

undergraduate student of mine at Sheffield Hallam University, who had been a miner in the South Yorkshire coalfields, was quizzed by his fellow students on the extent to which the book reflected the communities he grew up in: 'Well, yes, we used to wrestle, but we used to keep our clothes on'; an echo of Richard Hoggart's grandmother, the presumption being that doing 'normal' things with your clothes off was a bit 'lah-de-dah'.

Mavis, born in 1937, grew up in the colliery weigh station where her father was manager. Always decisive, Mavis knew exactly which book it was that had changed the way she thought:

> *Sons and Lovers*. It both led me on to a different level of adult fiction even if I didn't always pick up on the nuances but ... it made me see how people adapt, grow up, fall in and out of love – I think it went along with my development at the right age.

She was 14 when she read it, at the prestigious Sheffield Girls' High School which, as well as paying pupils, took scholarship girls, but only those with the highest marks, of whom Mavis was one. She dismissed any suggestion that it appealed to her because of her father's connection with the coal industry. 'Not at all... In a way, the miners in the family had moved up from the miners of Lawrence, from his father's.' Her uncles were deputies, mining engineers. 'They may have been miners but they weren't the sort of miners who went to the pit baths.' Nevertheless, the living conditions of miners were clearly familiar to Mavis.

> People read it now and hear about pit baths and baths in front of the fire, the lifestyle and, of course, it's totally alien, but it wasn't then. So, it was sufficiently familiar for me not to be brought up short by anything. Nor in *Lady Chatterley's Lover*, apparently.

At which Mavis laughed, because she recalled that the only reason she was not shocked by *Lady Chatterley* was that at 14 she hadn't a clue what was going on in the woods.

It was Mavis who read Lawrence in the spirit that I imagine he would have welcomed: not out of prurience (which he wrote against), nor out of a desire to have a peek at an alien class (which was not 'totally alien' to the majority of our readers), nor out of curiosity to map the past. Mavis read Lawrence because she felt his novels increased her knowledge of human nature, 'how people adapt, grow up, fall in and out of love'. She read *Sons and Lovers* in 1951, just on the cusp of adulthood; it was her present life that the book helped her explore.

One curious effect of the *Lady Chatterley* phenomenon is that it engaged readers with an author they didn't necessarily warm to. D.H. Lawrence's novels had this in common with the unappealing volumes of Walter Scott that were inflicted upon them at school in the 1930s; both authors 'must be read', as if *Lady Chatterley* was part of some unwritten syllabus. Like him or not, our readers were driven on to explore Lawrence because they 'had' to find those forbidden passages. In her eighties, Jean Ansdell reflected that this was a task to be completed: 'Do you know I haven't read *Lady Chatterley's Lover* and I must do.'

'Funny and not silly': the brighter side of the 1930s

It is difficult to find 'comedy' or 'humour' in the index of a history of 1930s literature. Nevertheless, the humorists of the 1920s and 1930s do figure in the memories of our readers. P.G. Wodehouse (discovered by adults) and Richmal Crompton (appealing to both adults and children) come up again and again. Many Wodehouse novels were to be found for sale in Boots catalogues of bargain books, books remaindered from its commercial library. The *Library Association Record* lists P.G. Wodehouse as the fourth most popular author in 1933 and the *Bookseller* lists him as the seventh most popularly bought author in 1935. It is clear from our readers that Wodehouse was equally available on the shelves of moneyed families, such as the wealthy David Flather (who found him 'old hat' in the 1940s), as he was on the shelves of the tuppenny libraries. His appeal bridged class and regional divides. The doings of Bertie Wooster and his friends were, perhaps, so totally apart from any society to which our readers were exposed that the mayhem to which Jeeves restored order left the reader free to survey this comic universe as just that: a separate world.

If, as Peter B rightly suggests, Lawrence was one of the first writers to represent the working class as having an interior life (our interviews contain no mention of James Hanley or Henry Green, who also offered such representations in the 1930s), our readers would have to wait even longer before reading accounts of the sorts of lives they led that made them laugh. Meanwhile many working-class readers seem to have had fun with Jeeves and Wooster, the Earl of Emsworth and the Empress of Blandings: Dorothy H: 'Yes, I liked Wodehouse. I liked the Blandings, the pig.'[24] Dorothy smiled as she recalled the Empress, but most of the women who mentioned Wodehouse either gave up on him or found him,

24 Dorothy H, born 1929, interviewed by Susan Roe, 7 May 2013.

as Anne did, 'a bit silly', a word often used by our female readers about a range of things, including their younger selves. What Eva liked was a writer who was 'not silly, but funny' and Wodehouse definitely fell into the silly category. Mary Wilkinson was not deterred by the silliness. She read him constantly in 1937, before she was married to Maurice Soar and before the outbreak of war. She also picked him up occasionally during the war itself as light relief from her serious, non-fiction reading.

Men were generally tolerant of Wodehouse's silliness; two at least found the 'silly ass' an attractive figure. Peter Mason, son of a mining engineer, unusually read Wodehouse as a child, probably his parents' copies, and said that what he liked about them was that the 'silly ass', with the help of Jeeves, 'always came out on top, with a smile'. An adult equivalent of the 'noodle' stories enjoyed in the early 1930s by Jean Mercer as a child. Though Chris Farris never read his father's copies of Wodehouse, at the end of his interview with us he decided that Wodehouse would be the first author to be loaded on to his recently acquired Kindle. It was always satisfying when, in the course of an interview, a resolution was made to read an author still unexplored: Jean to read *Lady Chatterley's Lover* or Chris to explore his father's taste for Wodehouse.

There were other comic writers mentioned by our readers: the American Betty Macdonald, Stella Gibbons, Compton Mackenzie and Jerome K. Jerome (with one mention of *Gentleman Prefer Blondes* by Anita Loos from the voracious Eva), but little reflection on why they were found funny. Only Wodehouse attracted significant comment from our readers, his greatest fans being Ken, attracted by the stylistic elegance of the writing, and Pat Cymbal, who was inspired by her Lithuanian father's love of wit and literary playfulness.

Keeping up to date

If our readers had set out to keep their reading up-to-date where would they have looked? The most recent writing readily available to our readers was to be found in the tuppenny libraries, which did indeed stock contemporary writing – genre fiction that did not deviate too disturbingly from the expectations of its readers. The Sheffield Poetry Society sounds as if might have been more promising. It was founded in 1923 'to refute the ancient taunt that Sheffield is unliterary'.[25] In 1932 it renamed itself the Sheffield Literary Society. In spite of its stated aim

25 'A Sheffield Poetry Club', *Sheffield Daily Telegraph*, 23 May 1923, 5.

to introduce 'famous modern poets to give readings of their works', this ambition does not seem to have been realised. In her research in the records of the society, Val Hewson has found no mention of poetry readings by any poets with a national reputation in the post-war period, 1944–54.[26] The closest encounter to the contemporary was a talk on T.S. Eliot.

Boots being out of the financial reach of most, the municipal libraries would have been the most likely source of contemporary literary works with a high critical reputation, but in the 1930s and 1940s librarians were not trained to act as literary mentors, and Chief Librarian Lamb, of course, hoped that readers would find their own ways of making reading choices. Custodians of cheap commercial libraries, on the other hand, made a point of responding to and guiding their customers' tastes. In a 1931 Mills and Boon romance by the bestselling Sophie Cole, much is made of the quicksilver way in which the well-educated lover of the heroine shifts the attention of the varied clientele of her tuppenny library from popular to more literary fiction or vice versa. By extending the customers' tastes he increases the profits of his beloved.[27]

Without such an adept guide, our readers might have looked to the book pages of the *Sheffield Daily Telegraph* which, as we have seen, was commonly read and would have been a source of thoughtful reviews of newly published books. But on these book pages there were few references to writers we now regard as epitomising the literary culture of the 1930s and 1940s. Ken would not have found such reviews in the *Sheffield Daily Telegraph*. Although Frederick Wood, its erudite and insightful reviewer in the 1930s and 1940s, did review modern fiction, between 1930 and 1950 he never reviewed novels by Graham Greene, for example.

A reader in pursuit of the new authors would have had a greater chance of reading reviews of a wide range of contemporary fiction in the national papers or literary magazines. Her father's job in the Town Hall enabled Shirley to access such publications in the 1940s. Her father was a council employee, so their house was full of magazines.

> In the treasury department ... they had a magazine club, and the men there subscribed, and therefore were able to buy a whole range of magazines, and they circulated in turn, you'd have them for so long then had to send them back. And I know – and I first was acquainted with *Punch* then, and with

26 Val Hewson, personal communication, 2022.
27 Sophie Cole, *Primrose Folly*, London: Mills and Boon, 1931.

Country Life, and the *London Illustrated News* – I'm very familiar with the format of those three.[28]

Access to metropolitan magazines is here clearly linked to clerkly employment, an occupational group that, as has been noted, formed a smaller proportion of Sheffield workers than it did in the cities of Leeds, Manchester and Birmingham.

Familiarity with the national rather than local press could itself be connected with political engagement of various sorts. Erica's father, an active Liberal and member of the Left Book Club, took 'the liberal paper', presumably the *News Chronicle*, while communists Ken and Kath read the *Guardian*. Frank's father, a Tory miner in a village south of Sheffield, took the *Daily Mail*.

Men's general preference for non-fiction over fiction was accompanied by a habit of newspaper reading, predominantly a male interest. If the *Sheffield Daily Telegraph* found its way into the home of a youngster growing up in the 1930s or 1940s it would usually have been the choice of a father. The father too would have had first dibs on the newspaper, which he would read in the evening after his tea. Maureen L describes the family kitchen in the evening as being the domain of her exhausted father. In the late 1940s he was a labourer who worked 12-hour shifts, six till six. From twenty past six in the evening, he ate, then read the paper and fell asleep. Once the newspaper had dropped from his hands, the family had a claim on it. Only four readers recall reading a newspaper in their teens, all men: David Flather in the late 1930s, who had learned to read by sharing the cricket results with his father, the owner of a steelworks; Ken, who in the early 1940s sought out the *Guardian* for its political views; Peter Mason, also in the early 1940s, who was encouraged by his father, a mining engineer, to take an interest in current affairs and used well-written articles to develop his own writing style. James Green was a young adult when, in the late 1950s, he sought out a paper very different from his father's *Daily Express*. He, like Ken, took the *Guardian*, which his mates at the steelworks thought was 'weird'.

> Through reading newspapers you'd get writers and critics that would dissect a certain book or books or a genre, and make you see things that you hadn't seen before. And you think, well that's not right, you know.

28 Shirley Ellins, born 1936, interviewed by Loveday Herridge, 22 November 2011.

Literature on the radio

It was unlikely our readers' awareness of contemporary fiction would have been increased by listening to the radio. Many interviewees described listening to news broadcasts as a family during the war but, as we have seen, Mary Wilkinson, who listened in her teens to spoken word features broadcasts with her father, was unusual. Throughout the 1930s and 1940s finding such programmes was not straightforward. Compared with music, these formed a tiny proportion of the BBC's National Service schedules, often at the least popular times of the day. Although there were intermittent attempts to introduce new writers to radio audiences, they were on nothing like the same scale as the crusade by the BBC's Edward Clark to initiate the British listener into the world of classical music, including works by modernist composers. Clark, a major influence in the BBC Music Department from 1924 to 1936, not only included examples of European modernist composers in BBC schedules, but encouraged British composers such as William Walton and other non-modernist contemporaries. While Sheffield readers with no access to metropolitan publications would have struggled to become aware of current literary figures, radio listeners throughout the 1930s would have been given as many opportunities to make their minds up about a new composer's work as a wealthy metropolitan concertgoer. Audrey Sainsbury, a future Oxford student of English who grew up in working-class Liverpool in the 1930s, said her family never listened to the spoken word. 'That wasn't what we listened to the radio for.'[29] Her father chose the programmes for the family and it was always tuned into music.

Even the news could be difficult to access. In the late 1940s a Lincolnshire grammar school boy, Keith Bolderson, did his National Service before going on to Cambridge.

> I don't think any of us were really conscious of what was going on in the outside world. The only newspaper we ever saw was probably the *Daily Mirror* which was not known for its news content. There was no wireless so no *Dick Barton* or *ITMA* – there was no such thing as a portable radio. There may have been a big wireless in the NAAFI but I didn't go to the NAAFI much. I was too busy running the theatre in the evenings.[30]

---

29 Audrey Sainsbury, personal communication, 23 January 2017.
30 Colin Shindler, *National Service: From Aldershot to Aden. Tales from the Conscripts, 1946–62*, London: Sphere, 2012, 22.

Our reader Ken, with his eclectic diet of the novels of Sholokhov and P.G. Wodehouse, and the essays of Quiller Couch, certainly dismisses the notion that the radio in wartime had any influence on what he read.

> But during the war that was all you could do, read books, with very little other entertainment. Certainly nothing like the radio or TV, as there is now, so you were thrown on to books and written material, newspapers.[31]

Ken had too many reading resources to feel deprived.

Clearly, spoken word broadcasting played little part in our readers' lives, but for those who did have listening opportunities, there was no shortage of Dickens dramatisations. He had more exposure on the radio than any other author we might now regard as classic, and his books were a surprisingly pervasive presence in our readers' homes.

Dickens in the 1930s

Dickens dominated the airwaves in the 1930s and had many lives in the imaginations of our readers. For those who encountered him on the Joint Matriculation Board syllabus which set the exams taken in the grammar schools of Sheffield in the 1930s and 1940s, he tended to be regarded as dull: associated with swotting up in preparation for an exam. His novels were set twice by the Joint Matriculation Board in the 1930s: *A Tale of Two Cities* in 1933 and *David Copperfield* in 1938. The sheer length of a Dickens novel, its physical weight, could be a deterrent. Judith found Dickens 'turgid' when a teenager in the 1940s: 'all right, he's descriptive, but you know, my God, get on with it! But when you read him afterwards you realise why it's a masterpiece.'[32] Television adaptations of his novels often prompted these reappraisals.

Ted as a teenager in the 1930s found the length of Dickens's novels oppressive as he 'wasn't fussy on the really weighty novels'. He conceded that the stories were probably 'splendid' but 'they were buried in a lot of print and to me I wanted it quick and easy'.[33] Frank never 'really got to grips' with his parents' set of Dickens in the 1940s.

> I couldn't stand three pages of, you know, a fellow started with what somebody ate for breakfast and then going on for the whole of his political

---

31 Ken, born 1925, interviewed by Clare Keen, 16 November 2011.
32 Judith G, born 1939, interviewed by Loveday Herridge, 14 February 2013.
33 Ted, born 1919, interviewed by Mary Grover, 19 February 2013.

opinions and prejudices and all the rest of it before we got on to the story again.[34]

Both Ted and Frank presented their negative response as purely personal, not a dismissal of Dickens himself. Mary Robertson, surrounded by the novels of Dickens that belonged to her husband, never had a taste for them and concluded that a Dickens novel was 'a man's book'. She was 92 when she was interviewed, and was astonished to hear that her female interviewer loved Dickens: 'Do you really? I should have given him a go shouldn't I? Given him a go. I think it is a bit too late now.' Just as Jean Ansdell, impressed by her interviewer's references to Lawrence, contemplated embarking on *Lady Chatterley*, Mary was ready to shed her prejudices against Dickens. Both responses are typical of the openness to new reading experiences on the part of most of our readers.

Although Judith, Frank and Ted found the weight of descriptive detail a barrier, for two of our readers this weight was wealth. Peter Mason valued this feature of Dickens's writing because he 'covered all facets of the Victorian period very well'. 'It gave you an insight into just how unfortunate some people were and how they lived. You get *Oliver Twist*, you get all the books. The class distinctions are very clear in those books.' Malcolm too, head teacher and historian, mined *Oliver Twist* with a particular purpose. In the 1990s, while a mature postgraduate student, he read it to compare with other sources when researching education in Sheffield's workhouses.[35]

Adele as a grammar school teenager in the 1950s devoured the lot, and the length of each book was a lure.

> I was an avid reader of very big books. I read all the Dickens. You know, when I think about my appetite for reading at sixteen, it was just amazing. And you've got the time, haven't you? Well, a lot more time in bed, for a start, as a teenager. So, you know, you just have an appetite and nothing else much to do really.[36]

For those craving to have their appetite sated, the weight of each book, the number of volumes, made Dickens ideal fodder. For some it was the Abbey School series, for others Dickens. Why not both?

Born in 1925, Eva started reading Dickens when she was seven years old. Although her father, a steelworker, read war books and her mother

34 Frank, born 1938, interviewed by Loveday Herridge, 21 August 2012.
35 Malcolm Mercer, born 1925, interviewed by Mary Grover, 10 August 2010.
36 Adele, born 1942, interviewed by Liz Hawkins, 19 July 2012.

romances, some of Dickens's novels were to be found in the house. Eva discovered *David Copperfield*, 'my favourite', in 1933. She then sought out all the rest on her own behalf at the local library: 'I was more interested in those sort than fairy tales and those sorts of books.'[37]

Her sense that Dickens was about the adult world is shared by the significant number of readers who identified with David Copperfield. He was the first of Dickens's characters to be discovered by Bob, born in 1940. Bob's father was a steelmaker and in the late 1940s the family moved to the vast new estate of Parson Cross being built on the hills to the north of the steel mills in the Don Valley. There was no library on the estate and few books in the home, so Bob hunted on his own: 'everything I did was on [*sic*] my own bat'. He walked the mile down the hill to Hillsborough Library. There he discovered Dickens and found '*David Copperfield*, and Charles Dickens on the whole, easy to read'.

> They were speaking my language, you know. Some of the older authors, more classical authors, were speaking not my language, you know, and I didn't want to keep looking in dictionaries to see what the words were or anything like that.

The character of David Copperfield still fascinates him: 'I had to be interested in people. I mean, you can't get a more interesting character than David Copperfield, you see.'[38] Self-identification with David Copperfield is often mentioned by the readers quoted by Jonathan Rose, for example the cricket and music commentator Neville Cardus, who, from a background every bit as precarious as Copperfield's, felt that 'David Copperfield so often behaved and thought as I behaved and thought that I frequently lost my own sense of identity in him'.[39]

The mature responses of these men, using Dickens's fiction to understand the shape of their own lives, is very much at odds with Q.D. Leavis's early view of Dickens as incapable of representing the complexities of human character and development. In her pioneering work *Fiction and the Reading Public*, Leavis sternly warns the serious reader of literature that the 'peculiarity of Dickens … is that his originality is confined to recapturing a child's outlook on the grown-up world, emotionally he is not only uneducated but also immature'.[40]

37 Eva, born 1925, interviewed by Susan Roe, 16 May 2012.
38 Bob W, born 1940, interviewed by Trisha Cooper, 19 February 2012.
39 Neville Cardus, *Second Innings*, London: Collins, 1950, 45–7.
40 Leavis, *Fiction and the Reading Public*, 157.

For years both the Leavises argued that Dickens was not worthy of his 'classic' status. In 1932, Q.D. Leavis asserted that those in possession of 'an alert critical mind' should check the facile emotions that might be prompted by what Dorothy H calls 'Dickens's tear-jerkers'.[41]

The way that Dickens's novels were represented on the radio may have fuelled the perception that he merely created caricatures aimed at provoking either tears or laughter. Throughout the 1930s the adventures of David Copperfield and the voices of characters such as Mr Micawber, Fagin, Pickwick or Magwitch could be heard on the wireless, in every kind of programme. Dickens featured in Children's Hour, schools' programmes and the early evening serial. In 1934 *Oliver Twist* was dramatised for both children's and adult programmes. The links between Dickens and the music hall were explicit in a 1930 programme entitled 'Vaudeville' which advertised Bransby Williams, 'the Famous Portrayer of Dickens Characters' in 'A Pickwick Party', a musical extravaganza subtitled 'A Dickens Dream Fantasy', with a 'Chorus of Dickens Dogs and Dainty Ducks' (just a touch of Disney).[42] *Pickwick Papers*, in particular, represented the Dickens whose chief function on the radio seemed to be to provide the nation with an endless supply of comic turns.

The absence of the darker works by Dickens from the broadcasting schedules would also have reinforced the popular image of him as entertainer. *Bleak House* or *Little Dorrit* would not have been chosen. These were, however, two of the first works to attract extensive literary-critical interest from the Leavises. In 1970, having previously anathematised all his novels except *Hard Times*, they published a complete collection of essays on Dickens in which they now conclusively recognised his literary qualities. The new appreciation was dependent on reading the novels in the way that the Leavises instructed. Q.D. Leavis's essay on *Great Expectations* is entitled threateningly, 'How we must read *Great Expectations*'.[43] There was not much tolerance of Dickens the humorist or entertainer.

Another reason for the equivocal way in which Dickens was regarded by modernists and Leavisites alike was his long-standing popularity among working-class readers. Working-class memoirs quoted by Jonathan Rose

41 Dorothy H, born 1929, interviewed by Susan Roe, 7 May 2013.
42 'A Dickens Dream Fantasy', broadcast on the BBC National Programme, 29 December 1930.
43 F.R. Leavis and Q.D. Leavis, *Dickens the Novelist*, London: Chatto and Windus, 1970.

demonstrate how accessible Victorian and Edwardian readers found Dickens.[44] Jean H was born in 1926 to clever parents who had had few educational opportunities. She 'loved Dickens'. She was well known in the elementary school that she attended for being able to recite poetry, her great love, but the novels of Dickens 'were the only books that stick in my mind somehow. I just borrowed them either from the library or wherever I could.'[45] Her favourite was *A Christmas Carol*, another staple of Christmas broadcasting. From 1923, the year when the British Broadcasting Company was launched, to 1950, 14 separate versions of *A Christmas Carol* were broadcast. So, Jean would have been able to spend nearly every Christmas of her childhood with her favourite author.

Was it the novel or one of Bransby Williams's readings that inspired Dorothy H to feel sorry for Oliver Twist, 'the way he was treated'? One of eight children, Dorothy, born in 1929, was not brought up in absolute poverty, but her father, a butcher in the working-class terraces in north Sheffield, would have negotiated daily the struggles of his customers to purchase enough meat to feed families as big as his own. Betty Newman is Dorothy's contemporary, born in 1935. She too responded to the tangible or credible in the fiction of Dickens's novels, so she read Dickens in spite of a dislike for novels in general. She supposes that Dickens 'was the nearest I got to fiction', then adds reflectively, 'I don't think he really is fiction.'[46] This is a reminder that Dickens came nearer to describing the economic realities of the industrial working class than any twentieth-century author our readers might have encountered.

The omnipresence of Dickens on the radio in the 1930s coincided with a tide of cheap editions of the complete novels. This deluge of uniform volumes must have reinforced prejudices against a writer whose excessive popularity was somehow linked to a substandard reading public whose tastes were governed by a commercial culture industry. Indeed, the rationale for such cheap editions was strictly commercial. In 1933 the conservative *Daily Mail*, liberal *News Chronicle* and left-wing *Daily Herald* engaged in a costly circulation war, using Dickens as bait for new readers. Over 300,000 complete sets of Dickens were purchased in the following twelve months. This is very likely the source of Frank's father's complete set. My father's family in South Wales acquired theirs, in its purpose-built oak bookcase, through the *News Chronicle*.

---

44 Rose, *The Intellectual Life of the British Working Classes*, 111–15.
45 Jean H, born 1926, interviewed by Mary Grover, 8 May 2012.
46 Betty Newman, born 1935, interviewed by Ros Witten, 13 October 2011.

24 My grandparents' set of Dickens, bought on subscription from the *News Chronicle*

It was through the *Daily Herald* in 1933 that Dickens entered the home of the 12-year-old Irene. Her grandfather had been illiterate and her mother had never been seen to read a book, but suddenly she found herself with a constant supply of brand-new editions of Dickens's novels for the exclusive use of herself and her family. Irene's father bought their set through the *Daily Herald* despite its politics.

> A man came round to the house getting you to buy the *Daily Herald*. My father said, 'We'll never use that newspaper because we don't agree with those politics', but eventually the man must have been good, because he signed up so I got the whole of Dickens's works with that newspaper.[47]

47 Irene Hailstone, born 1921, interviewed by Susan Roe, 28 February 2012.

The saving was immense even though the cost was considerable to a family unused to spending money on new books. The *Herald* offered registered readers the 16 volumes for four guineas (four pounds and four shillings), just under a month's wages for a skilled steelworker in the early 1930s. Mary Soar, as an unmarried teenager, was so tempted by one of the subscription offers advertised in *Woman's Weekly* that she still has the clipping, though it was never acted upon. On 14 March 1933, the day after the *Daily Herald* launched its offer, the Labour leader George Lansbury exulted in the success of the subscription offer in the paper's pages,

> I feel that the whole country owes the *Daily Herald*, a debt of gratitude for making it possible for every home in the land to possess its set of Dickens.
>
> You have performed a miracle.[48]

The sets of Dickens that entered working-class homes in the 1930s thanks to the newspaper subscription wars were an incalculable benefit to those who, otherwise, had few books in the home and who read little that related at all to their own lives. But the very omnipresence of his works fuelled intellectual disdain.

The most complex encounter we have between a young reader and Dickens is described by Jessie Robinson, born in 1906. As we have heard, the vicar's housekeeper rebuked the 14-year-old 'tweenie' in 1920 for reading the vicar's 'London papers'. Jessie was redirected to the housekeeper's own set of Dickens as more suitable reading matter for a girl of her class. It is rare that we found a reader who had access to a library belonging to a person whose educational background was so distant from her own. Not only was her employer a clergyman and a university graduate, but he was from London. The housekeeper herself was the guardian of cultural goods that would have been unavailable to the girl had she not entered domestic service. Curiously, this cultural gatekeeper regarded Dickens as enclosing the curious girl safely within her existing social class. Yet thirty years later, in the early 1950s, it was the works of both Dickens and Orwell that reinforced the growing conviction of the young James Green, initially prompted by reading the *Guardian*, that 'This ain't right.'

By the very fact of being a servant in a middle-class household, Jessie's class and cultural perspectives changed. When Adele reflected on the

---

48 Anon., '£4 4s Dickens Library: Special Message from Sir Henry Dickens: Amazing Response to "Herald" Offer', *Daily Herald*, 21 March 1933, 6.

way her parents tolerated her hours reading Dickens in the 1950s, she thinks that her mother's tolerance of her apparent idleness was born of her years as a domestic worker in wealthy homes:

> It was my mother who always said, 'No she's reading. Leave her.' And yet she was the least educated of my parents. She'd been in service, but I think she'd seen a different way of life and I think she'd been surrounded by books.

However, Dickens's cultural value was never stable. Rather than a devalued commodity only fit for 'tweenies', Dickens represented to Margaret G prestigious goods that she was not fit to consume. Margaret attended an intermediate grammar school in the 1930s, a tier down from the better-funded grammar schools in which pupils were given five not four years to prepare for the School Certificate. Although she would have sat the School Certificate in 1938 when *David Copperfield* was on the syllabus (less intimidating than some of the later novels), Margaret G shrank from even starting Dickens because 'I didn't think I was clever enough.'[49] Presumably, the way he was taught in preparation for the exam constructed a pedagogic apparatus which, sadly, acted as a barrier. The untutored working-class girls, Jessie and Jean, made Dickens their own in the 1920s and 1930s. Although they were judged ineligible to take a public examination, they did not consider themselves ineligible to enjoy Dickens. The interwar subscriptions unleashed sets of Dickens into communities, which helped bypass the prejudices and fears of what Dickens might represent and offered a gloriously long run of books that could be sampled in individual ways in many different kinds of home. Private ownership of Dickens's novels helped free their readers from evaluative barriers.

In the 1970s, when Dickens was firmly established as part of any university syllabus, his novels were still being devoured by those with little education because they were judged to be about 'ordinary' people and written for them.[50] Bob judged the language to be his own. The profile of Dickens's readership between the wars is unique. No other author was perceived in such a variety of apparently contradictory ways, and in ways that changed hugely over the first seventy years of the twentieth century.

The diverse ways in which our readers accessed both nineteenth- and twentieth-century authors, such as Dickens and Lawrence, demonstrate

---

49 Margaret G, born 1924, interviewed by Loveday Herridge, 31 October 2011.
50 'Dot', in Oxted, Surrey, in conversation with Mary Grover, 1985.

how the way a text is encountered shapes the way it is read. What is striking about our readers' responses to authors now regarded as in some sense 'canonical' is that those who had no higher education came at them unfettered by genre or cultural expectations. Not only did the vast majority of our readers not categorise the books they encountered as canonical or up-to-the minute, they did not categorise themselves as a certain type of reader or a book as 'my sort of book'. The contrast with the way in which readers are now directed by online marketing to reinforce reading tastes already established could not be sharper.

One of the freedoms born out of the very constraints upon our readers' reading choices was the freedom from fear that they might be perceived as ignorant, provincial or behind the times. It is significant that it was Margaret G, an attendee at an intermediate grammar school, already labelled as 'not good enough' for the higher-tier grammar school, who felt she might not be 'good enough' to read Dickens.

The Last Word of my book is given to those of our readers who did experience that moment of censure that can so easily blight the confidence of an aspirant reader. I hope the ways in which they dealt with these encounters with cultural gatekeepers will demonstrate the power of having established oneself as an indiscriminate and voracious reader before meeting the gorgons at the gate.

The Last Word

Born in 1937, Mavis was the daughter of the manager of Tinsley Colliery weigh station. There were three books in the house: the Bible, a copy of a novel by Dorothy L. Sayers and a book called 'Vigil', 'which I thought was Virgil till I thought he couldn't have been that bad and it turned out to be a book of prayers'. An uncle and honorary aunt lent her books from the libraries of schools where they taught. Another aunt let her loose on her piles of the *People's Friend*. 'I was a bit omnivorous and unselective.'

Mavis gained the highest pass among 11-plus candidates in 1947, winning a scholarship place at Sheffield Girls' High School. She managed to spend Friday afternoons in Sheffield Central Library during optional games periods. Mavis went on to study English at Leeds University and to teach in secondary schools all over England: in Harlow, Bolton, Kearsley and Carlisle. She did what every English teacher should be able to do: fostered reading for pleasure. She created groups in which every member read a different book and shared her opinions with her friends. No student was taught to be ashamed of ignorance.

When, at university, Mavis was temporarily abashed by how little she had learned at school about the Metaphysical poets, her response was characteristically matter of fact and entirely positive: 'I realised that I had very large gaps which was a good thing to know.'

I started this project angry: angry that people of my educational background had conspired throughout the twentieth century to undermine the confidence of men and women to read what and how they wanted. I had spent ten years writing about the nastiness of the rhetoric directed at the popular reader during the years when our readers were coming to adulthood. Thanks to the generosity of those who agreed to talk to 'Reading Sheffield', my anger towards those who dismissed the reading 'masses' no longer dogs me. I see now that, if there was a conspiracy to humiliate the reader of popular fiction, then for these Sheffield readers this conspiracy failed.

For the vast majority it failed because they were oblivious to the possibility that their private reading was being judged. We didn't ask them whether they felt that their reading had been evaluated until we had got far down our list of interviewer's prompts, and only then if we felt there was no danger of their mistakenly thinking that we were there to evaluate them. By far the majority were frankly puzzled when asked if there was any book that they might have been embarrassed to be seen reading. This majority were, to use the northerner J.B. Priestley's term, 'broadbrow': they had wide reading tastes. Half a dozen readers expressed themselves nervous of tackling books that were held to be 'classics' or were a bit of a reading stretch, but there was rarely a suggestion that our readers would avoid books that were off the limits of some kind of cultural map. No one used the words 'pretentious', or 'highbrow' to dismiss books that were regarded as difficult or belonging to an alien cultural world. Malcolm Mercer, head teacher and educational historian, said that he had only heard the word highbrow used to describe music.[1] The term 'middlebrow' was simply baffling. The only time we heard the word 'lowbrow' used, its user embraced it and called it his own. John D firmly identified himself as 'lowbrow' when asked what the words 'highbrow, middlebrow, lowbrow' meant to him.

> John: I like lowbrow things! My record collection was dance bands of the 30s and 40s and big bands. So in Britain you'd have Roy Fox, Ambrose, Lew Stone ... and that sort of thing.
>
> Mary: ... So would the word highbrow for you be a word of criticism or just not your thing?
>
> John: My motto has always been 'live and let live'. Let 'em live with it if they want it, that's them.[2]

1 Malcolm Mercer, born 1925, interviewed by Mary Grover, 10 August 2010.
2 John D, born 1927, interviewed by Mary Grover, 7 June 2013.

Some of our readers, of course, because of their cultural background or on entry to higher education, became aware that their tastes might be judged. Two in particular identified a particular moment when they were found wanting. From a wealthy background and privately educated at a prestigious girls' boarding school, and then evacuated to the South Coast in the war, Jocelyn was asked by an exasperated English teacher, 'Why are you reading such rubbish when you're capable of reading something so much better?' Although Jocelyn knew perfectly well what her teacher meant, she did not take these strictures to heart. She laughs as she reflects on how she should have responded:

> I suppose I should have said, 'Because that's all there is.' And I think that was in a way true, to a point. And I also think you need to read rubbish in order to find out what rubbish is and then you can form an opinion about what's worth it and what isn't. And if you're not feeling very well, rubbish is what you want!

Jocelyn was not going to be defined by her reading tastes or confine her reading to a socially acceptable canon, and none of our readers (in our presence) defined other people on the basis of shared or divergent reading tastes. The tastes of others were accepted, matter-of-factly on the whole. Alan's lack of success with Virginia Woolf ('I didn't get on with it') and his wife Anne's revulsion against *Jane Eyre* ('I just couldn't stick it') are typical. The statements are self-descriptive: personal and not directed at others.

A lack of awareness of literary prohibitions and an absence of literary guidance could lead to idiosyncratic modes of navigation. To have formed a set of reading tastes in a relatively solitary and unguided fashion could leave a voyager adrift in terrain where others were setting their course with the aid of an acceptably calibrated compass. When Mavis became aware in her university interview that she was judged off course, she dealt with the situation in a way that demonstrated a high degree of literary confidence and competence. This confidence was, in part, born of her years of indiscriminate reading. Generations of pupils taught by Mavis can be grateful that she herself was not deterred from studying English literature by the sneers and raised eyebrows of literary gatekeepers. In fact, she had to run the gauntlet twice.

Mavis's first university choice was King's College, London, where she hoped to study English Literature. At first her familiarity with the works of Osbert Sitwell appeared to interest her interviewers. She had discovered the Sitwells when reading a local newspaper article about speed traps in the Derbyshire village where the Sitwell family still live. They laid out their Italianate gardens on the hills above the coal mines they owned. Their artistic activities and generous patronage of the arts were built on profits from the mining industry. But familiarity with the Sitwells did not stand Mavis in good stead. The family were in fact 'an awful downfall'.

> I was asked what I thought of [Osbert's] father and I said I'd not have fancied him myself as a father, and I was asked didn't I think he was unusually peculiar. I said, no, he's just a posher version of an awful lot of other people in Yorkshire ... he was noughtie [*sic*], he was odd, there was a lot of people like that. He was just upper class but I'd met people a lot funnier than him. They clearly thought I was bonkers and all I got was, I was on the waiting list. I was so annoyed to be on the waiting list that when I got the offer in the summer I thought, 'Blow you, I'm not going there.'[3]

It was not necessary to travel as far as London to feel culturally insecure. The second time Mavis put herself at risk of not gaining a university place her vulnerability was exposed by the mode of transport used to attend the interview. Though she was aware that she shouldn't read *Woman's Own* on the bus when she was in high school uniform, it didn't occur to Mavis to think strategically about her reading choices on the train journey to her interview at Leeds University.

> It's only an hour, even then, and my mother, that's the one thing she would read was *Reader's Digest*. So, I brought a *Reader's Digest*. Interviewer: 'What did you read on the train?' So I said, '*Reader's Digest*' and I saw this expression and I thought, 'Ah' and I explained about my mother who wasn't a reader but she did enjoy the *Reader's Digest* and I explained to be honest I had never been on a train before and I was on a stopping train as the most suitable one and I didn't want to get into a book because [after Leeds] the train didn't stop until it reached the Scottish border and if I got into a book I might not have got off until I reached the Scottish border, and I thought, 'I hope I've got out of that one all right'. After that I was aware that there were things you didn't own up to but apart from magazines I don't think it would have ever occurred to me. I wasn't the most perceptive young person, I'm afraid.

She may not have regarded herself as perceptive but she was a quick learner. The uncharacteristically long and headlong sentence recalling the defence of her possession of the *Reader's Digest* suggests the energy

3 Mavis, born 1937, interviewed by Mary Grover, 12 March 2012.

and determination with which she pursued her university place. Once she had made that train journey to Leeds, not only did Mavis learn to map the status of her reading matter, she learned that she herself could be placed off-limits on the basis of her reading choices.

It was my first interviewee, Malcolm Mercer, who gently defused the anger that had fuelled my ten years of university research into the rhetoric of cultural disparagement and set me on a more open inquiry. Malcolm had left school at 14, went into shop work but, as a result of determined self-education and evening classes, became head teacher of a successful primary school serving a large estate built in post-war Sheffield; he is himself an educational historian.[4] When I tentatively asked Malcolm whether he had ever come across the term 'middlebrow' used by the communist Dwight Macdonald, the author Virginia Woolf and the critic Q.D. Leavis to anathematise the tastes of those whose culture they despised, he said no. After my explanation of the way this term was used he looked at me sternly: 'I think it was partly that if we had lived at your end of the city we would have [heard of it]... We were all sort of surrounded by working-class people.' We cannot change the end of the city where we came from or the terms of the debate that we inherit.

This book did not set out to defend or assess the value of what our readers read. The 'Reading Sheffield' project simply aimed to attend to readers whose tastes had been dismissed. Our readers' eloquence, discernment and sense of delight stand as a testament to the transformative power of books and of the act of making reading choices. These histories are full of opportunities lost and hopes unfulfilled. It is all the more remarkable that the dominant tone of our interviewees is one of wonder. The books our readers chose opened up intellectual and imaginative spaces that seemed for a time all their own, and the spaces in which they found those books were arenas of choice. This exceptional opportunity to exercise personal autonomy was as precious as the books they sought, the constraints to freedom of choice intensifying the thrill of exercising it.

4 Malcolm Mercer, *Schooling the Poorer Child: Elementary Education in Sheffield 1560–1902*, Sheffield: Sheffield Academic Press, 1996.

Interview Prompts

At the beginning of the interview, the details of interviewer and interviewee: 'This is an interview conducted by … [spell it out]. It is [date] … I am interviewing … [spell it out]. He/she was born in … on … and lived in … [area of Sheffield] between [dates]'

Did anyone read to you when you were young? How, when, who? What kind of books?

What were the first books you read that made you feel that you were now reading grown-up/adult books?

Where did you get them from? Family member, library, friend, school or… ?

Can you talk about any of the books you read as a young adult that made an impression on you? Why did they make an impression?

What kind of books did you really like? Why?

Tell me about where you got most of the books that you read as a teenager/young adult. *[Prompt: local library, college library, works library, bookshops – new or second-hand?]*

Did anyone encourage you to read?

Did anyone make you feel that reading was a waste of time?

Where and when did you find time to read?

Were you ever made to feel embarrassed about what you read – a guilty pleasure? Or did you ever read anything because you thought it would improve you in any way?

Which books did you read with pleasure when you were young that you wouldn't dream of reading again? Why not?

Do any of the following authors or books ring any bells with you? [Prompt: choose names from the list that seem to link with the kinds of books the reader has liked; encourage interviewee to reflect on what he/she liked about them.]

Are there any ways in which your reading has changed your life?

Informants and Interviewers

Readers who shared their memories informally with us

Maureen Burgin, born 1945, wife of 'Reading Sheffield' interviewee Frank Burgin

Jennifer Fox discussed the reading experiences of her parents, both born 1906

John Gilbert, born in the 1930s, discussed informal teaching of literacy to soldiers during National Service

Josie Hall, born in 1942, a 'Reading Sheffield' interviewee, was also interviewed on 5 December 2012 by a group of students from Sheffield Hallam University: Hannah Gorrill, James Hunter and Talia McGuinre

Diane Haswell (d.o.b. unknown), niece of 'Reading Sheffield' interviewee Wynne Wilson

Catherine Pinion, born 1941, librarian, Sheffield

Ruth Potts, born 1960, daughter of 'Reading Sheffield' interviewee David Flather

Muriel Pyle, born 1932, librarian, Knaresborough

Jessie Robinson, born 1906, 'tweenie' for the vicar of St John's Park

Frances Soar discussed the reading experiences of her mother, the 'Reading Sheffield' interviewee, Mary Soar

'Sue', born 1924, wife of Sheffield industrialist

Jude Warrender, born 1950, user of Firth Park Library as a child

Dorothy Wood, born 1935, librarian, Harrogate, Castleford and Knaresborough

Sheffield groups of retirees who shared their memories with us

Blenheim Court Residential Home

Dore Ladies Group
Ecclesall Library event
The Inner Wheel
Portland Works
Probus Club: Stumperlowe Branch
Ranmoor History Society
Ranmoor Lunch Club
Sheffield Libraries events attendees
Sheffield Parkinson's Support Group
Sheffield Town's Women's Guilds: three branches
Sheffield Women in Fellowship
The Slightly Sprightly Exercise Group, Wadsley
Soroptomists
Trefoil Guild
U3A Sheffield
The Venue group at Stocksbridge

The 'Reading Sheffield' interviewing team

Sahra Ajiba
Jan Chatterton
Trisha Cooper
Jean Gilmour
Mary Grover
Liz Hawkins
Loveday Herridge
Clare Keen
Sue Roe
Alice Seed
Mike Watson
Ros Witten

Bibliography

Archives

Boots UK archive, held by Walgreen Boots Alliance Archive, Nottingham
The British Newspaper Archive
The Joint Matriculation Board, JMB Regulations, Examination Papers and
    Examiners' Reports, held by AQA, Manchester University
Mass Observation Online, http://www.massobservation.amdigital.co.uk/
'Reading Sheffield' website, www.readingsheffield.co.uk
Sheffield City Archives
Sheffield Local Studies Library, minutes and papers of Sheffield Council's
    Education and Library committees
UK Reading Experience Database 1450–1945, http://www.open.ac.uk/Arts/
    RED/index.html
The Workers' Education Association Archives, Sheffield

Works in response to the 'Reading Sheffield' project

Brown, Eleanor, *White Ink Stains*, Hexham: Bloodaxe, 2019.
Tuckerman, Lizz, 'In Praise of Libraries', exhibition at Bank Street Arts,
    Sheffield, 2017.
Tuckerman, Lizz, 'The Making of In Praise of Libraries', post on the
    Reading Sheffield website, https://www.readingsheffield.co.uk/events/
    the-making-of-in-praise-of-libraries/ (accessed 3 June 2020).

Unpublished books and articles

Adsetts, Norman, 'My Life in Books and Films', unpublished memoir.
Grover, Mary, and Val Hewson, 'Running up Eyre Street: Sheffield
    Reading and the Second World War', paper presented at a conference
    at Leeds Library to celebrate its 250th anniversary, 21 September
    2018, https://www.readingsheffield.co.uk/wp-content/uploads/2018/09/

Running-Down-Eyre-Street10.8.18withPics-2.pdf (accessed 27 January 2023).

Hewson, Val, '"Even Edgar Wallace may be discovered...": The Fiction Policy of an English Public Library in the 1930s', paper given to 'The Auden Generation and After' conference, Sheffield Hallam University, 17 June 2016, https://www.readingsheffield.co.uk/research/even-edgar-wallace-may-be-discovered/ (accessed 3 June 2020).

Kelly, James R., 'An Oral History of Sheffield Public Libraries, 1926–1974', MA thesis, University of Sheffield, April 1983.

Longden, Roger, 'The History of Secondary Education in Sheffield 1902–1939', PhD thesis, University of Sheffield, 1976.

McIntosh, Tania, '"A Price Must be Paid for Motherhood": The Experience of Maternity in Sheffield, 1879–1939', PhD thesis, Department of History, University of Sheffield, 1997.

Roberts, John, 'The Sheffield Educational Settlement 1918–1955', Krebs Room thesis, 1961.

Sadler, M.E., *Report on Secondary and Higher Education*, Sheffield Local History Collection, 1903.

Seed, T. Alec, 'Croft House Settlement Operatic Society', 1951, www.crofttheatre.co.uk/sites/default/files/t-alec-seed-croft-house.pdf (accessed 19 February 2023).

Sheffield City Libraries, 'A Survey of Children's Reading', 1938, Local Pamphlets Collection 47 042 SST, Local Studies Library, Sheffield Central Library.

Sheffield City Libraries, 'Report of the Libraries Sub-Committee covering the period 1 April, 1939–31 March, 1947', 1947, Sheffield City Archives.

Spencer, E.B., 'Sister Edith', 'Reminiscences of Croft House Settlement, 1914–1953', undated, Sheffield City Archives, M.D. 3417.

Thurston, H.M., 'Report of His Majesty's Inspector of Schools, January 1935: Wisewood Council Senior Mixed School', 1935, Sheffield City Archives.

Thurston, H.M., 'Wybourn Council Senior Mixed School', 1934 [unclear whether this is a formal or interim report], Sheffield City Archives.

Books, articles and films

Adsetts, Norman, *A Man of Sheffield: The Adsetts Story*, Sheffield: RMC Media, 2017.

Albaya, Winifred, *Through the Green Door: An Account of the Sheffield Educational Settlement Shipton Street 1918 to 1955 Parts I and II*, Sheffield: Sheffield District Education Committee, 1980.

Alderson, Brian, 'Tracts, Rewards and Fairies: The Victorian Contribution to Children's Literature', in *Essays in the History of Publishing*, ed. Asa Briggs, London: Longman, 1974, 245–82.

Anon., 'A Sheffield Poetry Club', *Sheffield Daily Telegraph*, 23 May 1923, 5.

Anon., '£4 4s Dickens Library: Special Message from Sir Henry Dickens: Amazing Response to "Herald" Offer', *Daily Herald*, 21 March 1933, 6.

Anon., 'One Act Plays', *Sheffield Daily Telegraph*, 29 April 1950, 3.

Auchmuty, Rosemary, and Juliet Gosling (eds), *The Chalet School Revisited*, London: Bettany Press, 1994.

Badger, S.M., *Abbeydale Girls' Grammar School – Jubilee Year 1968*, Sheffield: Greenups, 1968.

Batty, Ronald F., *How to Run a Tuppenny Library*, London: John Gifford, 1938.

Bauer P.J., *Remembering the Times of Our Lives: Memory in Infancy and Beyond*, Mahwah, NJ: Laurence Erlbaum Associates, 2007.

Baxendale, John, *Priestley's England: J.B. Priestley and English Culture*, Manchester: Manchester University Press, 2007.

Beaven, Brad, *Leisure, Citizenship and Working-Class Men in Britain, 1850–1945*, Manchester: Manchester University Press, 2005.

Bennett, Tony, Michael Emmison and John Frow, *Accounting for Tastes*, Cambridge: Cambridge University Press, 1999.

Binfield, Clyde, Roger Harper, David Hey, Richard Childs, David Martin and Geoffrey Tweedale (eds), *The History of the City of Sheffield 1843–1993*, 3 vols, Sheffield: Sheffield Academic Press, 1993.

Bingham, Adrian, '"Putting literature out of reach"? Reading Popular Newspapers in Mid-Twentieth-Century Britain', in *The History of Reading, Volume 2: Evidence from the British Isles, c.1750–1950*, ed. Katie Halsey and W.R. Owen, Basingstoke: Palgrave Macmillan, 2011, 139–54.

Black, Alistair, 'The Library as Clinic: A Foucauldian Interpretation of British Public Library Attitudes to Social and Physical Disease, ca. 1850–1950', in *Libraries and Culture: Historical Essays Honoring the Legacy of Donald G. David, Jr.*, ed. Cheryl Knott Malone, Hermina G.B. Anghelescu and John Mark Tucker, Washington, DC: Library of Congress, The Center for the Book, 2006, 194–212.

The Board of Education, *Handbook of Suggestions for Teachers: 'For the Consideration of Teachers and Others Concerned in the Work of Public Elementary Schools'*, London: HM Stationery Office, 1937.

Boughton, John, *Municipal Dreams: The Rise and Fall of Council Housing*, London: Verso, 2019.

Bourdieu, Pierre, *Distinction: A Social Critique of the Judgement of Taste*, trans. Richard Nice, London: Routledge and Kegan Paul, 1986.

Bourke, Joanna, *Working-Class Cultures in Britain 1890–1960*, London: Routledge, 1994.

Brearley, Harry, *Stainless Pioneer: Autobiographical Notes*, Solihull: British Steel Stainless and the Kelham Island Industrial Museum, Sheffield, 1989.

Briggs, Asa, *The History of Broadcasting in the United Kingdom, Volume 3: The War of Words*, London: Oxford University Press, 1970.

Briggs, Asa, *The BBC: A Short History of the First Fifty Years*, Oxford: Oxford University Press, 1995.

Briggs, Asa (ed.), *Essays in the History of Publishing*, London: Longman, 1974.

Brown, Erica, and Mary Grover, *Middlebrow Literary Cultures: The Battle of the Brows, 1920–1960*, Basingstoke: Palgrave Macmillan, 2012.

Buckler, Warwick, 'This Film Lag', *Sheffield Daily Telegraph*, 18 October 1950, 2.

Cardus, Neville, *Second Innings*, London: Collins, 1950.

Carpenter, Louise, 'Ida and Louise', *Granta* 98, 2 July 2007, https://granta.com/ida-and-louise/ (accessed 12 January 2022).

Chapman, James, *British Comics: A Cultural History*, London: Reaktion, 2011.

Cole, Sophie, *Primrose Folly*, London: Mills and Boon, 1931.

Cook, Caldwell, *The Play Way: An Essay in Educational Method*, New York: Frederick A. Stokes, 1917.

Doctor, Jenny, *The BBC and Ultra-Modern Music, 1922–1936*, Cambridge: Cambridge University Press, 1999.

Entwistle, Dorothy, 'Sunday-School Book Prizes for Children: Rewards and Socialisation', *Studies in Church History*, vol. 31 (1994), 405–16. doi:10.1017/S0424208400013012.

Farrell, Stephen, and Malcolm Mercer, *A Portrait of the Manor in the 1930s: The Evolution of a Council Estate*, Sheffield: Pickard Publishing, 2002.

Feather, John, *A History of British Publishing*, London: Routledge, 1988.

Felsenstein, Frank, and James J. Connolly, *What Middletown Read: Print Culture in an American Small City*, Amherst, MA: University of Massachussetts Press, 2015.

Freeman, Arnold, *The Equipment of the Workers: An Enquiry by the St. Phillips Settlement Education and Economics Research Society into The Adequacy of the Adult Manual Workers for the Discharge of their Responsibilities as Heads of Household, Producers and Citizens*, London: George Allen and Unwin, 1919.

Gardiner, Juliet, *The Thirties: An Intimate History*, London: Harper Press, 2011.

Giddings, Robert, 'Radio in Peace and War', in *Literature and Culture in Modern Britain*, ed. Gary E. Day, vol. 2, London: Pearson Education, 1997, 132–62.

Great Britain Historical GIS Project, 'A Vision of Britain Through Time', https://web.archive.org/web/20110629044720/http://www.visionofbritain.org.uk/index.jsp (accessed 19 December 2020).

Greene, Graham, *Journey without Maps*, London: Heinemann, 1936.

Gross, John, *The Rise and Fall of the Man of Letters: English Literary Life Since 1800*, Harmondsworth: Penguin, 1991.

Grover, Mary, *The Ordeal of Warwick Deeping: Middlebrow Authorship and Cultural Embarrassment*, Madison, NJ: Fairleigh Dickinson University Press, 2009.

Grover, Mary, 'The View from the Middle: Godden and her Literary Landscape', in *Rumer Godden: International and Intermodern Storyteller*, ed. Lucy Le-Guilcher and Phyllis B. Lassner, Farnham: Ashgate, 2010, 23–38.

Grover, Mary, 'Firth Park Teacher Guiding Sheffield's Literary Taste', https://www.readingsheffield.co.uk/firth-park-teacher-guiding-sheffields-literary-taste/, 16 November 2016 (accessed 4 June 2020).

Hall, David, *Working Lives: The Forgotten Voices of Britain's Post-War Working Class*, London: Random House, 2012.

Hall, David, *Work Town: The Astonishing Story of the 1930s Project that Launched Mass-Observation*, London: Weidenfeld and Nicolson, 2015.

Halsey, Katie, '"Something light to take my mind off the war": Reading on the Home Front during the Second World War', in *The History of Reading, Volume 2: Evidence from the British Isles, c.1750–1950*, ed. Katie Halsey and W.R. Owen, Basingstoke: Palgrave Macmillan, 2011, 84–100.

Halsey, Katie, and W.R. Owen (eds), *The History of Reading, Volume 2: Evidence from the British Isles, c.1750–1950*, Basingstoke: Palgrave Macmillan, 2011.

Harris, Jose, *Private Lives, Public Spirit: Britain 1870–1914*, Harmondsworth; Penguin, 1994.

Hartley, Jenny, and Sarah Turvey, *Reading Groups*, Oxford: Oxford University Press, 2002.

Hattersley, Roy, *In Search of England*, London: Little, Brown, 2009.

Hawson, Keble, *Sheffield: The Growth of a City, 1893–1926*, Sheffield: J.W. Northend, 1968.

Herridge, Loveday, and Susan Roe, 'Sheffield Libraries and Private Book Clubs, 1771–1850', in *Before the Public Library: Reading, Community and Identity in the Atlantic World 1650–1850*, ed. Mark Towsey and Kyle B. Roberts, Leiden: Brill, 2017, 174–99.

Hewson, Val, blogposts on Sheffield Libraries, readingsheffield.co.uk (accessed 15 April 2020).

Hey, David, 'Sheffield Schools, 1918–60', in *The History of the City of Sheffield 1843–1993, Volume 2: Society*, ed. Clyde Binfield, Roger Harper, David Hey, Richard Childs, David Martin and Geoffrey Tweedale, Sheffield: Sheffield Academic Press, 1993, 316–23.

Higgins, Charlotte, *This New Noise: The Extraordinary Birth and Troubled Life of the BBC*, London: Guardian Books, 2015.

Hilliard, Christopher, *To Exercise Our Talents: The Democratization of Writing in Britain*, Cambridge, MA, Harvard University Press, 2006.

Hilliard, Christopher, *English as a Vocation: The 'Scrutiny' Movement*, Oxford: Oxford University Press, 2012.

Hilliard, Christopher, 'Popular Reading and Social Investigation in Britain, 1850–1940s', *The Historical Journal*, 57.1 (2014), 247–71.

Hilliard, Christopher, 'The Twopenny Library, the Book Trade, Working-Class Readers and "Middlebrow" Novels in Britain 1920–1942', *Twentieth Century British History*, 25.2 (2014), 199–220.

Hinton, James, 'The "Class Complex": Mass-Observation and Cultural Distinction in Pre-War Britain', *Past and Present*, 199 (May 2008), 207–36.

Hoggart, Richard, *The Uses of Literacy*, Harmondsworth: Penguin, 1958.

Hoggart, Richard, *A Local Habitation: Life and Times, Volume 1: 1918–40*, Oxford: Oxford University Press, 1989 [1988].

Holbrook, David, *People and Diamonds, Volumes 1 and 2*, Cambridge: Cambridge University Press, 1962.

Hopkins, Chris, *English Fiction in the 1930s: Language, Genre, History*, London: Continuum, 2006.

Hopkins, Chris, *Walter Greenwood's* Love on the Dole*: Novel, Play, Film*, Liverpool: Liverpool University Press, 2018.

Hoy, Grace, *Nineteenth Century Reformers, The University Settlement Movement and Education by Magic at the Sheffield Educational Settlement under Arnold Freeman*, Truro: Grace Hoy, n.d.

Hyndman, Michael, *Schools and Schooling in England and Wales: A Documentary History*, London: Harper and Row, 1978.

James, Robert, *Popular Culture and Working-Class Taste in Britain 1930–1939*, Manchester: Manchester University Press, 2010.

Jenkinson, A.J., *What Do Boys and Girls Read?*, London: Methuen, 1940.

Kaye Smith, Sheila, *All the Books of Our Lives*, London: Cassell, 1956.

Kelly, Thomas, *A History of Adult Education in Great Britain*, Liverpool: Liverpool University Press, 1992.

Kirk-Smith, H.A., *History of Wadsley, 1800–1957*, Sheffield: J.C. Short, 1957.

Knights, Ben, *Pedagogic Criticism: Reconfiguring University English Studies*, Basingstoke: Palgrave Macmillan, 2017.

Knights, L.C., 'Scrutiny of Examinations', *Scrutiny*, 4.2 (1933), 137–63.

Koven, Seth, *Slumming: Sexual Politics and Social Policies in Victorian London*, Princeton, NJ: Princeton University Press, 2006.

Kynaston, David, *Austerity Britain 1945–51*, London: Bloomsbury, 2007.

Lamb, J.P., 'Some Notes on Library Planning I: Sheffield', *The Library World Supplement*, 33.5 (1 October 1930), 145–60.

Lamb, J.P., 'Librarian when Young: Part 1', *The Librarian and Book World*, 45.1 (1956), 1–5.

Lamb, J.P., 'Librarian when Young: Part 2', *The Librarian and Book World*, 45.2 (1956), 34–6.

Lamb, J.P., *The City Libraries of Sheffield 1856–1956*, Sheffield: Sheffield Libraries, Art Galleries and Museums Committee, 1956.

Leader, Robert Eadon, 'The Sheffield Book Society: Some of its First Members', *Sheffield Daily Telegraph*, 5 January 1907, 8.

Leavis, F.R., and Q.D. Leavis, *Dickens the Novelist*, London: Chatto and Windus, 1970.

Leavis, Q.D., *Fiction and the Reading Public*, London: Bellew, 1990 [1932].

Light, Alison, *Common People*, Harmondsworth: Penguin, 2014.

Lukács, György, *History and Class Consciousness: Studies in Marxist Dialectics*, Cambridge, MA: MIT Press, 2000 [1923].

MacDonald, Dwight, 'A Theory of Mass Culture', in *Mass Culture: The Popular Arts in America*, ed. Bernard Rosenberg and David Manning White, New York: Macmillan, Free Press, 1964 [1957], 59–73.

Mackerness, E.D., *Somewhere Further North: A History of Music in Sheffield*, Sheffield: J.W. Northend, 1974.

Mangan, Lucy, *Bookworm: A Memoir of Childhood Reading*, London: Square Peg, 2018.

Martin, David, 'Arnold Freeman and the Sheffield Educational Settlement', *Transactions of the Hunter Archaeological Society*, 20 (1999), 71–80.

Mason, Charlotte, *Parents and Children*, London: Kegan Paul, 1897, https://amblesideonline.org/CMM/M2complete.html.

Mass-Observation, File Report 47, March 1940, 'Wartime Reading'.

Mass-Observation, 'Children's Reading at Fulham Library', File Report 96, 8 May 1940.

Mass-Observation, *The Press and its Readers: A Report Prepared by Mass-Observation for the Advertising Guild*, London: Art and Technics, 1949.

Mathers, Helen, 'The City of Sheffield 1893–1926', in *The History of the City of Sheffield 1843–1993, Volume 1: Politics*, ed. Clyde Binfield, Roger Harper, David Hey, Richard Childs, David Martin and Geoffrey Tweedale, Sheffield: Sheffield Academic Press, 1993, 53–84.

Mathers, Helen, *Steel City Scholars: The Centenary History of the University of Sheffield*, London: James and James, 2005.

Mathieson, Margaret, *The Preachers of Culture: A Study of English and Its Teachers*, London: George Allen and Unwin, 1975.

McAleer, Joseph, *Popular Reading and Publishing in Britain 1914–1950*, Oxford: Clarendon, 1992.

McKibbin, Ross, *Classes and Cultures: England 1918–1951*, Oxford: Oxford University Press, 1998.

Melrose, Elizabeth, 'J.P. Lamb, M.A., F.L.A', in *The Provision and Use of the Library and Documentation Service: Some Contributions from the University of Sheffield Postgraduate School of Librarianship*, vol. 4 of The International Series of Monographs in Library and Information Science, Oxford: Pergamon Press, 1966, 1–28.

Melville, Alan, *Weekend at Thrackley*, London: British Library, 2018 [1934].

'Mental Dramshops: Young Librarians' Contempt for Fiction', *Sheffield Daily Telegraph*, 18 September 1913.

Mercer, Malcolm, *Schooling the Poorer Child: Elementary Education in Sheffield 1560–1902*, Sheffield: Sheffield Academic Press, 1996.

Mercer, Malcolm, *A Portrait of the Manor in the 1930s: The Evolution of a Council Estate*, Sheffield: Pickard Publishing, 2002.

Morgan, Mary S., Iain Sinclair and the London School of Economics, *Charles Booth's London Poverty Maps: A Landmark Reassessment of Booth's Social Survey*, London: Thames and Hudson, 2019.

Mulhern, Francis, *The Moment of Scrutiny*, London: NLB, 1979.

The Newbolt Report: The Teaching of English in England, London: HM Stationery Office, 1921.

Ollé, James G., 'The Lost Libraries', *Library Review*, 20.7 (1966), 452–6.

Ollé, James G., 'J. P. Lamb: The Last of the Patriarchs', *Library Review*, 24.7 (1974), 295–300, https://doi.org/10.1108/eb012607.

O'Malley, Raymond, and Denys Thompson, *Rhyme and Reason*, London: Chatto and Windus, 1957.

Orwell, George, *The Road to Wigan Pier*, Harmondsworth: Penguin, 1989 [1937].

Orwell, George, 'Boys' Weeklies', *Horizon*, 3 (1940); reprinted in *Inside the Whale and Other Essays*, Harmondsworth: Penguin, 1957.

O'Sullivan, T., 'Listening Through: The Wireless and World War Two', in *War Culture: Social Change and Changing Experience in World War Two Britain*, ed. P. Kirkham and D. Thoms, London: Lawrence and Wishart, 1995, 173–85.

Owen, A.D.K., *A Survey of Juvenile Employment and Welfare in Sheffield*, Sheffield Social Survey Pamphlet no. 6, April 1933.

Pawley, Christine, *Reading Places: Literacy, Democracy, and the Public Library in Cold War America*, Amherst, MA: University of Massachusetts Press, 2010.

Pollard, Sidney, *A History of Labour in Sheffield*, Liverpool: Liverpool University Press, 1959.

Pollard, Sidney, 'Labour', in *The History of the City of Sheffield 1843–1993, Volume 2: Society*, ed. Clyde Binfield, Roger Harper, David Hey, Richard Childs, David Martin and Geoffrey Tweedale, Sheffield: Sheffield Academic Press, 1993, 260–78.

Pollard, Sidney, and Colin Holmes (eds), *Economic and Social History of South Yorkshire*, Barnsley: SYCC, 1976.

Poole, Edmund H., *The Teaching of Literature in the WEA*, London: British Institute of Adult Education, 1938.

Poole, Edmund H., 'English Literature as a Subject in WEA Classes', *Adult Education*, 12 (June 1940), 165–75.

Porter, W.S., *Sheffield Literary and Philosophical Society 1822–1832*, Sheffield: J.W. Northend, 1932.

Price, David, *Sheffield Troublemakers: Rebels and Radicals in Sheffield History*, Chichester: Phillimore, 2008.

Pybus, Sylvia (ed.), *'Damned Bad Place, Sheffield': An Anthology of Writing about Sheffield Through the Ages*, Sheffield: Sheffield Academic Press, 1994.

Reid, C., 'Middle Class Values and Working Class Culture in Nineteenth Century Sheffield: The Pursuit of Respectability', in *Economic and Social History of South Yorkshire*, ed. Sidney Pollard and Colin Holmes, Barnsley: SYCC, 1976, 275–95.

Richards, Jeffrey, and Dorothy Sheridan (eds), *Mass-Observation at the Movies*, London: Routledge and Kegan Paul, 1987.

Roberts, Robert, *The Classic Slum: Salford Life in the First Quarter of the Century*, Harmondsworth: Penguin, 1973 [1971].

Rodgers, P., *A lecture on the origin, progress and results of the Sheffield Mechanics' Institute*, Sheffield: J.H. Greaves, 1840.

Rose, Jonathan, *The Intellectual Life of the British Working Classes*, New Haven, CT: Yale University Press, 2001.

Rose, Jonathan, 'Arriving at a History of Reading', *Historically Speaking*, 5.3 (2004), 36–9.

Salt, J., 'The Creation of the Sheffield Mechanics' Institute: Social Pressures and Educational Advance in an Industrial Town', *Vocational Aspect*, 18 (1966), 143–9.

Samuel, Raphael, and Paul Thompson, *The Myths We Live By*, London: Routledge, 1990.

Scannell, Paddy, and David Cardiff, *A Social History of Broadcasting, Volume One: 1922–1939*, Oxford: Basil Blackwell, 1991.

Scott, W. Stuart, 'Amateur Actors' Duty to the Theatre', *The Daily Independent*, 17 January 1936, 4.

Seed, Alec T., *The Sheffield Repertory Theatre: A History*, Sheffield: The Sheffield Repertory Co., 1959.

Shayer, David, *The Teaching of English in Schools*, London: Routledge and Kegan Paul, 1972.

Sheffield City Council Libraries Committee, *Books in Hand* (film), 1956, https://www.yfanefa.com/record/2585 (accessed 27 January 2023).

Sheffield Libraries, Art Galleries and Museums Committee, *The City Libraries of Sheffield, 1856–1956*, 1956.

Shindler, Colin, *National Service: From Aldershot to Aden. Tales from the Conscripts, 1946–62*, London: Sphere, 2012.

Simpson, Margaret, 'A Sheffield Woman's Diary', *The Sheffield Telegraph*, 20 December 1939, 8.

Smith, Dennis, *Conflict and Compromise: Class Formations in English Society 1830–1914*, London: Routledge and Kegan Paul, 1982.

Spevack, Martin, 'The Golden Treasury: 150 Years On', eBLJ 2012, Article 2, https://bl.iro.bl.uk/concern/articles/97e9035b-7614-4463-b5e8-11de2fb57360?locale=en (accessed 26 January 2023).

Spufford, Francis, *The Child that Books Built*, London: Faber and Faber, 2002.

Stocks, M.D., *Fifty Years in Every Street*, Manchester: Manchester University Press, 1945.

Taylor, Helen, *Scarlett's Women: Gone with the Wind and its Female Fans*, London: Virago, 2014 [1989].

Taylor, Helen, *Why Women Read Fiction*, Oxford: Oxford University Press, 2020.

Thorpe, Andrew, 'The Consolidation of a Labour Stronghold 1926–1951', in *The History of the City of Sheffield 1843–1993, Volume 1: Politics*, ed. Clyde Binfield, Roger Harper, David Hey, Richard Childs, David Martin and Geoffrey Tweedale, Sheffield: Sheffield Academic Press, 1993, 85–118.

Todd, Selina, 'Poverty and Aspiration: Young Women's Entry to Employment in Inter-War England', *Twentieth Century British History*, 15.2 (2004), 119–42.

Todd, Selina, *The People: The Rise and Fall of the Working Class 1910–2010*, London: John Murray, 2014.

Turner, E.S., *Boys Will Be Boys: The Story of Sweeney Todd, Deadwood Dick, Sexton Blake, Billy Bunter, Dick Barton et al.*, Harmondsworth: Penguin, 1975 [1948].

Vaninskaya, Anna, 'Learning to Read Trash', in *The History of Reading, Volume 2: Evidence from the British Isles, c.1750–1950*, ed. Katie Halsey and W.R. Owen, Basingstoke: Palgrave Macmillan, 2011, 67–83.

Vickers, J. Edward, *A Popular History of Sheffield*, Sheffield: Applebaum Bookshop, 1987.

Walton, Mary, *Sheffield: Its Story and its Achievements*, Otley: Amethyst Press, 1948.

Walton, Mary, *A History of the Parish of Sharrow*, Sheffield: Author, 1968.

Walton, O.F., *A Peep Behind the Scenes*, London: The Religious Tract Society, 1877.

Wang, Qi, and Sami Gülgöz, 'New Perspectives on Childhood Memory', Special issue, *Memory*, 27.1 (2019), 1–5.

Watson, Victor, *Reading Series Fiction: From Arthur Rackham to Gene Kemp*, London: Routledge, 2000.

West, Rebecca, 'The Tosh Horse', in *The Strange Necessity: Essays and Reviews*, London: Jonathan Cape, 1928, 319–25.

Wheatley, D.E., *Apprenticeships in the United Kingdom*, Social Policies Services no. 30, Brussels: European Economic Union Collection Studies, 1978.

Wilson, Nicola, 'Boots Book-lovers' Library and the Novel: The Impact of a Circulating Library Market on Twentieth-Century Fiction', *Information and Culture: A Journal of History*, 49.4 (2014), 427–49.

Winter, Jackie, *Lipsticks and Library Books: The Story of Boots Booklovers Library*, Dorset UK: Chantries Press, 2016.

Woolf, Virginia, *The Death of the Moth and Other Essays*, London: Hogarth Press, 1942.

Index

General Index

Reading matter mentioned by Reading Sheffield interviewees